THE EVERYTHING®
U.S. CONSTITUTION BOOK

Dear Reader,

The first time I encountered the U.S. Constitution, half a century ago, just a week of our mandatory high school American History course was devoted to how a bill becomes a law, the three branches of government, and the Bill of Rights. Over the next ten years, studying the Constitution first as an undergraduate and later as a law student, my classmates and I never considered that anyone discussing the Constitution might have an agenda. The Constitution was the Constitution, or so we thought.

Today, as elections have become increasingly polarized, so have interpretations of what the Constitution was or was not intended to mean. People wave it as a banner, convinced *their* interpretations are the *only* interpretations.

In writing this book, I have tried to stick with the attitude of that earlier time when I first read the Constitution to rely on the law as it stands, without trying to say whether laws are good or bad—they simply *are*. The genius of the document that has governed the United States for two and a quarter centuries is that it has managed to evolve with the American people and reflect who they have become. The laws written to complement it may change, but even as new laws are written, or old ones are interpreted differently, the Constitution's basic functions and principles remain the same. The purpose of this book is to help you understand *how* it works, *why* it works that way, and how it has changed over the years.

Ellen M. Kozak

Welcome to the EVERYTHING. Series!

These handy, accessible books give you all you need to tackle a difficult project, gain a new hobby, comprehend a fascinating topic, prepare for an exam, or even brush up on something you learned back in school but have since forgotten.

You can choose to read an *Everything*® book from cover to cover or just pick out the information you want from our four useful boxes: e-questions, e-facts, e-alerts, and e-ssentials.

We give you everything you need to know on the subject, but throw in a lot of fun stuff along the way, too.

We now have more than 400 *Everything*® books in print, spanning such wide-ranging categories as weddings, pregnancy, cooking, music instruction, foreign language, crafts, pets, New Age, and so much more. When you're done reading them all, you can finally say you know *Everything*®!

QUESTION

Answers to common questions

FACT

Important snippets of information

ALERT

Urgent warnings

ESSENTIAL

Quick handy tips

PUBLISHER Karen Cooper

DIRECTOR OF ACQUISITIONS AND INNOVATION Paula Munier

MANAGING EDITOR, EVERYTHING® SERIES Lisa Laing

COPY CHIEF Casey Ebert

ASSISTANT PRODUCTION EDITOR Jacob Erickson

ACQUISITIONS EDITOR Lisa Laing

ASSOCIATE DEVELOPMENT EDITOR Hillary Thompson

EDITORIAL ASSISTANT Ross Weisman

EVERYTHING® SERIES COVER DESIGNER Erin Alexander

LAYOUT DESIGNERS Colleen Cunningham, Elisabeth Lariviere, Ashley Vierra, Denise Wallace

Visit the entire Everything® series at *www.everything.com*

THE EVERYTHING®

U.S. CONSTITUTION BOOK

An easy-to-understand explanation of the
foundation of American government

Ellen M. Kozak

A adamsmedia

Avon, Massachusetts

For my sisters

An Everything® Series Book.
Everything® and everything.com® are registered trademarks of F+W Media, Inc.

Contains material adapted and abridged from *The Everything® Founding Fathers Book*,
by Meg Greene, MA, MS, and Paula M. Stathakis, PhD, copyright © 2011 by F+W Media, Inc.,
ISBN 10: 1-4405-2586-2, ISBN 13: 978-1-4405-2586-5; *The Everything® Civil War Book, 2nd Edition*
by Brooke C. Stoddard and Daniel P. Murphy, PhD, copyright © 2009, 2000 by F+W Media, Inc.,
ISBN 10: 1-59869-922-9, ISBN 13: 978-1-59869-922-7; *The Everything® American History Book,
2nd Edition* by John R. McGeehan, MA, copyright © 2007, 2001 by F+W Media, Inc.,
ISBN 10: 1-59869-261-5, ISBN 13: 978-1-59869-261-7.

Published by Adams Media, a division of F+W Media, Inc.
57 Littlefield Street, Avon, MA 02322 U.S.A.
www.adamsmedia.com

ISBN 10: 1-4405-1274-4
ISBN 13: 978-1-4405-1274-2
eISBN 10: 1-4405-2561-7
eISBN 13: 978-1-4405-2561-2

Printed in the United States of America.

10 9 8 7 6 5 4 3 2 1

Library of Congress Cataloging-in-Publication Data
Kozak, Ellen M.
The everything U.S. Constitution book / Ellen M. Kozak.
p. cm.
Includes bibliographical references and index.
ISBN-13: 978-1-4405-1274-2 (alk. paper)
ISBN-10: 1-4405-1274-4 (alk. paper)
ISBN-13: 978-1-4405-2561-2 (e-book)
ISBN-10: 1-4405-2561-7 (e-book)
1. Constitutional law—United States—Popular works. 2. Law for laypersons I. Title.
KF4550.Z9K69 2011
342.7302—dc22
2011006246

This book is available at quantity discounts for bulk purchases.
For information, please call 1-800-289-0963.

Contents

Acknowledgments

So many to thank, so little space:

First and foremost, there was the late Phoebe Morrison, lawyer, judge, and professor, who inspired so many Barnard women to become lawyers in an era when women weren't welcome in "a man's profession";

The late Judge Myron L. Gordon, who hired me as his law clerk and gave me a chance to see the workings of a federal court from the inside;

My friend Marshall Segal, not only for being supportive, but also for having moved my admission to the U.S. Supreme Court;

Larry Church, for taking the time to supply a valuable jump-start;

Three Pams—Brown, Burden, and Lichtenstein—good friends all;

Sharon Jarvis, Sherman Stock, Bill Lemieux, Alice Kehoe, Reg Sprecher, Karla Benton, Patty Levine, and Jim and Judy Nortman, for their varied assistance and support;

Martha Andes Ziskind, Dee McGarity, and Ralph Ehlinger, for their insights and suggestions;

My more-than-patient editors, Lisa Laing and Hillary Thompson;

My sisters Carla Kozak and June Kozak Kane for kindnesses too numerous to list;

The Big Bang Theory and Owen O. for making me laugh;

Last but not least, Muffin, for finally learning to use the lawn rather than the living room floor (most of the time).

The Top 10 Things You May Not Know about the Constitution

1. The Constitution is an outline for running the government. It does not contain the laws that the government uses to run the country.

2. The Constitution restricts the powers of the government, rather than the rights of the people.

3. The Constitution replaced the Articles of Confederation that preceded it, but did not specifically revoke them.

4. Each state has equal representation in the Senate, although ultimately senators represent the people of their states as well as the states as a whole. The *people* of the United States are represented in the House of Representatives according to population numbers revealed by the census every ten years.

5. The states can and do make their own laws on most subjects such as inheritance, marriage, divorce, speed limits, and penalties for crimes committed within the state.

6. The Bill of Rights, which guarantees the people of the United States specific freedoms like freedom of speech, did not require the states to guarantee those rights until after the ratification of the Fourteenth Amendment in 1868.

7. Only one crime, treason, is defined in the Constitution.

8. The Constitution creates and defines the three branches of the federal government: legislative, executive, and judicial.

9. The Constitution is only 4,400 words long, although its twenty-seven Amendments add another 3,500 words.

10. You can see the original Constitution at the National Archives in Washington, D.C.

Introduction

AMERICAN LAW, LIKE THE British law from which it developed, is based on precedent. What a word meant before determines what it will mean today, and the way the law was applied to a certain set of facts determines how it will be applied to a set of facts today.

Well, almost. It is possible for laws to be rewritten, and it is possible for lawmakers and courts to reverse themselves—to decide they have been going down the wrong path and essentially admit they were wrong and start over. This doesn't happen often, and when it does, it is usually accompanied by extensive explanations—in the case of new laws, by much debate in Congress or legislatures, and in the case of judicial reinterpretations, by lengthy written opinions explaining why.

Lawmakers, lawyers, and ordinary citizens need those explanations, or the historic background of what has gone before, so they can rely on them in going about their daily business. You want to know that when you drive to work on the right side of the road, you won't suddenly find that the rules have been changed, that everyone is driving on the left, and you are suddenly headed into oncoming traffic.

The U.S. Constitution is one of the historical documents on which Americans base their actions. The Constitution declares itself—and is accepted as—the supreme law of the land. All other laws must mesh with it, but how? When is a law in conflict with the Constitution or its principles? When do the actions of government or of citizens step over the line?

The way to understand that—to understand what the Constitution means today—is to understand what it has meant over the years since it was created. It is part of a long historical tradition harking back to the Magna Carta of England, a document that a group of barons forced the king to sign to curtail some of his arbitrary acts. As the North American colonies came under British rule, they based their law on English precedent, and relied on it, assuming they possessed "the Rights of Englishmen." The curtailment of those rights prompted them to declare their independence with a document, the Declaration of Independence.

They followed that with a compact among the rebellious colonies—now calling themselves "states"—called the Articles of Confederation. What they set forth in those articles determined how they interacted for the first dozen years the United States existed.

The Constitution came after the Articles, and it was followed by amendments, and by laws that expanded on its principles, and by court cases that interpreted them.

Because of this tradition, if you want to understand the Constitution, you need to know where it came from—the Articles of Confederation, and the various state constitutions—and where it went, through laws that were passed and repealed, court decisions, and even a great war between those who held two different ideas of what the words of the Constitution meant.

Deciding things in court, rather than on the battlefield, is a way to keep the peace. Knowing the way the laws have been historically interpreted allows you to live your life without worrying whether the traffic flow will reverse itself; whether when you come home at night your house will still be where you live; whether when you go to work, you can rely on the fact that you will receive a paycheck; and whether, when you deposit that paycheck in a bank, you can rely on having that money in your account an hour or a day or a month later.

The Constitution has been referred to as a living document because it is constantly being reinterpreted, and sometimes even being revised. But it is also an historic document, one that relies on what came before for its current meaning. That is why you will find historical references throughout this book—some serious, some entertaining—telling you what the Constitution says, why those words were used, and how that has been applied in various factual situations.

The text of the original Constitution can be found after Chapter 2. Some words and phrases are emphasized in bold type to call your attention to them. This emphasis does not occur in the original document. The full text of all Amendments is reproduced in Appendix A.

CHAPTER 1

The Great Experiment

Before the thirteen colonies that rebelled against the British monarchy organized themselves into a country, most countries just *happened*. They grew out of a cluster of towns or were created when someone with charisma or an army or both declared a group of towns and the surrounding area to be under his power. Custom that evolved over time dictated what authority the leader would have, and a change in leadership was often effected either through inheritance or when someone else challenged the current ruler. It was only after rules and customs were established that they were (sometimes) documented. But to create a nation from scratch? The idea that a bunch of towns or states could come together to form a country in an organized manner was a new one, and when the colonies did just that, they did so by setting down the rules that would bind them together into their new nation.

The First Attempt: The Articles of Confederation

The Second Continental Congress, an assembly of delegates from the thirteen colonies, met in Philadelphia beginning on May 10, 1775. As relations with the "mother country," England, went from bad to worse, the Congress in June of 1776 appointed a committee to draft their Declaration of Independence from England's King George III.

FACT

The First Continental Congress met at Carpenters' Hall in Philadelphia from September 5 to October 26, 1774, to consider a response to the "Coercive Acts," the laws England used to attempt to punish the colonies, and more particularly Massachusetts, for the Boston Tea Party. Its primary achievements were calling for a boycott of British goods beginning that December, and summoning the colonies to participate in the Second Continental Congress the following May.

Shortly after creating the committee that would draft the Declaration, Congress appointed another committee to draft the rules under which the colonies would operate their new alliance. Although they had joined together in a common cause—rebellion against the English king—the states had not really decided how they would relate to each other. The rules under which they operated (and waged the Revolutionary War) came to be called the Articles of Confederation.

The Articles of Confederation

The Articles were agreed to by Congress on November 15, 1777; they were ratified by all thirteen colonies, and consequently went into effect as of March 1, 1781.

Preamble

To all to whom these Presents shall come, we the undersigned Delegates of the States affixed to our Names send greeting.

Whereas the Delegates of the United States of America in Congress assembled did on the fifteenth day of November in the Year of our Lord One Thousand Seven Hundred and Seventy seven, and in the Second Year of the Independence of America, agree to certain articles of Confederation and perpetual Union between the States of New Hampshire, Massachusetts-bay, Rhode Island and Providence Plantations, Connecticut, New York, New Jersey, Pennsylvania, Delaware, Maryland, Virginia, North Carolina, South Carolina and Georgia, in the words following, viz:

Articles of Confederation and **perpetual Union** between the States of New Hampshire, Massachusetts-bay, Rhode Island and Providence Plantations, Connecticut, New York, New Jersey, Pennsylvania, Delaware, Maryland, Virginia, North Carolina, South Carolina and Georgia.

ARTICLE I. The Stile of this Confederacy shall be "**The United States of America.**"

Although it first met in Philadelphia, starting in 1783, the Second Continental Congress met at various sites in New York, New Jersey, and Maryland. After the Articles were fully ratified by all of the states in 1781, the Second Continental Congress came to be known as the Confederation Congress or the Congress of the Confederation. Its official documents list their source as "The United States in Congress assembled."

Joining the Confederation created a *perpetual* union, something the Articles of Confederation mention half a dozen times. (The term "perpetual" does not appear in the U.S. Constitution.)

The Articles of Confederation established the name of the alliance, which became the name of the country.

ARTICLE II. Each state retains its **sovereignty, freedom, and independence**, and every Power, Jurisdiction, and right, which is not by this confederation expressly delegated to the United States, in Congress assembled.

ARTICLE III. The said States hereby severally enter into a firm league of friendship with each other, **for their common defense, the security of their liberties, and their mutual and general welfare**, binding themselves to assist each other, against all force offered to, or attacks made upon them, or any of them, on account of religion, sovereignty, trade, or any other pretense whatever.

ARTICLE IV. The better to secure and perpetuate mutual friendship and intercourse among the people of the different States in this union, the free inhabitants of each of these States, paupers, vagabonds, and fugitives from justice excepted, shall be entitled to all privileges and immunities of free citizens in the several States; and the people of each State shall have free ingress and regress to and from any other State, and shall enjoy therein all the privileges of trade and commerce, subject to the same duties, impositions, and restrictions as the inhabitants thereof respectively, provided that such restrictions shall not extend so far as to prevent the removal of property imported into any State, to any other State, of which the owner is an inhabitant; provided also that no imposition, duties or restriction shall be laid by any State, on the property of the united States, or either of them.

If any person guilty of, or charged with, treason, felony, or other high misdemeanor in any State, shall flee from justice, and be found in any of the united States, he shall, upon demand of the Governor or executive power of the State from

The issue of state sovereignty was very important at the time. While the Articles created an interdependent alliance for certain purposes, such as joint defense, each state guarded its autonomy from the others and from the country as a whole.

The words "common defense," "security of their liberties," and "general welfare" would later be echoed in the Preamble to the Constitution.

Women of Grace

Concert & Dessert

Featuring soloist
Sarah Van Drunen

Sarah provides innovative worship for young and old through hymns and inspirational songs.

Join us
Tuesday, October 25th
7:00pm
Grace Fellowship Church
Auditorium

Dessert following the concert in the gymnasium

Tickets are: $7 each

Purchase tickets at the women's table in the foyer.

Invite a Friend!

Grace Fellowship Church
15150 So. Oak Park Ave. Oak Forest, IL
708.535.1200

---

which he fled, be delivered up and removed to the State having jurisdiction of his offense.

Full faith and credit shall be given in each of these States to the records, acts, and judicial proceedings of the courts and magistrates of every other State.

ARTICLE V. For the most convenient management of the general interests of the united States, **delegates shall be annually appointed in such manner as the legislatures of each State shall direct**, to meet in Congress on the first Monday in November, in every year, with a power reserved to each State to recall its delegates, or any of them, at any time within the year, and to send others in their stead for the remainder of the year.

No State shall be represented in Congress by less than two, nor more than seven members; and **no person shall be capable of being a delegate for more than three years in any term of six years; nor shall any person, being a delegate, be capable of holding any office under the united States, for which he, or** another for his benefit, receives any salary, fees or emolument of any kind.

Each State shall **maintain** its own delegates in a meeting of the States, and while they act as members of the committee of the States.

In determining questions in the united States, in Congress assembled, **each State shall have one vote.**

Freedom of speech and debate in Congress shall not be impeached or questioned in any court or place out of Congress, and the members of Congress shall be protected in their persons from arrests or imprisonments, during the time of their going to and from, and attendance on Congress, except for treason, felony, or breach of the peace.

ARTICLE VI. **No State, without the consent of the united States in Congress assembled, shall send any embassy to, or receive any embassy from, or enter into any conference, agreement, alliance or treaty with any King, Prince or State;** nor shall any person holding any office of profit or trust under the united States, or any of them, accept any present, emolument, office or title of any kind whatever from any King, Prince or foreign State; nor shall the United States in congress assembled, or any of them, grant any title of nobility.

No two or more States shall enter into any treaty, confederation or alliance whatever between them, without the consent of the united States in congress assembled, specifying accurately the purposes for which the same is to be entered into, and how long it shall continue.

No State shall lay any imposts or duties, which may interfere with any stipulations in treaties, entered into by the united States in congress assembled, with any King, Prince or State, in pursuance of any treaties already proposed by congress, to the courts of France and Spain.

No vessel of war shall be kept up in time of peace by any State, except such number only, as shall be deemed necessary by the united States in congress assembled, for the defense of such State, or its trade; nor shall any body of forces be kept up by any State in time of peace, except such number only, as in the judgement of the united States, in congress assembled, shall be deemed requisite to garrison the forts necessary for the defense of such State; but every State shall always keep up a well-regulated and disciplined militia, sufficiently armed and accoutered, and shall provide and constantly have ready for use,

The idea behind Article VI was for the states to present a united front in negotiating with foreign governments. Those creating the Articles of Confederation were also still wary of foreign royals granting titles and thus undermining their independence, and of the newly united states somehow turning into a monarchy. They were careful to prohibit either from occurring.

The new alliance was wary of any states allying themselves with each other within the new country. This provision prevented such alliances from being created without the permission of the rest of the states—but in allowing for permission, made it possible for states to create joint ventures, such as a bridge over a river that ran between them.

in public stores, a due number of filed pieces and tents, and a proper quantity of arms, ammunition and camp equipage.

Because the timing of communication was limited to the speed a horse could travel in those days, provision was made for states to defend themselves in case of emergency without the consent of the central government. Militias were to be maintained for that purpose. However, standing armies (and navies) were forbidden without the permission of the Congress.

No State shall engage in any war without the consent of the united States in congress assembled, unless such State be actually invaded by enemies, or shall have received certain advice of a resolution being formed by some nation of Indians to invade such State, and the danger is so imminent as not to admit of a delay till the united States in congress assembled can be consulted; nor shall any State grant commissions to any ships or vessels of war, nor letters of marque or reprisal, except it be after a declaration of war by the united States in congress assembled, and then only against the kingdom or State and the subjects thereof, against which war has been so declared, and under such regulations as shall be established by the united States in congress assembled, unless such State be infested by pirates, in which case vessels of war may be fitted out for that occasion, and kept so long as the danger shall continue, or until the united States in congress assembled shall determine otherwise.

When army units were raised by the states for "the common defense," the officers of these units were appointed, and thus controlled, by the states. This continued as a common practice in sending troops to fight in the Civil War, and it wasn't until the mid-twentieth century that military units began to be intentionally integrated with members from varied states.

ARTICLE VII. When land forces are raised by any State for the common defense, **all officers of or under the rank of colonel, shall be appointed by the legislature of each State respectively,** by whom such forces shall be raised, or in such manner as such State shall direct, and all vacancies shall be filled up by the State which first made the appointment.

ARTICLE VIII. All charges of war, and all other expenses that shall be incurred for the common defense or general welfare, and allowed by the united States in congress assembled, shall be defrayed out of a common treasury, which shall be supplied by the several States in proportion to the value of all land within each State, granted or surveyed for any person, as such land and the buildings and improvements thereon shall be estimated according to such mode as the united States in congress assembled, shall from time to time direct and appoint.

The taxes for paying that proportion shall be laid and levied by the authority and direction of the legislatures of the several States within the time agreed upon by the united States in congress assembled.

This was a major stumbling block in the function of the government under the Articles of Confederation. The central government could not raise funds directly; money to cover its expenses had to be raised by the state governments, and they could—and often did—drag their heels.

ARTICLE IX. The united States in congress assembled, shall have the sole and exclusive right and power of determining on peace and war, except in the cases mentioned in the sixth article—of sending and receiving ambassadors—entering into treaties and alliances, provided that no treaty of commerce shall be made whereby the legislative power of the respective States shall be restrained from imposing such imposts and duties on foreigners, as their own people are subjected to, or from prohibiting the exportation or importation of any species of goods or commodities whatsoever—of establishing rules for deciding in all cases, what captures on land or water shall be legal, and in what manner prizes taken by land or naval forces in the service of the United States shall be divided or appropriated—of granting **letters of marque and reprisal** in times of peace—appointing courts for the trial of piracies and felonies committed on the high seas and establishing courts for receiving and determining finally appeals in all cases of captures, provided that no member of Congress shall be appointed a judge of any of the said courts.

Letters of marque and reprisal were authorizations for private ships to engage in boarding and taking the ships (including the private ships) of a country with which your country was at war. Those who held such authorizations were known as "privateers," and they and their actions were respected, as opposed to those who operated without such authorizations, who were reviled as pirates and subject to execution if caught.

The United States in Congress assembled shall also be the last resort on appeal in all disputes and differences now subsisting or that hereafter may arise between two or more States concerning boundary, jurisdiction or any other causes whatever; which authority shall always be exercised in the manner following. Whenever the legislative or executive authority

The manner of settling disputes between states, and of choosing who would settle them, was very carefully spelled out in the Articles of Confederation. It was clearly expected that such disputes would arise often enough to merit this careful planning.

or lawful agent of any State in controversy with another shall present a petition to Congress stating the matter in question and praying for a hearing, notice thereof shall be given by order of Congress to the legislative or executive authority of the other State in controversy, and a day assigned for the appearance of the parties by their lawful agents, who shall then be directed to appoint by joint consent, commissioners or judges to constitute a court for hearing and determining the matter in question: but if they cannot agree, Congress shall name three persons out of each of the United States, and from the list of such persons each party shall alternately strike out one, the petitioners beginning, until the number shall be reduced to thirteen; and from that number not less than seven, nor more than nine names as Congress shall direct, shall in the presence of Congress be drawn out by lot, and the persons whose names shall be so drawn or any five of them, shall be commissioners or judges, to hear and finally determine the controversy, so always as a major part of the judges who shall hear the cause shall agree in the determination: and if either party shall neglect to attend at the day appointed, without showing reasons, which Congress shall judge sufficient, or being present shall refuse to strike, the Congress shall proceed to nominate three persons out of each State, and the secretary of Congress shall strike in behalf of such party absent or refusing; and the judgement and sentence of the court to be appointed, in the manner before prescribed, shall be final and conclusive; and if any of the parties shall refuse to submit to the authority of such court, or to appear or defend their claim or cause, the court shall nevertheless proceed to pronounce sentence, or judgement, which shall in like manner be final and decisive, the judgement or sentence and other proceedings being in either case transmitted to Congress, and lodged among the acts of Congress for the security of the parties concerned: provided that every commissioner, before he sits in judgement, shall take an oath to be administered by one of the judges of the supreme or superior court of the State, where the cause shall be tried, 'well and truly to hear and determine the matter in question, according to the best of his judgement, without favor, affection or hope of reward': provided also, that no State shall be deprived of territory for the benefit of the United States.

All controversies concerning the private right of soil claimed under different grants of two or more States, whose jurisdictions as they may respect such lands, and the States which passed such grants are adjusted, the said grants or either of them being at the same time claimed to have originated antecedent to such settlement of jurisdiction, shall on the petition of either party to the Congress of the United States, be finally determined as near as may be in the same manner as is before prescribed for deciding disputes respecting territorial jurisdiction between different States.

The United States in Congress assembled shall also have the sole and exclusive right and power of regulating the alloy and value of coin struck by their own authority, or by that of the respective States—fixing the standards of weights and measures throughout the United States—regulating the trade and managing all affairs with the Indians, not members of any of the States, provided that the legislative right of any State within its own limits be not infringed or violated—establishing or regulating post offices from one State to another, throughout all the United States, and exacting such postage on the papers passing through the same as may be requisite to defray the expenses of the said office—appointing all officers of the land forces, in the service of the United States, excepting regimental officers—appointing all the officers of the naval forces, and commissioning all officers whatever in the service of the United States—making rules for the government and regulation of the said land and naval forces, and directing their operations.

Those who drafted the Articles of Confederation anticipated certain problems would arise, so the officers of the armed forces above the level of colonel and all naval officers were to be appointed by Congress. In addition, Congress was charged with establishing both standard weights and measures (essential to a society that was just on the cusp of becoming industrialized) and interstate post offices that could charge for postage in order to defray their expenses.

The Articles spelled out how the Congress should, from among the delegates, pick a presiding officer—hence the term "president." They also spelled out how, in the event of war, additional members of the armed forces could be raised in the event a state could not meet its quota.

On November 5, 1781, Charles Thompson, the secretary of the Congress, sent a letter to George Washington (who was in Virginia negotiating the surrender of General Cornwallis) informing him that John Hanson, a Maryland delegate, had been elected the first president of the Congress under the Articles of Confederation.

The United States in Congress assembled shall have authority to appoint a committee, to sit in the recess of Congress, to be denominated 'A Committee of the States', and to consist of one delegate from each State; and to appoint such other committees and civil officers as may be necessary for managing the general affairs of the United States under their direction—**to appoint one of their members to preside**, provided that no person be allowed to serve in the office of president more than one year in any term of three years; to ascertain the necessary sums of money to be raised for the service of the United States, and to appropriate and apply the same for defraying the public expenses—to borrow money, or emit bills on the credit of the United States, transmitting every half-year to the respective States an account of the sums of money so borrowed or emitted—to build and equip a navy—to agree upon the number of land forces, and to make requisitions from each State for its quota, in proportion to the number of white inhabitants in such State; which requisition shall be binding, and thereupon the legislature of each State shall appoint the regimental officers, raise the men and cloath, arm and equip them in a solid-like manner, at the expense of the United States; and the officers and men so cloathed, armed and equipped shall march to the place appointed, and within the time agreed on by the United States in Congress assembled. But if the United States in Congress assembled shall, on consideration of circumstances judge proper that any State should not raise men, or should raise a smaller number of men than the quota thereof, such extra number shall be raised, officered, cloathed, armed and equipped in the same manner as the quota of each State, unless the legislature of such State shall judge that such extra number cannot be safely spread out in the same, in which case they shall raise, officer, cloath, arm and equip as many of such extra number as they judge can be safely spared. And the officers and men so cloathed, armed, and equipped, shall march to the place appointed, and within the time agreed on by the united States in congress assembled.

The united States in congress assembled shall never engage in a war, nor grant letters of marque or reprisal in time of peace, nor enter into any treaties or alliances, nor coin money, nor regulate the value thereof, nor ascertain the sums and expenses necessary for the defense and welfare of the United States, or any of them, nor emit bills, nor borrow money on the credit of the united States, nor appropriate money, nor agree upon the number of vessels of war, to be built or purchased, or the number of land or sea forces to be raised, nor appoint a commander in chief of the army or navy, **unless nine States assent to the same**: nor shall a question on any other point, except for adjourning from day to day be determined, unless by the votes of the majority of the united States in congress assembled.

The congress of the united States shall have power to adjourn to any time within the year, and to any place within the united States, so that no period of adjournment be for a longer duration than the space of six months, and **shall publish the journal of their proceedings monthly, except such parts thereof relating to treaties, alliances or military operations, as in their judgement require secrecy**; and the yeas and nays of the delegates of each State on any question shall be entered on the journal, when it is desired by any delegates of a State, or any of them, at his or their request shall be furnished with a transcript of the said journal, except such parts as are above excepted, to lay before the legislatures of the several States.

ARTICLE X. The committee of the States, or any nine of them, shall be authorized to execute, **in the recess of congress**, such of the powers of congress as the united States in congress assembled, by the consent of the nine States, shall from time to time think expedient to vest them with; provided that no power be delegated to the said Committee, for the exercise of which, by the articles of confederation, **the voice of nine States in the Congress of the United States assembled be requisite.**

For specific purposes, like those enumerated in this paragraph, or when the Congress was not in session, the agreement of nine states out of thirteen was sufficient to do things like coining money or declaring war. However, to alter or correct the Articles, all the states had to agree.

The transparency arguments of Wikileaks notwithstanding, it was recognized as early as the Articles of Confederation that some of the work of government would at times require secrecy. Except for those matters, the Congress was charged with maintaining a record of its proceedings. This provision, which was incorporated into the Constitution as well, forms the basis for keeping records of Congressional proceedings since the country began, and for their actual publication, as the *Congressional Record*, since 1873.

The Articles of Confederation require a vote of nine states, or two-thirds of the thirteen members, for passage of most important matters. But there is no provision for changing this number should the number of states increase.

This provision was an open invitation for the English-speaking provinces of Canada to join the United States without requiring a vote of the Congress. Any other territory that wanted to join would require the approval of the delegates from nine states.

The Congress obligated itself to pay the debts of the United States, but did not give itself the authority to raise the funds with which to pay them. It could assess the states for these funds, but the states would have to raise them and pay them over.

The Articles of Confederation could not be altered except by an agreement in the Congress, which was then submitted for ratification by the legislatures of *all* the member states. This created an inherent problem with the reference to the number "nine," rather than a two-thirds majority, for congressional action. The U.S. Constitution avoided such finite numbers, making it easier for the country to grow without extensive technical corrections to the basic governing document.

ARTICLE XI. Canada acceding to this confederation, and adjoining in the measures of the united States, shall be admitted into, and entitled to all the advantages of this union; but no other colony shall be admitted into the same, unless such admission be agreed to by nine States.

ARTICLE XII. All bills of credit emitted, monies borrowed, and debts contracted by, or under the authority of congress, before the assembling of the united States, in pursuance of the present confederation, shall be deemed and considered as a charge against the United States, for payment and satisfaction whereof the said united States, and the public faith are hereby solemnly pledged.

ARTICLE XIII. Every State shall abide by the determination of the united States in congress assembled, on all questions which by this confederation are submitted to them. And the Articles of this confederation shall be inviolably observed by every State, and the union shall be perpetual; nor shall any alteration at any time hereafter be made in any of them; unless such alteration be agreed to in a congress of the united States, and be afterwards confirmed by the legislatures of every State.

And Whereas it hath pleased the Great Governor of the World to incline the hearts of the legislatures we respectively represent in Congress, to approve of, and to authorize us to ratify the said articles of confederation and perpetual union. Know Ye that we the undersigned delegates, by virtue of the power and authority to us given for that purpose, do by these presents, in the name and in behalf of our respective constituents, fully and entirely ratify and confirm each and every of the said articles of confederation and perpetual union, and all and singular the matters and things therein contained: And we do further solemnly plight and engage the faith of our respective constituents, that they shall abide by the determinations of the united States in congress assembled, on all questions, which by the said confederation are submitted to them. And that the articles thereof shall be inviolably observed by the States we respectively represent, and that the union shall be perpetual.

In Witness whereof we have hereunto set our hands in Congress. Done at Philadelphia in the State of Pennsylvania the ninth Day of July in the Year of our Lord one thousand seven Hundred and Seventy-eight, and in the Third Year of the independence of America.

On the part and behalf of the State of New Hampshire:

Josiah Bartlett

John Wentworth Junr. August 8th 1778

Josiah Bartlett, who also signed the Declaration of Independence, served as governor of New Hampshire, and also served as a judge and as a member of the New Hampshire Supreme Court. However, he was not a lawyer, but a practicing physician for almost half a century. The fictional president on the television series *The West Wing* was named for him, and was ostensibly his descendant.

On the part and behalf of The State of Massachusetts Bay:

John Hancock

Samuel Adams

Elbridge Gerry

Francis Dana

James Lovell

Samuel Holten

John Hancock, as president of the Continental Congress from 1775 to 1777, was the first to sign the original copy of the Declaration of Independence (and later the official printed version, or "engrossed copy" on which all the delegates' signatures also appeared).

Samuel Adams, one of the leaders of the American Revolution, also signed the Declaration of Independence. Among the offices he held in his native Massachusetts was the post of governor of Massachusetts from 1793 to 1797.

Elbridge Gerry, who also signed the Declaration of Independence, later refused to sign the Constitution because it did not contain a bill of rights. He served as governor of Massachusetts, and his name is forever associated with manipulative redistricting because one electoral district created during his term looked so much like a lizard that it gave rise to the term "gerrymander."

On the part and behalf of the State of Rhode Island and Providence Plantations:

William Ellery

Henry Marchant

John Collins

William Ellery also signed the Declaration of Independence. A lawyer who served on the Rhode Island Supreme Court, he was appointed collector of customs for the Newport District by President George Washington in 1790, a post he held for the rest of his life. He also served as clerk of the Rhode Island General Assembly.

On the part and behalf of the State of Connecticut:

Roger Sherman

Samuel Huntington

Oliver Wolcott

Titus Hosmer

Andrew Adams

Roger Sherman affixed his signature to the Declaration of Independence, the Articles of Confederation, and the Constitution. He later represented Connecticut in both the U.S. Senate and the U.S. House of Representatives.

Samuel Huntington also signed the Declaration of Independence. He served as president of the Continental Congress from 1779 to 1781.

Oliver Wolcott was also a signer of the Declaration of Independence. He was a Federalist, and served as the fourth governor of the state of Connecticut.

On the Part and Behalf of the State of New York:

James Duane

Francis Lewis

Wm Duer

Gouv Morris

Francis Lewis also signed the Declaration of Independence. A native of Wales, he moved to the colony of New York in 1734 when he was twenty-one.

On the Part and in Behalf of the State of New Jersey, November 26, 1778.

Jno Witherspoon

Nath. Scudder

John Witherspoon, a native of Scotland, emigrated to New Jersey in 1768 to become president of what would later be known as Princeton University. He signed both the Articles of Confederation and the Declaration of Independence, and was the only active clergyman to do so.

Robert Morris, born in Liverpool, England, came to the colonies at the age of thirteen. He became a merchant in Philadelphia, and was signatory to the Declaration of Independence, the Articles of Confederation, and the Constitution. He later served as a U.S. senator from Pennsylvania.

Thomas McKean was also a signatory of the Declaration of Independence. He was a delegate to the Continental Congress from Delaware, and served six months as president of the Continental Congress. He later served Pennsylvania as chief justice and then as governor.

John Dickinson, who served both as president of Delaware and president of Pennsylvania, represented first Pennsylvania and later Delaware in the Continental Congress. Believing that America's dispute was with parliament, rather than with the king, he did not sign the Declaration of Independence, but later signed both the Articles of Confederation and the Constitution.

Daniel Carroll was one of five men to sign both the Articles of Confederation and the U.S. Constitution. He then participated actively in the ratification process in Maryland, and later served in the First Congress as a representative from Maryland.

On the part and behalf of the State of Pennsylvania:

Robt Morris

Daniel Roberdeau

John Bayard Smith

William Clingan

Joseph Reed 22nd July 1778

On the part and behalf of the State of Delaware:

Tho Mckean February 12, 1779

John Dickinson May 5th 1779

Nicholas Van Dyke

On the part and behalf of the State of Maryland:

John Hanson March 1 1781

Daniel Carroll

On the Part and Behalf of the State of Virginia:

Richard Henry Lee

John Banister

Thomas Adams

Jno Harvie

Francis Lightfoot Lee

On the part and Behalf of the State of No Carolina:

John Penn July 21st 1778

Corns Harnett

Jno Williams

On the part and behalf of the State of South Carolina:

Henry Laurens

William Henry Drayton

Jno Mathews

Richd Hutson

Thos Heyward Junr

On the part and behalf of the State of Georgia:

Jno Walton 24th July 1778

Edwd Telfair

Edwd Langworthy

Richard Henry Lee served in the Second Continental Congress and there moved that the colonies declare their independence from England. He was a signatory to the Declaration of Independence as well as the Articles of Confederation. He later served as a U.S. senator from Virginia, and while doing so, served six months as president pro tempore of the U.S. Senate.

Francis Lightfoot Lee was the younger brother of Richard Henry Lee and like him, was a signatory to both the Declaration of Independence and the Articles of Confederation. Francis Lightfoot Lee served as a member of the Virginia House of Burgesses as well.

These Articles went through several drafts and were finally ratified by the Continental Congress on November 15, 1777; they were then sent to the states for ratification. In the meantime, the Continental Congress conducted its business as though the rules had been ratified. After Maryland, the last state to do so, ratified the Articles on March 1, 1781, they became the legal basis for the alliance of states that termed itself the United States of America.

What Ratifying the Articles of Confederation Meant

Joining the Confederation created, according to the document, a *perpetual* union. Future states could join, although the affirmative votes of at least nine member states were required for their admission. The document was clear that each state retained its autonomy and could create—or continue to operate under—its own laws.

In stressing the autonomy of the states, the seeds were sown for some of the political battles that sparked the Civil War and continue, to a certain extent, into the twenty-first century. The Constitution would lean more heavily toward a strong central government, though it still notes (in the Tenth Amendment) that the powers not specifically granted by the Constitution to that central government are reserved to the states (or to their people).

The Articles of Confederation created a Congress that would loosely govern the alliance. In that Congress, each state had only one vote, although it was allotted at least two and no more than seven members.

What the Articles Required of the States

The Articles of Confederation provided that there would be free entry of people from one state to another (except for "paupers, vagabonds, and fugitives from justice"). The citizens of one state possessed the freedoms granted to citizens of any state into which they crossed, but criminals escaping across state lines could be subject to extradition back to the state in which their crime had been committed.

The Articles also provided for "full faith and credit" of government and judicial rulings of one state in all the others. There was also a guarantee of free speech in the Articles, but it specified that it was for things said in Congress.

Powers of the Central Government under the Articles

Only the Congress—the central government created by the Articles of Confederation—was allowed to declare war or to conduct foreign *policy*, but this Congress had no power to regulate foreign or interstate *trade*. It could contract for and pay the country's debts, and the war debts that had been incurred by the fledgling country were specifically affirmed, but the national Congress didn't have the power to raise that money through taxes. It could, instead, call for funds to be raised by the various state legislatures, but it had no power to enforce such requests. The share of the national debt that each state owed was to be apportioned according to the value of the land in that state.

Operating as an alliance of states instead of as a nation, and with that alliance governed by a committee (the Congress), the United States did not function efficiently, and people began to call for revisions of the Articles. Eventually, there was a call for a convention to assemble on May 14, 1787, in Philadelphia, to address defects in the Articles. However, it was two weeks after that date before a quorum of seven states was present. In the interim, the delegates from Virginia who were already there put together a plan for drafting a wholly new constitution for the country.

The American Tradition of Written Charters

Many of the earliest American colonies were business ventures, or were created under royal grant. Most of the earliest colonists were literate men who expected to have written documentation of their right to settle in the new land in the same way someone today would expect a lease for an apartment or a deed for a house. When they arrived—or sometimes before—they often created written agreements among themselves.

In the case of the Mayflower Compact, this was just a bare-bones document by which the forty-one males settling in Plymouth Colony agreed to abide by such rules as they would make, together, for the good of all members. They felt they needed a written agreement because their point of landing was on shaky legal grounds: They had a land patent from the London Virginia Company to settle at the mouth of the Hudson River, but had been blown off course beyond the area to which the London Virginia Company had any claim.

ESSENTIAL

The Mayflower Compact was an agreement that the colony would be governed like an English town. It did not really resolve the legal right of the colonists to settle where they had landed, but having a document seemed to make those who were nervous about settling in Massachusetts feel better about doing so.

Contracts, compacts, and royal grants were not the only documents under which the colonies operated. Petitions, such as the Flushing Remonstrance (to Peter Stuyvesant, Governor of New Amsterdam, who had banned Quaker worship in the Dutch colony he ran) were common as well, as were written protests and appeals to the companies in Europe that had sponsored various settlements. (Colonists in New Amsterdam often went over Stuyvesant's head, writing to his bosses, the Dutch West India Company, back in Holland.) So the idea that the British colonies in North America would first write their Declaration of Independence and then the mutual agreement—the Articles of Confederation—that would bind them to each other in a defense pact and commercial alliance, was totally in character.

Britain's Unwritten Constitution

The British system of government does not have a basic central document to which it can refer, so it is often termed an "unwritten constitution." In truth, it consists of a body of writings going back a thousand years. These documents include written court decisions, acts of Parliament, and the various versions of the Magna Carta.

The Magna Carta (Latin for "Great Charter") created a committee of barons who could confiscate the king's castles if he failed to comply with the other conditions of the charter, and hold them until he had complied. Among those provisions were such things as the king not compelling a widow to marry, not requiring minors to pay interest during their minority on debts they inherited from their parents, and not requiring the children of barons to buy their inheritance from the crown. But the primary rights it granted were:

- Independence to the Church of England (at that time, still the Catholic church) from the king's interference.
- "Ancient liberties and customs" to the City of London and such other towns and boroughs that had been governing themselves according to custom.
- Due process for freemen (and, of course, nobles). In other words, no freeman could be deprived of life, liberty, or property without a trial by a jury of his peers.

Though kings almost immediately began to re-establish their royal prerogative against the barons' council, the main points guaranteed by the Magna Carta, and many of the lesser ones, became codified as laws.

FACT

The group of English barons who forcibly persuaded King John to sign the Magna Carta were looking to curtail the arbitrary nature of his reign—but only as it applied to nobles and the freemen they wanted to back them up. Serfs did not gain any rights under this "Great Charter."

When the American colonists began to stand up to the crown, they initially demanded "the rights of Englishmen"—those rights that had stemmed from the Magna Carta and had since become established parts of the laws of England, either through codification or from written legal decisions. Since many of those colonists had originally come from—or descended from people who had come from—the British Isles, they were not happy to be deprived of those rights merely by virtue of having traveled overseas to a new land.

Operating Under the Articles of Confederation

Coming hard on the heels of the Declaration of Independence, the Articles of Confederation governed the fledgling United States from the time they were drafted until the Constitution was ratified. There were thirteen Articles and a Preamble that together provided the basic rules for the alliance of states.

Unlike the Preamble to the Constitution, which sets forth the purposes of that document, the preamble to the Articles of Confederation merely stated the names of the thirteen colonies and that they were joining together in confederation and perpetual union. Any statement of purpose is not set forth until Article III, which speaks of joining together for common defense, security of their liberties, and "mutual and general welfare" against any attacks.

The states—that term was used by the former British colonies in the sense of "nation" rather than of a subdivision of a nation—were particularly jealous of their own authority, and were not willing to surrender it to any central government. After all, many of them believed that it was the crown and parliament—the epitome of "central government"—that had deprived them of their rights. So directly after that first Article (the one that gave the nascent country its name), the second Article (which was, perhaps, first in order of importance to those who drafted it) declared the rights that the states would be keeping: "Each State retains its sovereignty, freedom, and independence, and every power, jurisdiction, and right, which is not by this confederation expressly delegated to the United States."

FACT

Individual liberties were less important to the drafters of the Articles of Confederation than were the rights of the states. Indeed, individual liberties are almost never mentioned, although Article IV establishes open borders between states by providing for freedom of movement for the citizens of one state to move to any other. It also provides that citizens of one state, while in another state, would have the rights that anyone living there would have.

The Articles of Confederation were primarily devoted to defining the roles of the central government in relation to the states. The central government was "the united States in congress assembled," and everything was governed by consensus of that Congress (a vote of at least nine of the thirteen states was usually required, and sometimes—such as for the ratification of amendments—unanimity). When the Congress was in recess, which could happen for up to six months out of any year, the country would be governed by a committee consisting of one delegate from each state that the Congress had appointed from among the delegates and empowered to act in its stead.

ALERT

The Articles of Confederation used the word "congress" to mean assembling as a group. Thus "the united States in congress assembled" meant the states had, by their representatives, gathered together to conduct the business of government. The term "congress" eventually came to mean the legislative assembly of the government itself, as opposed to the fact that its members had gathered.

The Articles of Confederation did set forth a number of exclusive areas of responsibility of the central government that eventually found their way into the Constitution. These included declaring war, making foreign policy, and negotiating treaties, including peace treaties. The Congress was the sole authority for judging disputes between states. It had the right to fix standards of weights and measures, establish post offices, and regulate trade with Indians who were not members of any states—in other words, with the tribes of the frontier and any who had not assimilated. The Congress also was directed to publish a journal of its proceedings (except for secret treaty negotiations), including a record of its votes.

FACT

However, most of the Articles of Confederation set forth the rights and duties of the states as opposed to those of the Congress of states. The one thing that it stressed was that this alliance was perpetual, wording that does *not* find its way into the Constitution.

Arguments for and Against a Federal System

During the decade that the newly independent country operated under the Articles of Confederation, a number of problems arose that revealed flaws in that document. Founding Father (and later U.S. President) James Madison set down a number of them in his *Vices of the Political System of the United States*, published in April of 1787. Among the problems:

- Changes to the Articles required the unanimous approval of all of the state legislatures, which was almost impossible to achieve.
- Congress had no independent source of income, so it could not effectively borrow money from foreign countries. It asked for the right to collect duties on imports, but the state legislatures did not grant that.
- Congress did not have the right to regulate foreign trade, so it could not counter the discriminatory policies of other countries (particularly Britain) against U.S. merchants.

Federalist Arguments

The Federalists favored the idea of a functioning central government, strong enough to act on behalf of the American states in foreign relations (including trade policy and regulation), with the power to raise armies, wage war, and pay for all those things through tax levies and borrowing (often by means of bonds). They argued for a federal court system, a strong executive, and a separate legislative branch, each of which would be independent of the other two. Interestingly, the Federalists often argued against a bill of rights out of fear that these might come to be interpreted as being a *limiting* list of individual rights. This is the basis for the Ninth Amendment.

ALERT

The term "Federalist" takes on different meanings over the first half-century or so of the nation's existence. In the beginning, it meant those who supported the Constitution, favoring a strong central government. Later, it became the name of a party that existed from approximately 1792 to 1820. Many of those who had favored the passage of the Constitution later broke with each other over other policy disputes, and often because of personality conflicts.

Among the most prominent Federalists (when the term is used to mean those who favored the adoption of the Constitution) were James Madison, Alexander Hamilton, and John Jay. The three of them, writing under the joint pen name Publius, were the authors of the Federalist Papers. These essays—arguments for the ratification of the Constitution and the endorsement of the federal system created by the Constitution—are often cited in legal arguments as to the original intent of the framers, but they are not legal documents and do not have the power of law.

While it is often assumed that George Washington appeared to favor a Federalist philosophy, he refused to ally himself with any political faction or party during his term as president. The Federalist Party, dominated by the economic policies of Alexander Hamilton, faded away by around 1820. John Adams was the only Federalist president.

Anti-Federalist Arguments

The Anti-Federalists feared that a strong central government would become a threat to the rights of individuals. They were also concerned that a strong executive would take on the powers of a monarch and act to shrink or destroy individual liberties. The term they used at the time was "tyrant," although today they might express similar fears of dictators or strongmen.

Although ratification of the Constitution had to be on an up or down vote, with no qualifying language, Anti-Federalist sentiments influenced a large number of the states. As a result, ratification was frequently accompanied by a recommendation that a statement of individual rights be incorporated into the Constitution. The result was that the Amendments that became the Bill of Rights were proposed and sent to the states for ratification almost as soon as the Constitution itself was ratified.

Among the noted Anti-Federalists were George Mason, Patrick Henry, Samuel Adams, Richard Henry Lee, and future president James Monroe.

The Constitutions of the States

The constitutions of the fifty states that make up the United States of America are unique documents. They often cover many more areas of everyday life than does the Federal Constitution. State constitutions may, for example, designate cabinet departments where the U.S. Consitution does not. There are many areas that the United States Constitution does not address, leaving them to be covered by laws or regulations, rather than the core document. A state constitution may express a philosophy or define categories of crimes, or even specify requirements for marriages and divorces.

And while the constitutions of the states may follow the federal pattern of a bicameral legislature, an executive branch, and a judiciary, they are not required to do so. Indeed, while the Constitution requires that the United States guarantee a "republican form of government" to each of the states, there is some question as to what "republican" (with a lowercase *r*) actually means, other than that the people (or some of them) control the government, and that the president serve for a fixed term and be selected for, rather than inherit, the post.

FACT

Nebraska has a unicameral legislature—there is only one chamber, rather than an upper and lower house. Its members call themselves "senators" but it has no senate, just a body termed the "legislature." It is also unique in that its members are elected without identifying their party affiliation.

Some states, like Vermont and New Hampshire, have had their state constitutions almost as long as the federal government. (The constitution of Massachusetts is even older than the U.S. Constitution, dating from 1780!) Some states, like Wisconsin, Arizona, and Hawaii, have had the same constitution since their admission to the Union. Other states, like Connecticut, Georgia, and Louisiana, have replaced earlier constitutions in recent years.

Written Constitutions: Now an International Norm

The idea of creating a national government from scratch, with all of the details of how to run it in the form of a basic charter, was a novel one when the United States first attempted it. Written charters gave the United States the basic premises on which it has functioned for more than two centuries, after only one do-over, which was the replacement of the Articles of Confederation by the Constitution. (France has tried to function under more than a dozen constitutions over approximately the same period of time.)

Today, most countries are governed by core documents that give rise to the rest of their laws. Whenever a country obtains its independence or undergoes a change of governmental philosophy, it is likely to create a written constitution under which it will function. The United States Constitution has been the inspiration for these documents, even those that do not follow its construction.

A constitution can be whatever a country wants it to be. But what it always does, at base, is set up the rules by which the people who live under it have—at least in name—agreed to be governed.

CHAPTER 2

The Preamble

The Preamble to the U.S. Constitution sets forth the reasons for the creation of the document. Since the Constitution replaces but does not specifically revoke the Articles of Confederation, you should read it as a document that builds on, and reacts to, the Articles. If you look at it that way—even though the Constitution stands alone—you can understand why the drafters would have used a phrase like "a more perfect union," or why speaking of "people" rather than of "states" is important to consider.

The Preamble reads as follows:

We the People of the United States, in Order to form a more perfect Union, establish Justice, insure domestic Tranquility, provide for the common defence, promote the general Welfare, and secure the Blessings of Liberty to ourselves and our Posterity, do ordain and establish this Constitution for the United States of America.

Who Were the "United States"?

The original thirteen British colonies that rebelled against the Crown and formed the United States were Connecticut, Delaware, Georgia, Maryland, Massachusetts, New Hampshire, New Jersey, New York, North Carolina, Pennsylvania, South Carolina, Rhode Island, and Virginia. What is today the state of Maine was part of Massachusetts when the country was formed. The Articles of Confederation had made provision for the colonies of Eastern Canada to join the United States, but none chose to do so.

FACT

Separated from Massachusetts by New Hampshire, the state of Maine was admitted to the Union in 1820 as part of the Missouri Compromise of that year. By admitting Maine as a free state and Missouri as a slave state, parity between the number of free states and of slave states was retained.

The Constitution was created in the name of the *people* of the United States and not of the states themselves. This wording suggests a shift from emphasis on the states (in the Articles of Confederation) to emphasis on the citizens (in the Constitution). Despite this shift, the fact that the Senate represents the *states*, rather than the people, is a carryover from what came before. If you think of it that way, you can see how sometimes the states are more interested in their own standing than that of their citizens, and you can see that the seeds of the Civil War—fought partially in the name of states' rights—lay in the very fabric of the Constitution.

The Constitutional Convention

On February 21, 1787, the Continental Congress called for "a Convention of delegates," who would be appointed by the individual states they represented, to meet in Philadelphia on the "second Monday in May" (May 14) "for the sole and express purpose of revising the Articles of Confederation." In the end they did not revise them, but actually replaced them with a whole new document, the Constitution.

Twelve of the states sent a total of fifty-five delegates (Rhode Island declined to send any delegates), but not all attended the entire session. Only thirty-nine signed the new Constitution.

QUESTION

Who was Jonathan Dayton?
New Jersey's Jonathan Dayton was, at twenty-six, the youngest delegate to the Constitutional Convention. He had fought in the Revolutionary War, afterward becoming a lawyer and serving in the New Jersey Assembly. An ardent Federalist, he was a member of the House of Representatives from 1791 to 1799, rising to Speaker before serving a term in the Senate. He was later indicted, but never tried, for treason for conspiring with Aaron Burr.

The Convention's actual work—theoretically to revise the Articles of Confederation but actually much more drastic—began on May 25, 1787. However, from the outset, the Federalists, led by Alexander Hamilton and James Madison, sought to totally restructure the government of the new country. They prevailed, and the resulting Constitution was signed on September 17, 1787. The Constitution then was sent to the states for ratification by the state legislatures.

A *More Perfect* Union

One of the reasons for drafting the Constitution was "to form a more perfect union." This is a concession from the outset that the original union of the states was less than perfect. It also sets forth five other goals:

- Establishing justice
- Insuring domestic tranquility
- Providing for the common defense
- Promoting the general welfare
- Preserving liberty

In creating the Preamble, the framers were both pledging themselves to lofty goals and acknowledging that problems had occurred under the Articles of Confederation. The aims of the two documents were not so very different. As set forth in Article III of the Articles of Confederation, the states had pledged to "enter into a firm league of friendship with each other, for their common defense, the security of their liberties, and their mutual and general welfare." With the Constitution, they now added the establishment of justice and the preservation of domestic tranquility to that list—and didn't limit the application of those goals to the states.

Establishing Justice

The Articles had been silent as to the establishment of a court system, providing only that the Congress of the Confederation could itself, or by appointing a commission to do so, decide disputes between the states. Although each state had its own court system, there was suspicion that a state court might favor its own citizens against citizens of other states. The Constitution would remedy this by establishing a Supreme Court and allowing for the creation of a system of federal courts to deal with such situations, thus affirming that in the United States, disputes would be settled in courts rather than by government fiat or by individuals taking action on their own.

FACT

Benjamin Franklin of Pennsylvania was the oldest delegate to the Constitutional Convention. Born in 1706, he was eighty-one years old. He suffered from gout and needed to be carried into the chamber in a sedan chair. Despite his age and his declining health, he nevertheless participated actively in the convention that produced the Constitution.

The Articles of Confederation had not given the central government the power to enforce its decisions, nor to raise the money to pay for enforcing them. In their effort to avoid any possible emergence of royal power, they had left a void in the areas of resolving disputes and dealing with crime. The new Constitution would seek to fill this void by creating and funding a judicial system.

Domestic Tranquility

The first article of the Articles of Confederation—after the one that created the name, "the United States"—dealt with the autonomy of the states. It noted specifically that the states would retain any powers not granted to the central government by the Articles.

It is perhaps difficult to believe, looking back from the twenty-first century, how invested in the fortunes of their states the people of the eighteenth century and even the first half of the nineteenth century were. Today, you might resent it when the quarterback from your home team departs for a team in the next state, but you wouldn't think of going to war over it.

QUESTION

What is "domestic tranquility"?
While the phrase may seem a lofty goal, you cannot have a functioning (or "tranquil") society if you cannot rely on established rules by which everyone abides. The desire for this is expressed in that phrase. Where the rule of law prevails, people can rely on basic rights, without being subject to the arbitrary whims of a monarch.

States' rights may still be a rallying cry, but in the modern world, it appears to be more about trying to keep control over some things that the federal government seems to have taken upon itself. But if you were traveling to the next state on vacation, would it really make you happy if you weren't sure whether the aspirin you bought in a store there contained the same formula as the aspirin you normally buy at home? Would you really be happier if you couldn't rely on the safety of a bridge, or the safety in your workplace, while those one state over were totally protected?

The Constitution provided a way to regulate the relationships of the states. And in reality, although the Articles of Confederation were considered more state-centric, some phrases were taken virtually intact from the older document and put into the newer one—for example, the phrase "Full Faith and Credit shall be given in each State to the public Acts, Records, and judicial Proceedings of every other State" in the Constitution is almost identical to a similar phrase in the Articles ("Full faith and credit shall be given, in each of these States, to the records, acts, and judicial proceedings of the courts and magistrates of every other State"). This means that one state must recognize things like legitimate sales, marriages, and judgments that occur in other states.

Providing for the Common Defense

This was part of the reason for the original alliance among the states, and is included in Article III of the Articles of Confederation: "The said States hereby severally enter into a firm league of friendship with each other, for their common defence . . . binding themselves to assist each other against all force offered to, or attacks made upon them, or any of them. . . ." They knew that if they didn't stand together against England—or the established military might of any of the other European powers, for that matter—their independence wouldn't last long. And they knew that any one state might need assistance from the others in defending itself from attacks by Native Americans on the borders.

Promoting the General Welfare

The General Welfare clause of the Preamble is echoed in the enumeration of the powers of Congress in Article I, Section 8, where it says that "The Congress shall have Power To . . . provide for the common Defence and general Welfare of the United States . . . ." This was the basis for much of the social legislation enacted in the twentieth century, and there are those who argue that such legislation is not among the powers the Constitution grants to Congress. However, the final enumerated clause of Section 8 says that Congress can "make all Laws which shall be necessary and proper for carrying into

Execution the foregoing Powers, and all other Powers vested by this Constitution in the Government of the United States. . . ."

Is "providing for the general welfare" a modern concept?
It can be argued that "providing for the general welfare" covers things as basic as providing lighthouses, bridges, levees, and ferry boats—or the poorhouses and madhouses of Victorian England. It can also be argued that when, according to the Old Testament, Pharaoh laid in a supply of grain over the "seven fat years" to last his people for the "seven lean years" that were coming, he was "providing for the general welfare," carrying the tradition back thousands of years.

There are few who challenge the provision of "common defence" in the same introductory clause in Section 8, although the enumerated powers that follow only allow for raising and supporting *armies* and providing and maintaining a *navy*. An air force and things like missile defense and a coast guard are both things the enumerated powers don't provide for, but by using the "common defence" provision, it can be argued that these things—and even the CIA—are authorized. The establishment of the Department of Homeland Security is really based in this clause.

So too with the "general welfare" provisions, under which things like the regulation of food and drugs, and the domestic services of the FBI, as well as food stamps and Pell grants for education, not to mention Social Security, probably fall. It can be argued that the general welfare of the American people is premised on such regulations, and that spending on the National Institutes of Health, the Department of Veterans Affairs, the Centers for Disease Control, and the Department of Education is as valid as defense spending, which is authorized in the same sentence.

Securing the Blessings of Liberty

The Articles of Confederation had been drafted with the interests of the separate states in mind. The idea was to preserve the autonomy of the states as opposed to empowering the central government, since the only real experience they'd had with a central government was with an often arbitrary king and the distant Parliament (in which they had no representation) that did his bidding. By the time the Constitution was written, barely a decade later, the drafters were beginning to be as concerned with the rights of individuals as with the autonomy of states. While not surrendering that autonomy, they focused on the role and function of a central national government so that the states, joined together, would form a country, rather than an alliance. Part of what that central government could do, the founders saw, would be to protect individuals rather than persecute them, as kings had often done.

In drafting the Articles of Confederation, the framers had been very wary of creating a central executive with the vast and arbitrary powers of a monarch. Therefore, the Constitution would create an executive branch with the powers equal to and balanced against the Congress and the judiciary.

The specifics of the relationship between individuals and the state emerge in the Constitution. This was not so with the Articles. For example, the Constitution says, "Treason against the United States, shall consist only in levying War against them, or in adhering to their Enemies, giving them Aid and Comfort." It goes on to say that "No Person shall be convicted of Treason unless on the Testimony of two Witnesses to the same overt Act, or on Confession in open Court." This eliminated the kind of secret courts that had been created from time to time in England—and the monarch's "off with his head" attitude.

Indeed, the Constitution, in granting that "The Congress shall have Power to declare the Punishment of Treason," at the same time protects individuals by saying that "no Attainder of Treason shall work Corruption of Blood, or Forfeiture except during the Life of the Person attainted." In other words, there can't be a special bill declaring one particular person guilty of treason, and even if a person is found guilty of treason, the punishment for the sins of a father may not be exacted from his children. This was a very modern concept in the eighteenth century.

A Bare-Bones Outline

The U.S. Constitution is, by word count, the shortest operative Constitution in use today. It was meant to be that way, creating broad statements that would define the new country's governing philosophy while allowing for the creation of laws and regulations—more easily changed as times and circumstances required—to address the details of day-to-day life.

FACT

The Constitution does not contain any references to crimes, except to define treason, and to say that you can't be prosecuted for acts made criminal after you committed them. It contains no reference to marriage, other than saying that each state shall grant "full faith and credit" to the legal acts, like a marriage or adoption—or a sale of goods—conducted in another state. Such matters are left to laws passed by the states or, if there is a Constitutional provision authorizing them, the Congress.

The Constitution serves as the spinal column of the nation. Its published laws (created by Congress under the authority of the Constitution) serve as its bones, while its flesh is composed of a written body of cases decided by courts that have applied those broad principles to individual circumstances. In doing so, these cases provide examples—not unlike Biblical parables—from which people can extrapolate to determine the meanings and precise applications of various broad laws. The average citizen doesn't have to know a thousand little rules in order to function; you just need to understand the general principles and think about how they would apply in any given situation. Trials and other judicial proceedings exist to determine whether the general principle was applied correctly.

The Bill of Rights and Individual Freedoms

Individual freedoms were very important to the drafters of the Constitution, but debating the breadth of the freedoms an individual should possess threatened to hold up the passage of the document as a whole. As part of the argument for a bare-bones structure, the Federalists maintained that the powers of the government were limited to those granted by the Constitution. Thus they saw no need to list the rights that anyone should have—a citizen of the United States had every right the Constitution hadn't granted to the government.

QUESTION

Who was George Mason?
George Mason, a delegate to the Constitutional Convention from Virginia, had helped create Virginia's Declaration of Rights. Although he was an activist who favored the adoption of the Federal Constitution, he was so concerned by the absence of a bill of rights in the original document that he refused to sign it.

The Anti-Federalists—the faction that was more wary of a strong central government—thought there ought to be guarantees of certain rights in the Constitution. To remedy what they and even some Federalists had seen as a glaring lack, the first Congress under the new Constitution immediately drafted a series of amendments to the Constitution that became the Bill of Rights sent out to the states for approval. There were twelve proposed amendments. Ten of them were ratified by the states within two years. An eleventh was ratified some 200 years later, becoming the Twenty-Seventh Amendment, which says, in essence, that a congressional pay raise will apply to the next Congress, not to the Congress that passes it. (The twelfth one, dealing with the ratio of constituents to representatives, has never been ratified.)

The ten amendments that have been part of the supreme law of the land since 1791 guarantee, among other things, freedom of speech, religion, the press, and assembly, and the right against self-incrimination. They are as succinct as the rest of the Constitution, and their interpretation by various courts has often expanded on how they apply under various circumstances, such as weighing when their use by one person may impinge on the rights of another. Their existence makes up another part of the difference between the Articles of Confederation and the Constitution.

The Constitution of the United States of America

We the People of the United States, in Order to form a more perfect Union, establish Justice, insure domestic Tranquility, provide for the common defence, promote the general Welfare, and secure the Blessings of Liberty to ourselves and our Posterity, do ordain and establish this Constitution for the United States of America.

Article. I.

SECTION. 1.
All legislative Powers herein granted shall be vested in a Congress of the United States, which shall consist of a Senate and House of Representatives.

SECTION. 2.
The House of Representatives shall be composed of Members chosen every second Year by the People of the several States, and the Electors in each State shall have the Qualifications requisite for Electors of the most numerous Branch of the State Legislature.

No Person shall be a Representative who shall not have attained to the Age of twenty five Years, and been seven Years a Citizen of the United States, and who shall not, when elected, be an Inhabitant of that State in which he shall be chosen.

Unlike the Declaration of Independence, which was drafted in the name of "one people" (a nation) that intends to dissolve its bonds with another, or the Articles of Confederation, which were drafted by the representatives of the states (nations) that were uniting in an alliance, the Constitution is declared to have been created by the *people* who make up the United States.

Although all three branches of the government were meant to check and balance each other, the Founders listed the legislative branch first and devoted the most detail to it.

The House of Representatives consists of representatives of the people, serving for short, two-year terms, whose electors are the same people who elect members of the state legislature. These are the "citizen representatives," meant to be chosen by the people from among themselves, to act in their interest.

Representatives and direct Taxes shall be apportioned among the several States which may be included within this Union, according to their respective Numbers, which shall be determined by adding to the whole Number of free Persons, including those bound to Service for a Term of Years, and excluding Indians not taxed, three fifths of all other Persons. The actual Enumeration shall be made within three Years after the first Meeting of the Congress of the United States, and within every subsequent Term of ten Years, in such Manner as they shall by Law direct. The Number of Representatives shall not exceed one for every thirty Thousand, but each State shall have at Least one Representative; and until such enumeration shall be made, the State of New Hampshire shall be entitled to chuse three, Massachusetts eight, Rhode-Island and Providence Plantations one, Connecticut five, New-York six, New Jersey four, Pennsylvania eight, Delaware one, Maryland six, Virginia ten, North Carolina five, South Carolina five, and Georgia three.

When vacancies happen in the Representation from any State, the Executive Authority thereof shall issue Writs of Election to fill such Vacancies.

The House of Representatives shall chuse their Speaker and other Officers; and shall have the sole Power of Impeachment.

SECTION. 3.
The Senate of the United States shall be composed of two Senators from each State, chosen by the Legislature thereof for six Years; and each Senator shall have one Vote.

Immediately after they shall be assembled in Consequence of the first Election, they shall be divided as equally as may be into three Classes. The Seats of the Senators of the first Class shall be vacated at the Expiration of the second Year, of the

This section was voided by the Fourteenth Amendment, passed in 1866 and ratified in 1868. The "three-fifths" clause was a euphemism so that the word "slave" would not find its way into the charter of a country that had declared itself to exist on the premise that "all men are created equal" with the right to "life, liberty, and the pursuit of happiness."

The Constitution was ratified in 1787, and the census has been counted every year that ends in a zero since 1790. Having an accurate count of the population assures that the allotment of representatives will be as fair as possible.

The members of the House—not just of the majority party—choose the Speaker and such other officers, like sergeant at arms, as they decide they need. There is no mention of political parties in the Constitution.

The Seventeenth Amendment, passed in 1912 and ratified in 1913, provided for direct election of senators. When vacancies occur, replacements are to be chosen by special elections scheduled according to state law, although governors may make interim appointments so that the state is fully represented until an election can take place.

second Class at the Expiration of the fourth Year, and of the third Class at the Expiration of the sixth Year, so that one third may be chosen every second Year; and if Vacancies happen by Resignation, or otherwise, during the Recess of the Legislature of any State, the Executive thereof may make temporary Appointments until the next Meeting of the Legislature, which shall then fill such Vacancies.

No Person shall be a Senator who shall not have attained to the Age of thirty Years, and been nine Years a Citizen of the United States, and who shall not, when elected, be an Inhabitant of that State for which he shall be chosen.

The Vice President of the United States shall be President of the Senate, but shall have no Vote, unless they be equally divided.

The members of the Senate choose their own officers, and again, no mention is made of political parties, which are not referenced in the Constitution.

The Senate shall chuse their other Officers, and also a President pro tempore, in the Absence of the Vice President, or when he shall exercise the Office of President of the United States.

There have been only two presidential impeachment trials, one of Andrew Johnson in 1868, and one of William Clinton in 1999, so the chief justice has been required to preside only over those two trials. Chief Justice Rehnquist had a special robe created for him to wear during the Clinton impeachment trial. Inspired by a costume he had seen in a Gilbert and Sullivan operetta, it had gold stripes on the sleeves.

The Senate shall have the sole Power to try all Impeachments. When sitting for that Purpose, they shall be on Oath or Affirmation. **When the President of the United States is tried, the Chief Justice shall preside:** And no Person shall be convicted without the Concurrence of two thirds of the Members present.

Judgment in Cases of Impeachment shall not extend further than to removal from Office, and disqualification to hold and enjoy any Office of honor, Trust or Profit under the United States: but the Party convicted shall nevertheless be liable and subject to Indictment, Trial, Judgment and Punishment, according to Law.

SECTION. 4.
The Times, Places and Manner of holding Elections for Senators and Representatives, shall be prescribed in each State by the Legislature thereof; but the Congress may at any time by Law make or alter such Regulations, except as to the Places of chusing Senators.

The Congress shall assemble at least once in every Year, and such Meeting shall be on the **first Monday in December**, unless they shall by Law appoint a different Day.

SECTION. 5.
Each House shall be the Judge of the Elections, Returns and Qualifications of its own Members, and a Majority of each shall constitute a Quorum to do Business; but a smaller Number may adjourn from day to day, and may be authorized to compel the Attendance of absent Members, in such Manner, and under such Penalties as each House may provide.

Each House may determine the Rules of its Proceedings, punish its Members for disorderly Behaviour, and, with the Concurrence of two thirds, expel a Member.

Impeachment trials are not limited to presidents; anyone holding appointive or elective office in the United States can be impeached by the House and then tried by the Senate. If the Senate finds someone guilty, the only thing it can do is remove that person from office. However, impeachment is not a bar to an ordinary criminal trial afterward.

Because travel was so difficult in colonial times, there was originally a thirteen-month gap between the elections and the mandatory date Congress had to convene. In fact, a new Congress traditionally convened in March. The Twentieth Amendment, passed in 1932 and ratified in 1933, shortened that to the 3rd of January, only two months after the election.

There is no mention of things like filibusters, cloture, or supermajorities in the Constitution. These things stem from the rules the two houses have created for themselves under this provision, and they can be changed if the members want to change them.

This is a carryover from the Articles of Confederation, and it is the basis for the existence of the *Congressional Record*. The proceedings of all sessions of Congress can be accessed through the Library of Congress, in person or via its website.

The two houses of Congress are required to meet at the same site, and neither house may adjourn for more than three days during a term without the consent of the other—although as a rule, they adjourn for long periods of time throughout the year (with each other's consent).

Unlike members of Parliament, who also serve as "ministers" (the British equivalent of American cabinet officers), members of Congress must resign their seats if they accept another government office.

Each House shall keep a Journal of its Proceedings, and from time to time publish the same, excepting such Parts as may in their Judgment require Secrecy; and the Yeas and Nays of the Members of either House on any question shall, at the Desire of one fifth of those Present, be entered on the Journal.

Neither House, during the Session of Congress, shall, without the Consent of the other, adjourn for more than three days, nor to any other Place than that in which the two Houses shall be sitting.

SECTION. 6.

The Senators and Representatives shall receive a Compensation for their Services, to be ascertained by Law, and paid out of the Treasury of the United States. They shall in all Cases, except Treason, Felony and Breach of the Peace, be privileged from Arrest during their Attendance at the Session of their respective Houses, and in going to and returning from the same; and for any Speech or Debate in either House, they shall not be questioned in any other Place.

No Senator or Representative shall, during the Time for which he was elected, be appointed to any civil Office under the Authority of the United States, which shall have been created, or the Emoluments whereof shall have been encreased during such time; and no Person holding any Office under the United States, shall be a Member of either House during his Continuance in Office.

SECTION. 7.

All Bills for raising Revenue shall originate in the House of Representatives; but the Senate may propose or concur with Amendments as on other Bills.

Every Bill which shall have passed the House of Representatives and the Senate, shall, before it become a Law, be presented to the President of the United States: If he approve he shall sign it, but if not he shall return it, with his Objections to that House in which it shall have originated, who shall enter the Objections at large on their Journal, and proceed to reconsider it. If after such Reconsideration two thirds of that House shall agree to pass the Bill, it shall be sent, together with the Objections, to the other House, by which it shall likewise be reconsidered, and if approved by two thirds of that House, it shall become a Law. But in all such Cases the Votes of both Houses shall be determined by yeas and Nays, and the Names of the Persons voting for and against the Bill shall be entered on the Journal of each House respectively. If any Bill shall not be returned by the President within ten Days (Sundays excepted) after it shall have been presented to him, the Same shall be a Law, in like Manner as if he had signed it, unless the Congress by their Adjournment prevent its Return, in which Case it shall not be a Law.

Every Order, Resolution, or Vote to which the Concurrence of the Senate and House of Representatives may be necessary (except on a question of Adjournment) shall be presented to the President of the United States; and before the Same shall take Effect, shall be approved by him, or being disapproved by him, shall be repassed by two thirds of the Senate and House of Representatives, according to the Rules and Limitations prescribed in the Case of a Bill.

Although the president may propose a budget, authorization for it must originate in the House of Representatives. However, once the House creates an appropriations bill, the Senate can propose changes to it.

Section 8 of Article I deals with the powers of Congress, but Congress has other powers that can be found elsewhere—for example, in Article III, Section 3.

SECTION. 8.

The Congress shall have Power To lay and collect Taxes, Duties, Imposts and Excises, to pay the Debts and provide for the common Defence and general Welfare of the United States; but all Duties, Imposts and Excises shall be uniform throughout the United States;

To borrow Money on the credit of the United States;

To regulate Commerce with foreign Nations, and among the several States, and with the Indian Tribes;

To establish an uniform Rule of Naturalization, and uniform Laws on the subject of Bankruptcies throughout the United States;

To coin Money, regulate the Value thereof, and of foreign Coin, and fix the Standard of Weights and Measures;

To provide for the Punishment of counterfeiting the Securities and current Coin of the United States;

To establish Post Offices and post Roads;

To promote the Progress of Science and useful Arts, by securing for limited Times to Authors and Inventors the exclusive Right to their respective Writings and Discoveries;

To constitute Tribunals inferior to the supreme Court;

To define and punish Piracies and Felonies committed on the high Seas, and Offences against the Law of Nations;

To declare War, grant Letters of Marque and Reprisal, and make Rules concerning Captures on Land and Water;

To raise and support Armies, but no Appropriation of Money to that Use shall be for a longer Term than two Years;

To provide and maintain a Navy;

To make Rules for the Government and Regulation of the land and naval Forces;

To provide for calling forth the Militia to execute the Laws of the Union, suppress Insurrections and repel Invasions;

To provide for organizing, arming, and disciplining, the Militia, and for governing such Part of them as may be employed in the Service of the United States, reserving to the States respectively, the Appointment of the Officers, and the Authority of training the Militia according to the discipline prescribed by Congress;

To exercise exclusive Legislation in all Cases whatsoever, over such District (not exceeding ten Miles square) as may, by Cession of particular States, and the Acceptance of Congress, become the Seat of the Government of the United States, and to exercise like Authority over all Places purchased by the Consent of the Legislature of the State in which the Same shall be, for the Erection of Forts, Magazines, Arsenals, dock-Yards, and other needful Buildings; -And

This paragraph authorizes the creation of what would become the District of Columbia.

To make all Laws which shall be necessary and proper for carrying into Execution the foregoing Powers, and all other Powers vested by this Constitution in the Government of the United States, or in any Department or Officer thereof.

Congress has the broad power to pass whatever laws may be needed in order to carry out the other powers granted to Congress by the Constitution.

The writ of habeas corpus, which requires that a person who has been arrested or detained be brought into a court so that the legality of that arrest or detention can be determined, is one of the most important American civil liberties, and is guaranteed by the Constitution except in extreme circumstances.

This provision prohibits Congress from passing two kinds of oppressive laws the British Parliament had used. Bills of attainder were laws naming specific people as criminals (as opposed to finding them guilty in court) and often naming their punishment as well. Ex post facto laws did not name specific people, but they did make certain actions illegal *after the fact.* Thus, even if something had been perfectly legal when you did it, you could be found guilty of a crime under an ex post facto law that was passed afterward.

Capitation means a direct tax on people. Until 1913, when the Sixteenth Amendment passed—as under the Articles of Confederation—*states* were taxed in proportion to their populations. The Sixteenth Amendment, passed in 1909 and ratified four years later, opened the door for income taxes by giving Congress the power to tax people directly.

In creating a nationwide duty-free zone covering the entire United States for products from all the other states, the Constitution promoted the growth of interstate commerce and gave rise to the country's continent-wide economic power.

SECTION. 9.

The Migration or Importation of such Persons as any of the States now existing shall think proper to admit, shall not be prohibited by the Congress prior to the Year one thousand eight hundred and eight, but a Tax or duty may be imposed on such Importation, not exceeding ten dollars for each Person.

The Privilege of the Writ of Habeas Corpus shall not be suspended, unless when in Cases of Rebellion or Invasion the public Safety may require it.

No Bill of Attainder or ex post facto Law shall be passed.

No Capitation, or other direct, Tax shall be laid, unless in Proportion to the Census or enumeration herein before directed to be taken.

No Tax or Duty shall be laid on Articles exported from any State.

No Preference shall be given by any Regulation of Commerce or Revenue to the Ports of one State over those of another; nor shall Vessels bound to, or from, one State, be obliged to enter, clear, or pay Duties in another.

No Money shall be drawn from the Treasury, but in Consequence of Appropriations made by Law; and a regular Statement and Account of the Receipts and Expenditures of all public Money shall be published from time to time.

No Title of Nobility shall be granted by the United States: And no Person holding any Office of Profit or Trust under them, shall, without the Consent of the Congress, accept of any present, Emolument, Office, or Title, of any kind whatever, from any King, Prince, or foreign State.

SECTION. 10.
No State shall enter into any Treaty, Alliance, or Confederation; grant Letters of Marque and Reprisal; coin Money; emit Bills of Credit; make any Thing but gold and silver Coin a Tender in Payment of Debts; pass any Bill of Attainder, ex post facto Law, or Law impairing the Obligation of Contracts, or grant any Title of Nobility.

No State shall, without the Consent of the Congress, lay any Imposts or Duties on Imports or Exports, except what may be absolutely necessary for executing it's inspection Laws: and the net Produce of all Duties and Imposts, laid by any State on Imports or Exports, shall be for the Use of the Treasury of the United States; and all such Laws shall be subject to the Revision and Controul of the Congress.

No State shall, without the Consent of Congress, lay any Duty of Tonnage, keep Troops, or Ships of War in time of Peace, enter into any Agreement or Compact with another State, or with a foreign Power, or engage in War, **unless actually invaded, or in such imminent Danger as will not admit of delay.**

The drafters of the Constitution had just managed to free themselves from the rule of an inherited monarchy. Despite their admiration for George Washington (whom some wanted to appoint president for life), the idea of creating peerage in the United States was something most found extremely distasteful, and they nipped it in the bud with this provision.

In general, permission of Congress could override many of the prohibitions of Article I of the Constitution, but in a day when the best horses on the best roads could travel only about thirty miles in a day, provision had to be made for legalizing actions taken in the event of an emergency. This is just such a provision.

Article. II.

SECTION. 1.

The executive Power shall be vested in a President of the United States of America. He shall hold his Office during the Term of four Years, and, together with the Vice President, chosen for the same Term, be elected, as follows:

Each State shall appoint, in such Manner as the Legislature thereof may direct, a Number of Electors, equal to the whole Number of Senators and Representatives to which the State may be entitled in the Congress: but no Senator or Representative, or Person holding an Office of Trust or Profit under the United States, shall be appointed an Elector.

The Electors shall meet in their respective States, and vote by Ballot for two Persons, of whom one at least shall not be an Inhabitant of the same State with themselves. And they shall make a List of all the Persons voted for, and of the Number of Votes for each; which List they shall sign and certify, and transmit sealed to the Seat of the Government of the United States, directed to the President of the Senate. The President of the Senate shall, in the Presence of the Senate and House of Representatives, open all the Certificates, and the Votes shall then be counted. The Person having the greatest Number of Votes shall be the President, if such Number be a Majority of the whole Number of Electors appointed; and if there be more than one who have such Majority, and have an equal Number of Votes, then the House of Representatives shall immediately chuse by Ballot one of them for President; and if no Person have a Majority, then from the five highest on the List the said House shall

The term "president" comes from the verb "to preside." That meaning holds over in the title of "president pro tempore" of the Senate, the officer who presides when the vice president can't. But the "executive Power" that is vested in the president under the Constitution is far broader than merely presiding over the Congress, which had been the president's job under the Articles of Confederation.

in like Manner chuse the President. **But in chusing the President, the Votes shall be taken by States, the Representation from each State having one Vote; A quorum for this purpose shall consist of a Member or Members from two thirds of the States, and a Majority of all the States shall be necessary to a Choice. In every Case, after the Choice of the President, the Person having the greatest Number of Votes of the Electors shall be the Vice President. But if there should remain two or more who have equal Votes, the Senate shall chuse from them by Ballot the Vice President.**

The Congress may determine the Time of chusing the Electors, and the Day on which they shall give their Votes; which Day shall be the same throughout the United States.

No Person except a natural born Citizen, or a Citizen of the United States, at the time of the Adoption of this Constitution, shall be eligible to the Office of President; neither shall any Person be eligible to that Office who shall not have attained to the Age of thirty five Years, and been fourteen Years a Resident within the United States.

In Case of the Removal of the President from Office, or of his Death, Resignation, or Inability to discharge the Powers and Duties of the said Office, the Same shall devolve on the Vice President, and the Congress may by Law provide for the Case of Removal, Death, Resignation or Inability, both of the President and Vice President, declaring what Officer shall then act as President, and such Officer shall act accordingly, until the Disability be removed, or a President shall be elected.

This provision was negated by the Twelfth Amendment, passed in 1803 and ratified in June of 1804, well before the presidential election that year, to enable the members of the Electoral College to make it very clear which candidate they wanted for president and which for vice president. They weren't about to risk repeating the debacle of 1800, when there had been a tie between the top two candidates, Thomas Jefferson and Aaron Burr, both Democratic-Republicans. The Democratic-Republican electors had meant to elect Jefferson president and Burr vice president.

The Constitution specifies that only a "natural born Citizen" can be president, but the Naturalization Act of 1790 clarified the fact that children of American citizens are citizens even if they are born outside the country.

This paragraph was replaced by the Twenty-Fifth Amendment, passed in 1965 and ratified in 1967, which now governs presidential succession. After the assassination of President John F. Kennedy, the country was without a vice president for almost fourteen months. The Twenty-Fifth Amendment also defines succession in the event a president is unable or unwilling to continue in office. This was tested less than a decade later, when Vice President Spiro Agnew and President Richard Nixon both resigned within the first two years of their second term.

The founders provided for compensation, so that the presidency would not attract only the wealthy, but also provided that the compensation could not increase during a president's term, nor could a president mine the office to create great personal wealth by picking up a little extra money on the side from the federal or any state government.

Legend has it that George Washington added the words "so help me God" to the end of the oath, but there is no more proof of that than of the legend of the cherry tree. As to whether all other presidents have added it since, it is likely that Thomas Jefferson did not. However, now that inaugurations are broadcast, presidents omit it at their peril, since the public expects it.

In this grab-bag list of presidential powers, the fact that the president is commander in chief of the armed forces places the military firmly under civilian control.

The President shall, at stated Times, receive for his Services, a Compensation, which shall neither be increased nor diminished during the Period for which he shall have been elected, and he shall not receive within that Period any other Emolument from the United States, or any of them.

Before he enter on the Execution of his Office, he shall take the following Oath or Affirmation:—"I do solemnly swear (or affirm) that I will faithfully execute the Office of President of the United States, and will to the best of my Ability, preserve, protect and defend the Constitution of the United States."

SECTION. 2.
The President shall be Commander in Chief of the Army and Navy of the United States, and of the Militia of the several States, when called into the actual Service of the United States; he may require the Opinion, in writing, of the principal Officer in each of the executive Departments, upon any Subject relating to the Duties of their respective Offices, and he shall have Power to grant Reprieves and Pardons for Offences against the United States, except in Cases of Impeachment.

He shall have Power, by and with the Advice and Consent of the Senate, to make Treaties, provided two thirds of the Senators present concur; and he shall nominate, and by and with the Advice and Consent of the Senate, shall appoint Ambassadors, other public Ministers and Consuls, Judges of the supreme Court, and all other Officers of the United States, whose Appointments are not herein otherwise provided for, and which shall be established by Law: but the Congress may by Law vest the Appointment of such inferior Officers, as they think proper, in the President alone, in the Courts of Law, or in the Heads of Departments.

The President shall have Power to fill up all Vacancies that may happen during the Recess of the Senate, by granting Commissions which shall expire at the End of their next Session.

Originally intended to allow an office to be filled while the Senate was in recess—often for six months in the early days of the country—recess appointments have been used even during short breaks by recent presidents when the Senate has refused to hold hearings on an appointment.

SECTION. 3.

He shall from time to time give to the Congress Information of the State of the Union, and recommend to their Consideration such Measures as he shall judge necessary and expedient; he may, on extraordinary Occasions, convene both Houses, or either of them, and in Case of Disagreement between them, with Respect to the Time of Adjournment, he may adjourn them to such Time as he shall think proper; he shall receive Ambassadors and other public Ministers; he shall take Care that the Laws be faithfully executed, and shall Commission all the Officers of the United States.

The mandate for the president to report to the Congress on "the State of the Union" is used by modern presidents as a chance to lay out an agenda for the coming year and, because it is televised, to bring that agenda before the American people. The real requirement is just what it says—to report from time to time on how the president thinks the country is doing, and how the union of the states is holding up.

SECTION. 4.

The President, Vice President and all civil Officers of the United States, shall be removed from Office on Impeachment for, and Conviction of, Treason, Bribery, or other high Crimes and Misdemeanors.

"Impeachment" means, in essence, to indict, or make a formal accusation concerning an officeholder's official duties. Only after the House of Representatives decides there is merit to any charges does a trial take place in the Senate. "All civil Officers of the United States" can be removed from office using this process; members of the military are, instead, tried by courts martial.

Article III.

SECTION. 1.

The judicial Power of the United States shall be vested in one supreme Court, and in such inferior Courts as the Congress may from time to time ordain and establish. **The Judges, both of the supreme and inferior Courts, shall hold their Offices during good Behaviour, and shall, at stated Times, receive for their Services a Compensation, which shall not be diminished during their Continuance in Office.**

This is the basis for the "independent judiciary" in America. So long as judges conduct themselves with "good Behaviour," they cannot be removed from office during their lifetime, nor forced out by having their salaries reduced.

SECTION. 2.

The judicial Power shall extend to all Cases, in Law and Equity, arising under this Constitution, the Laws of the United States, and Treaties made, or which shall be made, under their Authority;—to all Cases affecting Ambassadors, other public Ministers and Consuls;—to all Cases of admiralty and maritime Jurisdiction;—to Controversies to which the United States shall be a Party;—to Controversies between two or more States;—**between a State and Citizens of another State,**—between Citizens of different States,—between Citizens of the same State claiming Lands under Grants of different States, and between a State, or the Citizens thereof, and foreign States, Citizens or Subjects.

The Eleventh Amendment, passed in 1794 and ratified in 1795, negated this phrase, and reinstated traditional "sovereign immunity" for the states. The Constitution, as amended, now prohibits suing a state unless the state consents to be sued.

In all Cases affecting Ambassadors, other public Ministers and Consuls, and those in which a State shall be Party, the supreme Court shall have original Jurisdiction. In all the other Cases before mentioned, the supreme Court shall have appellate Jurisdiction, both as to Law and Fact, with such Exceptions, and under such Regulations as the Congress shall make.

Cases where the Supreme Court has "original jurisdiction" go there directly. All other cases must wend their way up through the appeals process ("appellate jurisdiction"). Even then, the Court is not obligated to hear all appeals, but can pick and choose among those submitted.

55

The Trial of all Crimes, except in Cases of Impeachment, shall be by Jury; and such Trial shall be held in the State where the said Crimes shall have been committed; but when not committed within any State, the Trial shall be at such Place or Places as the Congress may by Law have directed.

Along with the writ of habeas corpus and the rights guaranteed by the Fifth Amendment, the right to trial by jury in criminal cases is part of the guarantee of due process for those accused of crimes.

SECTION. 3.

Treason against the United States, shall consist only in levying War against them, or in adhering to their Enemies, giving them Aid and Comfort. No Person shall be convicted of Treason unless on the Testimony of two Witnesses to the same overt Act, or on Confession in open Court.

The Congress shall have Power to declare the Punishment of Treason, but no Attainder of Treason shall work Corruption of Blood, or Forfeiture except during the Life of the Person attainted.

The crime of treason is very narrowly defined in the Constitution. Because of this, the basis for prosecuting acts that do not meet this precise definition—even acts like terrorism that is not state sponsored, or the publication of classified government documents—must be found in the wording of other laws, not "treason."

The Constitution forbids passing laws declaring specific individuals guilty of crimes, or penalizing the descendants of someone found guilty of treason.

Article. IV.

SECTION. 1.

Full Faith and Credit shall be given in each State to the public Acts, Records, and judicial Proceedings of every other State. And the Congress may by general Laws prescribe the Manner in which such Acts, Records and Proceedings shall be proved, and the Effect thereof.

This is an expanded version of a paragraph in Article IV of the Articles of Confederation. The second sentence gives Congress powers it did not have under the previous version, in essence allowing Congress to pass laws determining how, and even whether, acts legal in one state will be enforced in another.

SECTION. 2.

The Citizens of each State shall be entitled to all Privileges and Immunities of Citizens in the several States.

The version of this clause in the Articles of Confederation granted this privilege to the "free inhabitants" of each state; this version instead mentions "citizens."

A Person charged in any State with Treason, Felony, or other Crime, who shall flee from Justice, and be found in another State, shall on Demand of the executive Authority of the State from which he fled, be delivered up, to be removed to the State having Jurisdiction of the Crime.

This euphemistically phrased section was voided by the Thirteenth Amendment, passed and ratified in 1865, which bars slavery or involuntary servitude.

No Person held to Service or Labour in one State, under the Laws thereof, escaping into another, shall, in Consequence of any Law or Regulation therein, be discharged from such Service or Labour, but shall be delivered up on Claim of the Party to whom such Service or Labour may be due.

SECTION. 3.

Maine was formed from a disconnected portion of Massachusetts, but with the consent of that state. West Virginia is the only state that was carved out of another state, when its northwestern counties opposed Virginia's secession from the Union. The resolution admitting Texas as a state allows it to petition to be divided into five states, but only if Texas and Congress consent.

New States may be admitted by the Congress into this Union; but no new State shall be formed or erected within the Jurisdiction of any other State; nor any State be formed by the Junction of two or more States, or Parts of States, without the Consent of the Legislatures of the States concerned as well as of the Congress.

The Congress shall have Power to dispose of and make all needful Rules and Regulations respecting the Territory or other Property belonging to the United States; and nothing in this Constitution shall be so construed as to Prejudice any Claims of the United States, or of any particular State.

SECTION. 4.

The United States shall guarantee to every State in this Union a Republican Form of Government, and shall protect each of them against Invasion; and on Application of the Legislature, or of the Executive (when the Legislature cannot be convened), against domestic Violence.

Article. V.

The Congress, whenever two thirds of both Houses shall deem it necessary, shall propose Amendments to this Constitution, or, on the Application of the Legislatures of two thirds of the several States, shall call a Convention for proposing Amendments, which, in either Case, shall be valid to all Intents and Purposes, as Part of this Constitution, when ratified by the Legislatures of three fourths of the several States, or by Conventions in three fourths thereof, as the one or the other Mode of Ratification may be proposed by the Congress; Provided that no Amendment which may be made prior to the Year One thousand eight hundred and eight shall in any Manner affect the first and fourth Clauses in the Ninth Section of the first Article; and that no State, without its Consent, shall be deprived of its equal Suffrage in the Senate.

Article. VI.

All Debts contracted and Engagements entered into, before the Adoption of this Constitution, shall be as valid against the United States under this Constitution, as under the Confederation.

This Constitution, and the Laws of the United States which shall be made in Pursuance thereof; and all Treaties made, or which shall be made, under the Authority of the United States, shall be the supreme Law of the Land; and the Judges

The term "Republican" in this paragraph does not have anything to do with the Republican party, which was not even formed until more than half a century after the Constitution was written. As used here, it means a representative government without a monarch.

Although it is easier than the unanimous vote required by the Articles of Confederation, amending the Constitution is much more difficult than passing laws. This keeps a philosophy of the moment—which may be abandoned as social attitudes change—from becoming part of the supreme law of the land.

This is known as the Supremacy Clause. When the laws of any state are found by a court to be in conflict with the Constitution or any laws passed under its authority, the Constitution trumps the other law or ruling.

in every State shall be bound thereby, any Thing in the Constitution or Laws of any State to the Contrary notwithstanding.

The Senators and Representatives before mentioned, and the Members of the several State Legislatures, and all executive and judicial Officers, both of the United States and of the several States, shall be bound by Oath or Affirmation, to support this Constitution; but no religious Test shall ever be required as a Qualification to any Office or public Trust under the United States.

Article. VII.

The Ratification of the Conventions of nine States, shall be sufficient for the Establishment of this Constitution between the States so ratifying the Same.

The Word, "the," being interlined between the seventh and eighth Lines of the first Page, the Word "Thirty" being partly written on an Erazure in the fifteenth Line of the first Page, The Words "is tried" being interlined between the thirty second and thirty third Lines of the first Page and the Word "the" being interlined between the forty third and forty fourth Lines of the second Page.

This paragraph contains a general reference to what must be covered in an oath of office, but does not prescribe the actual words. The presidential oath is the only one actually spelled out in the Constitution. As a result, many oaths for very minor offices are much longer than the one the president takes.

The Articles of Confederation had required that any alteration to them had to be by ratification of the legislatures of all of the states. If the Constitution was an "alteration," using the nine states formula did not meet that standard. Eventually, though, conventions in all thirteen colonies ratified the Constitution, so the point became moot. This is the only place where a specific number of votes, rather than a percentage, is used.

This paragraph was inserted so that there would be no question about any obvious insertions or corrections evident in the copy of the Constitution that was being signed. Similar statements can often be found even today, for example in wills, indicating how many pages are in the document, and how many lines are above the signature, so no one can sneak anything in, and alterations in wills and contracts are normally initialed by the signer and all witnesses (though not in the Constitution).

Attest William Jackson Secretary

done in Convention by the Unanimous Consent of the States present the Seventeenth Day of September in the Year of our Lord one thousand seven hundred and Eighty seven and of the Independance of the United States of America the Twelfth In witness whereof **We have hereunto subscribed our Names,**

G°. Washington
Presidt and deputy from Virginia

Delaware

Geo: Read

Gunning Bedford jun

John Dickinson

Richard Bassett

Jaco: Broom

Maryland

James McHenry

Dan of St Thos. Jenifer

Danl. Carroll

Virginia

John Blair

James Madison Jr.

William Jackson, who served as secretary of the Constitutional Convention, had been an officer in the Continental army and had served on General George Washington's staff. He later served as one of Washington's personal secretaries while Washington was president.

Three of the delegates to the Constitutional Convention refused to sign the Constitution because they believed it failed to address the issue of individual rights sufficiently. They were George Mason and Edmund Randolph of Virginia and Elbridge Gerry of Massachusetts. Gerry had previously signed both the Declaration of Independence and the Articles of Confederation.

George Washington had been unanimously elected president of the Constitutional Convention. As presiding officer, he did not participate in the debates, but became a strong advocate for ratification once the Constitution was signed.

James McHenry, a physician who had served on Washington's staff during the Revolutionary War, was appointed by Washington as the third secretary of war, and continued in that office under President John Adams. Ft. McHenry, whose shelling inspired Francis Scott Key to write "The Star-Spangled Banner," was named for him.

Known as "the father of the Constitution," James Madison was its principal author, and after it was ratified, served in the House of Representatives, as secretary of state, and as the fourth president of the United States.

North Carolina

Wm. Blount

Richd. Dobbs Spaight

Hu Williamson

South Carolina

J. Rutledge

Charles Cotesworth Pinckney

Charles Pinckney

Pierce Butler

Georgia

William Few

Abr Baldwin

New Hampshire

John Langdon

Nicholas Gilman

Massachusetts

Nathaniel Gorham

Rufus King

Connecticut

Wm. Saml. Johnson

Roger Sherman

Roger Sherman, part of the "Committee of Five" that drafted the Declaration of Independence, signed all three documents—the Declaration, the Articles of Confederation, and the Constitution. He later served in both the House and the Senate.

New York

Alexander Hamilton

Alexander Hamilton, who had served as aide-de-camp to George Washington during the Revolutionary War, became the first secretary of the treasury under Washington. He was a principal advocate for the Constitution and wrote many of the Federalist Papers supporting it. He was a founder of the Federalist Party.

New Jersey

Wil: Livingston

David Brearley

Wm. Paterson

Jona: Dayton

Pennsylvania

B Franklin

Thomas Mifflin

Robt. Morris

Geo. Clymer

Thos. FitzSimons

Jared Ingersoll

James Wilson

Gouv Morris

Benjamin Franklin was the oldest of the delegates at the Constitutional Convention. His signature appears on both the Constitution and the Declaration of Independence (he was serving as America's representative, and later ambassador, to France when the Articles of Confederation were signed).

George Clymer of Philadelphia was an early supporter of independence from England. In addition to signing the Constitution, he was also one of the signers of the Declaration of Independence.

CHAPTER 3

Constitutional Rules on How to Use the Constitution

Of the seven articles that comprise the U.S. Constitution, four of them deal with how to use the document. Article IV discusses how to apply the Constitution, Article V discusses how to amend it, and Article VI discusses what its position is relative to other laws that may exist or come to exist in the United States. Article VII discusses the procedure for ratification of the Constitution. While these are the last four sections of the Constitution proper, there is a trick to understanding a legal document that lawyers learn early in law school: Read the rules for using a law before you try to understand the law itself. These articles will be discussed first, so that you can understand where the Constitution applies, and when—in other words, how to use it.

The Supreme Law of the Land

The second paragraph of Article VI of the Constitution may be the most important one in the entire document (with the possible exception of the Preamble). It reads:

> *This Constitution, and the Laws of the United States which shall be made in Pursuance thereof; and all Treaties made, or which shall be made, under the Authority of the United States, shall be the supreme Law of the Land; and the Judges in every State shall be bound thereby, any Thing in the Constitution or Laws of any State to the Contrary notwithstanding.*

You can't make a more sweeping statement than that: The Constitution is the supreme law of the land. All laws and treaties that are created under its authority are, by their association with the pursuance of constitutional ends, also the supreme law of the land. Any dealings you have with the United States or under the jurisdiction of the United States hark back to this document, and are determined by its parameters.

And while the laws and treaties that are, by extension, part of the law of the land may change according to formulas set forth in the Constitution, the Constitution itself can only be changed by amendment, a lengthy and difficult process. When the application of a law is not clear, you can bring the matter before a court, and a judge—after hearing testimony from both sides and reading the relevant cases, and even by reading the *Congressional Record* to see the arguments that accompanied its passage—can attempt to ascertain what the meaning of the law probably is. *The Constitution establishes its own priority over all other laws.*

The Rest of Article VI

The Constitutional Convention, in drafting this document, knew that the fledgling government of the United States still had debts to pay off from the Revolutionary War.

These were many of the same people who, a little more than a dozen years earlier, had pledged "our Lives, our Fortunes, and our sacred Honor" to explaining why they were declaring their independence from the British

Crown, because of "a decent respect to the opinions of mankind." These men were not about to renege on those debts; doing so would cause them to lose all credibility in the community of nations, not to mention those Americans to whom they still owed money. So the first paragraph of Article VI confirms the obligations of the country:

> *All Debts contracted and Engagements entered into, before the Adoption of this Constitution, shall be as valid against the United States under this Constitution, as under the Confederation.*

Validating the Revolutionary War debt was also part of the Federalist agenda, because in doing so, the government established a legitimate reason for levying the taxes with which they hoped to ultimately fund the new federal government. In addition, those to whom this money was owed would have a reason for supporting the new government, because it had both the obligation and the ability to pay them.

State Officers Are Also Bound

Just in case there were some employees of the states out there who thought their first loyalty was to their states, the third paragraph of Article VI makes it clear that they too, in taking office, must pledge to support the Constitution:

> *The Senators and Representatives before mentioned, and the Members of the several State Legislatures, and all executive and judicial Officers, both of the United States and of the several States, shall be bound by Oath or Affirmation, to support this Constitution; but no religious Test shall ever be required as a Qualification to any Office or public Trust under the United States.*

In other words, if you hold public office under the United States—any office, whether state or federal, in any capacity, whether legislative, executive, or judicial—you are bound when you take your oath of office, to support the Constitution, and from that, the government created by it. There are no split loyalties: Your first obligation as a citizen is to the United States.

Perhaps because America is such a mobile society, state loyalties no longer carry the day for most Americans. But one example of the old ways was General Robert E. Lee, a West Point graduate who had fought for the United States and believed in the Union. Although not really a supporter of secession, he nevertheless resigned his commission when Virginia seceded, because he felt his first loyalties were to his state.

Although it was probably not something many people considered, imposing a pledge of loyalty to the Constitution on state officeholders does remind them, at least on the day they are sworn in, of the primacy of the Constitution. This is clearly part of that shift from the state-centric tone of the Articles of Confederation to the vision of the Constitution, which is more nation-centric while still allowing for state loyalties.

Before the Civil War, it was common to use a plural verb with the name of the country—for example, saying "The United States are . . ." This clearly indicates that you are speaking for the individual states. After the Civil War, there was a shift in attitude, and people would instead say, "The United States is . . . " indicating a nation rather than an alliance.

The last sentence of Article VI is a repudiation of religious tests for holding public office. Such tests had been common in Europe. Where they existed in America, they were often holdovers from the religious origins of many of the colonies. Religion was a very personal matter to many of the framers, and they chose to insert this statement that religious beliefs should not ever be a qualification for holding public office well before the Bill of Rights was drafted. It can, and should, be read along with the First Amendment as proof that the framers did not believe in religious litmus tests, but rather the opposite.

Obligations and Rights of the States

Article IV of the Constitution discusses the relationship of the states to each other, and the way they have to treat the citizens of other states. The first paragraph, not unlike a similar paragraph in the Articles of Confederation, obligates them to give "full faith and credit" to the laws of other states.

> *Full Faith and Credit shall be given in each State to the public Acts, Records, and judicial Proceedings of every other State. And the Congress may by general Laws prescribe the Manner in which such Acts, Records and Proceedings shall be proved, and the Effect thereof.*

Here's how the full faith and credit requirement works. To enforce acts and proceedings of one state in another, generally, all you need is acceptable proof of a judgment you'd like to enforce (something like a certified copy from the court where the judgment was entered) or a marriage or divorce certificate (to prove your marital status).

The second state will then recognize that you are the custodial parent if you have your divorce certificate saying that is the case. If you need access to the safe-deposit box of someone who is deceased, a copy of the will authorizing you to be the personal representative (or a court order appointing you) plus a death certificate will usually get you access.

ALERT

The Defense of Marriage Act of 1996 allows one state to disregard the legality of a marriage that is legal in another state in defiance of the full faith and credit requirement. It does so under the authority of the part of the paragraph that allows Congress to "prescribe . . . the Effect thereof"—that is, of the law. Does this mean that Congress can negate the duty of a state to give full faith and credit to a marriage in another? The Supreme Court may ultimately be called upon to decide this.

The Rights of Individual Citizens

As was the case under the Articles of Confederation, citizens of one state traveling to or residing in another have all the privileges that a citizen of the state to which they had traveled would enjoy. The law reads:

> *The Citizens of each State shall be entitled to all Privileges and Immunities of Citizens in the several States.*

As used here (and often in the Constitution), the word "several" means "separate" or "individual." You have the same rights, in traveling to another state, that you would if you were a citizen of that state. This does not mean that you would bring with you the rights you had at home when you entered a new state (although the second state must recognize legal documents from the first state). Nevertheless, you would have the same rights as any other person in the new state. Before the Civil Rights Act of 1964, even though you had the right to eat at a lunch counter in your native Illinois, you might not have had that right—because of your race—in Alabama, if Alabama citizens of your race did not have that right.

The second paragraph of this clause allows for the extradition of criminals from one state to another:

> *A Person charged in any State with Treason, Felony, or other Crime, who shall flee from Justice, and be found in another State, shall on Demand of the executive Authority of the State from which he fled, be delivered up, to be removed to the State having Jurisdiction of the Crime.*

Even with this provision of the Constitution, extradition requires "due process." While many criminals, once caught, waive extradition hearings in order to shorten the trial process, it is possible to fight removal to the originating state.

Fugitive Slaves

The third paragraph of this clause was negated by the ratification of the Thirteenth Amendment, but it is part of American history. The Constitution avoided the words "slave" or "slavery," using instead euphemisms like "held to Service or Labour." This provision allowed for slaves who escaped to free states to be returned to their owners.

> *No person held to Service or Labour in one state, under the Laws thereof, escaping into another, shall, in Consequence of any Law or Regulation therein, be discharged from such Service or Labour, but shall be delivered up on Claim of the Party to whom such Service or Labor may be due.*

In other words, this, like the extradition of a criminal, was an exception to the first paragraph guaranteeing "privileges and immunities." If you were a slave and escaped to a free state, you didn't get the privileges and immunities of citizens of that state. On the assertion of your owner's claim, you would be returned.

Adding New States

The Constitution provides for the addition of new states to the Union, but it doesn't really provide for the addition of new territory from which those states can emerge. Its silence on the acquisition of territory gave President Thomas Jefferson pause when he made the Louisiana Purchase. Of course, once he bought that vast tract of land from France, the precedent for such acquisitions was set.

Here's how a state gets admitted:

> *New States may be admitted by the Congress into this Union; but no new State shall be formed or erected within the Jurisdiction of any other State; nor any State be formed by the Junction of two or more States, or Parts of States, without the Consent of the Legislatures of the States concerned as well as of the Congress.*

And here's how territories of the United States that are not states are to be governed:

The Congress shall have Power to dispose of and make all needful Rules and Regulations respecting the Territory or other Property belonging to the United States; and nothing in this Constitution shall be so construed as to Prejudice any Claims of the United States, or of any particular State.

This power of Congress is not listed under the other powers of Congress in Section 8 of Article I, but is instead found in Article IV, which describes how a territory that is claimed by the United States but is not part of any state (except for the District of Columbia) is to be governed. The District of Columbia is covered by a separate provision in Article I, Section 8, that deals with a "district" that shall "become the seat of the Government."

Until 1787, most of the states did not have western borders, but just continued westward into unsettled territory. The Northwest Ordinance of 1787 (passed by the Congress of the Confederation while the Constitution was still being drafted), dealt with the lands west of the Appalachians that had been ceded to the United States by the states.

The U.S. Congress affirmed this ordinance in 1789. The land it covered ultimately became the states of Ohio, Indiana, Illinois, Michigan, and Wisconsin.

FACT

In addition to the District of Columbia, other nonstate territories currently held by the United States include Puerto Rico, the U.S. Virgin Islands, the Northern Mariana Islands, and Guam as well as American Samoa and Wake Island. The United States holds Guantanamo Bay under a perpetual lease.

Congress began to create rules for governing the Northwest Territory almost as soon as it convened—among them, a law giving the president the right to appoint territorial governors, with the advice and consent of the Senate. But the acquisition of additional territory isn't really covered in the Constitution, so when Thomas Jefferson had the opportunity to make the Louisiana Purchase from France, he hesitated, because he wasn't sure such a purchase would be legal. After he had done so and Congress had confirmed the purchase, the precedent was set.

The legislative authority of Congress to make rules for the territories was used in order to, among other things, outlaw plural marriage in the Utah territory. West Virginia—created out of counties that seceded from Virginia after Virginia seceded from the United States during the Civil War—may not have been a legal admission under this provision, since the consent of Virginia had not been obtained. However, in time of war, and with the rest of the state in rebellion, no one challenged the state's admission to the Union.

ESSENTIAL

The act admitting Texas to the Union allows it to be broken up into as many as four "new states of convenient size in addition to . . . Texas." It also notes that only the territory north of the "Missouri Compromise Line must become free states. There is no sunset on this option, though the possibility of any being slave states was negated by the Thirteenth Amendment."

The Question of Secession

Under the Articles of Confederation, joining the union was *perpetual*. This word does not appear in the Constitution. And while the Constitution discusses how a state gets admitted, it is silent on whether a state can leave. The best answer on this subject might well be that since the Constitution replaced the Articles, but retained the "stile" of the United States of America, and since the country still has the same name, perpetual membership is an obligation held over from the first version.

The omission in the Constitution of any right to withdraw from the union left room for argument that it might be possible. New York, Virginia, and Rhode Island, in ratifying the Constitution, retained a right to secede, although the precedent of having joined a perpetual union would seem to have negated that. In addition, ratification of the Constitution was supposed to be on an up or down vote, so the validity of such a qualifying resolution is questionable. However, the ratifications were accepted without objection, which suggests that the qualifying resolutions were acceptable too. If those three states could legitimately secede, it could follow that all states might have that right, because all states ostensibly have rights equal to each other.

In addition, the Tenth Amendment, which holds that rights not reserved to the federal government or *forbidden* to the states belong to the states, seems to imply that since secession isn't reserved or forbidden, it is a right of the states.

Pursuant to U.S. custom and law, the appropriate place to have decided this would have been in the courts, rather than on all those bloody battlefields. This was never done. The closest anyone came was the 1869 case of *Texas v. White*. In that case, the Supreme Court ruled that the secessionist government of Texas had not had the authority to sell bonds belonging to the state of Texas. *Dicta* (side language) in the case says that entering the union is and was permanent and perpetual. That's as close as anyone has come to legally ruling on whether a state can withdraw from the union after it has joined it.

The Coup Preventer

The United States, and the power of the states joined together to form it, can be mustered to protect individual states that are suffering from riots or disaster. Troops can be called in to shore up a levee, to fight a forest fire, or to quell a riot. The general welfare provisions, and Article IV, Section 4, are where the United States finds the authority to do such things:

> *The United States shall guarantee to every State in this Union a Republican Form of Government, and shall protect each of them against Invasion; and on Application of the Legislature, or of the Executive (when the Legislature cannot be convened), against domestic Violence.*

The Constitution doesn't define what a "Republican Form of Government" is, but it is pretty certain that if there were a military coup in one of the states, the federal government could step in to quell it. The term "republican form of government" has nothing to do with the Republican party. Several parties have used the name "Republican," and all were created after the Constitution was drafted.

By most definitions, a republican form of government generally means one in which the governed can choose representatives who will govern them, and one that is led by someone who has been chosen by the governed, rather than a monarch who inherited the right to rule. Beyond that, there are so many variations that it is hard to say just what it is that the Constitution guarantees to every state, other than the right of its citizens to participate in choosing those who govern them, and the absence of a king.

Fixing What's Broken

The Articles of Confederation required unanimous consent to amend the articles. The wording was: "nor shall any alteration at any time hereafter be made in any of them, unless such alteration be agreed to in a congress of the united States, and be afterwards confirmed by the legislatures of every State." This made it virtually impossible to amend the Articles. But everyone makes mistakes, especially when trying to second-guess the future of a new system of government. And times and circumstances change, so that even the best-laid plans can become outdated. As a result, provisions for amending the Constitution were made, and can be found within Article V.

The bar is set fairly high, though not as high as the Articles set it. Two-thirds of each house of Congress must pass any proposed amendment, and then it must be submitted to the states for ratification. Only when three-quarters of the states have ratified it does an amendment become part of the Constitution.

An alternative procedure allows for the legislatures of two-thirds of the states to call for a constitutional convention, but amendments passed by such a convention also require ratification by three-quarters of the states. Ratification must be by both houses of bicameral legislatures, or, if Congress has so mandated it, by conventions called for that purpose as specified by Congress.

There are twenty-seven amendments that have made it through the entire procedure and are now part of the Constitution. Here is the specific wording authorizing amendments:

The Congress, whenever two thirds of both Houses shall deem it necessary, shall propose Amendments to this Constitution, or, on the Application of the Legislatures of two thirds of the several States, shall call a Convention for proposing Amendments, which, in either Case, shall be valid to all Intents and Purposes, as Part of this Constitution, when ratified by the Legislatures of three fourths of the several States, or by Conventions in three fourths thereof, as the one or the other Mode of Ratification may be proposed by the Congress; Provided that no Amendment which may be made prior to the Year One thousand eight hundred and eight shall in any Manner affect the first and fourth Clauses in the Ninth Section of the first Article; and that no State, without its Consent, shall be deprived of its equal Suffrage in the Senate.

Restrictions on Amendments

An odd provision near the end of Article V forbids the passage, before 1808, of any amendment restricting the importation of slaves. This was included because the South Carolina and Georgia delegations to the Constitutional Convention thought that being allowed to import slaves for another twenty years might help their states recover from economic losses incurred during the Revolutionary War. (As was typical in the Constitution, they managed to avoid using the words "slave" or "slavery.") As soon as the restriction expired, the importation of slaves to the United States was banned.

Representation of States in Congress

There is one other piece of the Constitution that can never be amended. It is the equal representation of the states in the Senate. This means that there will always be one house of Congress that will be elected on the basis of political units, rather than by population.

Ratification of the Constitution

The Articles of Confederation had required a two-thirds vote for passage of almost everything, and—to amend the Articles—a unanimous one. When it did act, it lacked the authority to follow through. The Constitutional

Convention was having none of that. Majorities, and occasionally superma-jorities, would be the rule under the new Constitution, but not unanimity. However, in giving each house of Congress the right to make its own rules, the Senate gave itself the filibuster, which used to mean that a senator had to take the floor and keep on talking in order to prevent the passage of a bill. Nowadays, they only have to threaten to do that; a filibuster can only be stopped by a three-fifths majority, currently sixty votes. Even though it isn't a constitutional rule, no one in the Senate seems willing to end this practice, or even to reduce the number of senators required to break a filibuster.

The Constitution set out its own rules for ratification in Article VII:

The ratification of the Conventions of nine States, Shall be sufficient for the Establishment of this Constitution between the States so ratifying the same.

The Federalists were determined to push the Constitution through, and what better way to do that than to bypass the legislatures, many of which were jealous of granting any of their power to the federal government? State conventions were organized, and the committee insisted on an up-or-down vote: Either you were with the Constitution or you were against it. There were to be no exceptions, no modifications.

FACT

Doubtless the elder statesman, Benjamin Franklin, articulated senti-ments that each of the delegates of the Constitutional Convention shared in one way or another. He said: "Thus I consent, Sir, to this Constitution, *because I expect no better, and because I am not sure it is not the best.*"

Numerical Problems

Legally, there were several problems with the way the Constitution was ratified. There was that nine-vote minimum. Was the Constitutional Conven-tion empowered to make the change from ratification by every state to ratifi-cation by nine out of thirteen? If they were still operating under the Articles of Confederation (which they were until the new Constitution was ratified), and if the Constitution could be construed as the "revisions" they'd been charged with making, they probably couldn't change the rules. The ratification should have been unanimous, rather than by nine states. However, once the nine states had ratified the Constitution, the others were virtually forced into joining, because, by its own rules, the Constitution was now operative. And once they *all* had ratified it, the argument that this had been done by fewer states than the Articles mandated was no longer valid.

Finally, Ratification

As for that up or down vote, at least three states submitted their ratifications with a separate memo reserving the right to secede. Others demanded some kind of a bill of rights, or even submitted their own drafts of such a bill. And of course, there was the need to ratify the Constitution by state conventions called for that purpose, rather than the legislatures. Again, the Articles of Confederation did not allow for this procedure, but the Constitution met the criteria it had spelled out. Having passed its own tests, it was deemed ratified.

There it was: The Constitution was ratified and was now the law of the land. All that remained was to elect the members of the House and Senate and a president, let them choose the members of the prescribed "one supreme Court" and "such inferior courts" as they found appropriate, and get on with the business of governing.

A new, three-branched government awaited them. The real experiment was about to begin.

CHAPTER 4

The Executive Branch

The powers, duties, and qualifications of the president are set forth in Article II of the Constitution, along with the rules for presidential elections and impeachments. The president is the head of state, commander in chief of the armed forces, and is in charge of executing and enforcing the laws written by Congress. The president's cabinet assists in enforcing these laws as well. The vice president must be ready to assume the presidency if needed, and serves as president of the United States Senate.

Defining the Chief Executive

Article II begins by naming the office: "The executive Power shall be vested in a President of the United States of America." It seems a simple enough statement, but half a dozen years after the Constitution was signed, Alexander Hamilton noticed that the wording defining each of the three branches of government was different. Article I says, "All legislative Powers herein granted shall be vested in a Congress. . . . " Article III says, "The judicial Power of the United States shall be vested in one supreme Court. . . . " But this article begins, "The executive Power shall be vested in a President. . . . "

It is typical of the detailed, nuanced way that lawyers and constitutional scholars read every word and punctuation mark in the Constitution that this difference in wording seems to signify a philosophical difference in the source of the three powers: The legislative powers are "granted" by the Constitution itself; the judicial power "of the United States" belongs to the Supreme Court—but the executive power simply exists, without qualifying language.

To a nonlawyer, this is an accident of drafting. To a lawyer or a constitutional scholar, there are no accidents.

If executive power simply exists (a monarchal concept if ever there was one, although the drafters were trying to get as far away as they could from the concept of a monarch), it could be deemed to come from some outside source, rather than from the *people* who had ordained and established the constitution.

FACT

Barack Obama is the forty-fourth president of the United States, and the first bi-racial president. John F. Kennedy, the thirty-fifth president, was the first and only Catholic to hold that office.

In England, the prime minister is often termed the "first among equals." As James Madison discussed in No. 51 of the Federalist Papers, the three branches of the government of the United States were supposed to be as equal in power and as independent of each other as was possible. So what could be read into the different introductory phrases? Does this phrasing make the executive branch first among the three equal branches? Did it make any difference that the legislative branch was discussed in Article I, before the executive or judicial branches? This kind of discussion is one of the best examples of why interpreting the Constitution is never as simple as it seems.

The Powers of the President

The Constitution sets forth the powers of the president in a rather concise statement in Section 2 of Article II:

> *The President shall be Commander in Chief of the Army and Navy of the United States, and of the Militia of the several States, when called into the actual Service of the United States; he may require the Opinion, in writing, of the principal Officer in each of the executive Departments, upon any Subject relating to the Duties of their respective Offices, and he shall have Power to grant Reprieves and Pardons for Offences against the United States, except in Cases of Impeachment.*
>
> *He shall have Power, by and with the Advice and Consent of the Senate, to make Treaties, provided two thirds of the Senators present concur; and he shall nominate, and by and with the Advice and Consent of the Senate, shall appoint Ambassadors, other public Ministers and Consuls, Judges of the supreme Court, and all other Officers of the United States, whose Appointments are not herein otherwise provided for, and which shall be established by Law: but the Congress may by Law vest the Appointment of such inferior Officers, as they think proper, in the President alone, in the Courts of Law, or in the Heads of Departments.*
>
> *The President shall have Power to fill up all Vacancies that may happen during the Recess of the Senate, by granting Commissions which shall expire at the End of their next Session.*

Mindful of the fact that an executive with powers that were too narrow would be ineffective and that one with powers that were too broad could develop monarchal tendencies or become a dictator, the framers of the

Constitution, while giving the president "executive" power, also created a basic list of what the president can do. All other presidential powers would have to be granted by the Congress or found in the writings of various courts.

The president can do the following things *without* the consent of Congress:

- The president is commander in chief of the armed forces of the United States, including the state militias when they are called into action on behalf of the country.
- The president has the authority to require reports from the heads of the "executive departments," principally meaning the cabinet.
- The president may grant pardons from convictions or reprieves from sentences (except in cases of impeachment).
- The president can convene or adjourn both houses of Congress, something that normally must be done by agreement between them, if such an agreement can't be reached by them.
- The president can receive ambassadors from other countries.
- The president commissions all officers of the United States.
- The president reports to Congress, from time to time, on "the state of the Union." (This originally meant exactly what it said—how the alliance between the states was going.)
- The president is in charge of making sure that the laws of the United States are "faithfully executed."

In addition, the president has another set of powers that can only be executed *with* the "advice and consent of the Senate." These are the power to make treaties and the power to appoint ambassadors, judges, and other officers. Further, the signature of the president is required before a bill can become a law, with certain exceptions that are outlined in Article I of the Constitution, which discusses the powers of Congress.

Because the powers of Congress include the right to make laws that expand on the responsibilities of the president as set forth in the Constitution, much of what the president is charged with doing is actually detailed in laws and regulations. The laws of the United States originate in Congress and are found in the United States Code. Regulations, which have the power of law but are created by other departments of the government under authority granted by Congress, can usually be found in the Code of Federal Regulations.

FACT

Under their enforcement power, presidents from time to time issue executive orders. Since only Congress can pass laws, these executive orders mandate action by officers of the United States, but not the population as a whole. The Emancipation Proclamation was such an order; so was the notorious Executive Order 9066, which forced all people of Japanese descent living on the West Coast into "relocation camps" in 1942.

The president's duty of enforcement extends to laws and regulations; the president does not personally enforce the laws, but delegates that enforcement to members of the military and of the executive departments of the government.

Commander in Chief

One of the areas that is covered by laws rather than by constitutional amendments is the execution of presidential authority as commander in chief. The Constitution specifies the army and navy. It does not name the marine corps, the air force, or the coast guard, but the president is commander in chief of these branches as well.

ESSENTIAL

The fact that the president, a civilian elected by the people, is commander in chief of the armed forces means that in the United States, the military is under civilian control. If it were to attempt to overthrow the president, as happens in many other countries, the military could never make a case for the legitimacy of that action, since it would be, by definition, mutiny.

As for state militias, they still exist, many under the term "state guard," and the president is the ultimate commander of these forces, and of the National Guard. All of these divisions of the military operate under Title 10 of the United States Code, which contains the law that governs the armed forces, and whatever regulations the Department of Defense or the separate military branches may create.

For example, the policy known as "Don't ask, don't tell" (the actual law is found at 10 U.S.C.A. §654), which governed homosexuals in the military, was passed by Congress in 1993, but its day-to-day enforcement was based on regulations of the various branches of the military as well as court rulings applying to specific cases. As commander in chief of the armed forces, the president—or, by delegation, the secretary of defense or various officers of the military—could decide how much knowledge constituted enough knowledge of homosexual or bisexual activity to take action under "Don't ask, don't tell." This policy was repeated in 2010.

All actions of the military, from the design of the uniforms to the length of deployments to what constitutes a military funeral, ultimately come under the authority of the president.

The Executive Departments

The executive departments include the cabinet departments and the various agencies that operate under the executive branch of the government, as well as the people who work in various capacities for the White House and the vice president. There are fifteen cabinet-level executive departments:

- Agriculture
- Commerce
- Defense (historically known as the War Department)
- Education
- Energy
- Health and Human Services
- Homeland Security
- Housing and Urban Development
- Interior
- Justice
- Labor

- State
- Transportation
- Treasury
- Veterans Affairs

The heads of these departments are known—except for the attorney general—as secretaries, and the appointment by the president of each of them requires Congressional confirmation before they can take office. These departments were established by laws passed by Congress under the authority of the Constitution, but they are not mentioned in the Constitution except by general reference: "[The President] shall nominate, and by and with the Advice and Consent of the Senate, shall appoint . . . public Ministers . . . and all other Officers of the United States . . . ." The size and complexity of the Executive Departments was not foreseen by the framers of the Constitution, but the system that has developed has made it possible for these departments to operate under the authority of the executive branch.

ESSENTIAL

The Department of Justice should not be confused with the judiciary branch of government. The Department of Justice is a part of the executive branch of the government and essentially serves as the government's law firm. The judiciary branch of the government consists of courts where federal cases are tried.

In addition, the executive branch includes independent agencies that range from AMTRAK and the CIA through the Federal Deposit Insurance Corporation (FDIC) and the Federal Reserve to the General Services Administration (which oversees the maintenance and upkeep of government buildings), NASA, the Peace Corps, the Securities and Exchange Commission (SEC), and the Social Security Administration. There is also an extensive list of boards, commissions, and committees that come under the executive branch.

Further adding to the list of departments administered by the executive branch of the government are agencies that are part of executive departments. These include the Census Bureau and the Patent and Trademark Office (both part of the Commerce Department), the Secret Service (now part of Homeland Security), the Bureau of Indian Affairs and National Park Service (both part of the Department of the Interior), and the U.S. Mint (part of the Department of the Treasury). At the higher levels, the people who work for these departments are appointed by the president with the Senate's concurrence. At lower levels—including White House staff positions—hiring does not require Senate approval.

Appointing and Receiving Ambassadors

The president appoints ambassadors with the advice and consent of the Senate. The president is also charged with "receiving" ambassadors from other countries. In theory, this allows the president to decide whether to recognize the ambassador of a government that has been overthrown, or of a province that has declared its independence from another country.

Appointing Judges

The Constitution says that the president shall have the power to appoint "judges of the supreme Court" with the advice and consent of the Senate. Supreme Court judges are now called justices, but the same clause section that gives the president this power to appoint "all other Officers of the United States" also with the advice and consent (technically, a majority vote) of the Senate is used to appoint judges to the lower U.S. courts using the same procedure. This section of the Constitution allows Congress to delegate this power to appoint lower court judges "to the President alone," or to the courts, or "to the heads of departments." As a rule, the president appoints judges to the federal courts, but certain lower-level judges—bankruptcy court judges and magistrate judges, for example—occupy positions that have been created by Congress pursuant to Article I of the Constitution. They are appointed by panels of district court judges (or sometimes by the heads of the agencies they serve) for limited, rather than lifetime, terms pursuant to this section of the Constitution.

The Term of Office

Presidents and vice presidents are elected for terms of four years. When this found its way into the Constitution, it was a departure from the more typical one-year term then served by chief executives of most of the states (and by the presiding officer chosen by the Congress under the Articles of Confederation). Presidents are elected at the same time as all members of the House of Representatives and one-third of the Senate. Technically, this means that in any given presidential year, the only holdovers from previous governments would be two-thirds of the Senate, but in fact, many presidents are re-elected to a second term, as are a large number of the members of the House.

FACT

Because the first elections after the Constitution was created took place in 1788, virtually all presidential elections take place in leap years. There is no leap year at the turn of any century that is not divisible by 400, but there is still a presidential election in those years.

In the United States, federal elections take place only in even-numbered years unless there is a vacancy in Congress to be filled. But in many other countries, elections of the president are staggered, with some terms running an odd number of years. If elections seem never-ending under the current system, imagine what they'd be like if people ran for different offices virtually every year.

There were no limits on the number of times anyone could serve in any federal office, including that of the president, in the original Constitution. George Washington chose to serve only two terms, as did the third and fourth presidents, Jefferson and Madison. (The second president, John Adams, served only one term, having lost his bid for re-election in 1800 to Thomas Jefferson.) Thus began a tradition that continued until 1940, when Franklin Delano Roosevelt, a Democrat, was elected to a third term and then was elected a fourth time in 1944. He died in office in 1945, and so, although elected to four terms, he actually served less than thirteen years.

In 1947, the Republican party won both houses of Congress for the first time in more than a dozen years. Almost immediately, the Republican-dominated Congress passed what would become the Twenty-Second Amendment, which essentially limits presidents to two terms. This Amendment was ratified in 1951, shortly before Dwight David Eisenhower, commander of the Allied forces in World War II, became the first Republican to win the presidency since 1932. As a war hero, he was extremely popular, but the new amendment foreclosed the possibility that he could run for a third term.

ESSENTIAL

In 1880, four years after the end of his second term, Ulysses S. Grant, a Republican, threw his hat into the ring for a third term, but was not nominated by his party. In 1912, Theodore Roosevelt (who was Franklin Delano Roosevelt's cousin), also sought a third term on the Republican ticket after being out of office for four years. He, too, was denied his party's nomination; he ran anyway, as the nominee of the newly organized Progressive (or Bull Moose) party, but was not elected.

Although over the course of American history only one president has served more than two terms, a dozen served only one, either because they did not choose to run for re-election, or were not elected when they did so. Nine presidents have failed to serve out the terms for which they were elected, eight of whom died in office of natural causes or were assassinated, and one of whom resigned—Richard Nixon, in 1974, under threat of impeachment.

Vice Presidential Succession

In Article II, Section 1, the Constitution provides for a vice president and states, "In Case of the Removal of the President from Office, or of his Death, resignation, or inability to discharge the Powers and Duties of the said Office, the Same shall devolve on the Vice President." The first time that provision was used was in 1841, when William Henry Harrison died a month after his inauguration.

What had seemed up till then to be a perfectly clear provision almost caused a constitutional crisis. People were not sure if Vice President John Tyler should become president, or just serve in that capacity while retaining the title "Vice President," or perhaps "Acting President." If he retained his title of vice president while fulfilling the duties of the president, should he continue to preside over the Senate and resolve tie votes? Or should he be barred from that position once he took over the job of the president, even if he didn't have the title? And if he were to serve as president, should it be for the full term to which he and the president had been elected, or should there be an emergency election to fill the presidential vacancy? No one knew, and the Constitution wasn't totally clear.

This is because the rest of that paragraph reads:

> . . . and the Congress may by Law provide for the Case of Removal, Death, Resignation or Inability, both of the President and Vice President, declaring what Officer shall then act as President, and such Officer shall act accordingly, until the Disability be removed, or a President shall be elected.

Suddenly, people wondered what "or a President shall be elected" meant. Should the country wait for the next regular election, or hold one sooner? If the latter, who would schedule it, and how would that affect the term of the person elected?

The Twelfth Amendment

The Twelfth Amendment, which had been ratified in 1804, clarified some of these points but only added to the confusion in others. For example, the amendment states that in the event of an election being thrown into the House of Representatives and not resolved before the scheduled Inauguration Day (at the time, March 4), "then the Vice-President shall act as President, as in the case of the death or other constitutional disability of the President." But which vice president? If members of the House hadn't been able to choose a new president, would they have been able to choose a new vice president? Did this mean the *outgoing* one? And did it mean that he (only men were eligible at the time) would only *act* as president, rather than *be* the president?

The Twentieth and Twenty-Fifth Amendments

This wasn't resolved until 1933, with the ratification of the Twentieth Amendment, Section 3 of which provides for the vice president to actually become the president, and the vice-president elect to do so in the event of the death of the president-elect. If no one had qualified for either office, Congress was empowered to create laws that would cover this, although that appeared to be a clear violation of the separation of powers.

The Twenty-Fifth Amendment, ratified in 1967, finally added some clarification to what should happen when death, resignation, or incapacity leaves the office of vice president vacant, but there are still some holes in the procedure. If there is a vacancy in the vice presidency, the president nominates a replacement vice president who takes office if he is approved by a majority vote of both houses of Congress—but only to the end of that term. Under the Twenty-Fifth Amendment, Congress has the power to specify how vacancies should be filled, but an ill-timed, massive disaster could create some very difficult quandaries.

FACT

Richard Nixon was the first president to make use of the Twenty-Fifth Amendment when he nominated Congressman Gerald R. Ford to replace Vice President Spiro T. Agnew, who had resigned in disgrace. Ford then became president after Nixon's resignation. Ford chose New York Governor Nelson Rockefeller to fill the vice presidential vacancy, and for the rest of Ford's term, both the offices of president and vice president were held by men who had never been elected to either post.

Even though the Constitution provides for the removal of the president from office for "inability," no one knew what the procedure for that should really be until the passage of the Twenty-Fifth Amendment. In addition to the amendment's provisions concerning vice presidential succession, Congress is empowered to pass laws that deal with succession in the event both the president and vice president—and perhaps even more officials in line for the office—are unable, for whatever reasons, to perform the duties of the office.

Qualifications of the President

The Constitution sets forth the basic qualifications for serving as president of the United States:

> *No Person except a natural born Citizen, or a Citizen of the United States, at the time of the Adoption of this Constitution, shall be eligible to the Office of President; neither shall any Person be eligible to that Office who shall not have attained to the Age of thirty five Years, and been fourteen Years a Resident within the United States.*

The term "natural born Citizen" probably meant something different to the framers than it means today. No one anticipated artificial insemination, egg donors, or surrogate parents, and there probably was no intent to exclude people born by Cesarean section (so named because Julius Caesar was born by that method). The Constitution authorized Congress to create naturalization laws, and the first one was passed in 1790. In theory, once someone is naturalized, that person has all the rights of a citizen. However, Article II of the Constitution prohibits naturalized citizens from becoming president.

Automatic Citizens

Over the years, Congress has passed laws defining who is automatically a citizen of the United States. The Fourteenth Amendment says, "All persons born or naturalized in the United States, and subject to the jurisdiction thereof, are citizens of the United States and of the State wherein they reside." Being born in the United States makes you a citizen, even if your parents are in the United States illegally at the time of your birth. And the child of a tourist, or of someone in the United States on a student visa, also qualifies under this section.

But you don't have to actually be born in the United States to qualify for automatic citizenship. If a U.S. citizen is serving outside the United States in the military or as an ambassador, that person's child—even though born outside the country—is still a citizen of the United States. So is the child of someone who is out of the country on vacation. If at least one of your parents is a citizen of the United States at the time of your birth, chances are you qualify as a citizen from birth even if you were born outside the country.

Residency

But more than being a "natural born citizen," someone who aspires to the presidency must be over the age of thirty-five and have been a U.S. resident for at least fourteen years. But official residency and actual residency are not the same thing. Official residency can be claimed in one place by someone living elsewhere if there is a valid reason for the claim.

FACT

Rahm Emanuel, who had served in Congress while retaining (as all members of Congress do) his home district residency, resigned his House seat to serve as President Barack Obama's chief of staff. He left that job and returned to Chicago in 2010 intending to run for mayor, but another candidate sued to remove his name from the ballot because he hadn't *resided* in Chicago while working in the White House. The Illinois Supreme Court ruled that under the circumstances, he hadn't forfeited his Chicago residency and could run. He was elected.

Thomas Jefferson, the third president of the United States, served as U.S. minister to France and lived there from 1785 to 1789. He was elected president in 1800, which was less than fourteen years after his sojourn in Paris—but since his official residence was his home in Virginia, he was not deemed ineligible for the office.

Similarly, people today with homes in two or more states, even if they travel between them, choose one as their official residence. Someone serving on the International Space Station still maintains resident status back on Earth. You vote, pay taxes, and can be called to serve on a jury based on your declared residence, not on the space you are temporarily occupying.

Electing a President

A large part of Article II is devoted to how to elect a president. It is a complex procedure that has been fine-tuned when problems have arisen, and whether it should be further reformed is still subject to debate.

The Constitution's original method of choosing a president and vice president involved the presidency going to the person who got the top number of votes in the Electoral College, with the vice presidency going to the runner-up. The advent of political parties within the first dozen years of the country's existence resulted in a constitutional crisis by the fourth presidential election: The Democratic-Republicans, Jefferson's party, had meant to elect him president in 1800, and elect Aaron Burr vice president, but they neglected to withhold one vote for Burr, so he tied Jefferson, throwing the vote into the House of Representatives.

The Electoral College

The convoluted system of electing a president that was created by the original language of the Constitution began with a two-step process. Voters would choose electors, and the electors—members of the Electoral College—would actually choose the president. Here's what the Constitution said before it was amended:

> *Each State shall appoint, in such Manner as the Legislature thereof may direct, a Number of Electors, equal to the whole Number of Senators and Representatives to which the State may be entitled in the Congress: but no Senator or Representative, or Person holding an Office of Trust or Profit under the United States, shall be appointed an Elector.*

It noted further: "The Congress may determine the Time of chusing the Electors, and the Day on which they shall give their Votes; which Day shall be the same throughout the United States."

The number of electors for each state was, and still is, equal to the combined total of senators and representatives. Members of the Electoral College cannot be senators, representatives, or hold any other United States office. But it was state legislatures that determined how the electors would be chosen and who would actually get to vote for them.

The Constitution also specified, "The Congress may determine the Time of chusing the Electors, and the Day on which they shall give their Votes; which Day shall be the same throughout the United States." For the first half century of the country's existence, Congress permitted electors to be chosen at any time within a thirty-four-day period before the first Wednesday of December in an election year; that was the date set for the Electors to meet in their home states to cast their ballots for president and vice president. However, as communications improved, it became evident that states voting later in this period would be alerted to the leading candidates and that knowledge could have undue influence on the outcome of a presidential election. Further, there were complaints that some people had voted in more than one state, because there was enough time between different states' election days.

In 1845, Congress set the election day as the first Tuesday after the first Monday in November in years divisible by four; this remains the presidential election day throughout the country.

The advent of optional early and absentee voting has had an effect on voting that hasn't really been discussed; while it may not seem significant, voting early forecloses voters from taking into account information that may surface in the last days of a campaign.

The election of the president by electors was the result of compromise on the part of the framers, who had considered both direct election of the president and election by state legislatures. As every scenario presented itself, the possibility of corruption of the process seemed apparent. If the president were to be chosen by the legislatures, the larger states might dominate the choice of president. If the choice were to be made by members of the Congressional delegations, cronyism might prevail—and the separation of powers might be in doubt. It was both feared and desired, depending on whose argument you ascribed to, that presidents could wind up representing the states rather than the people. A requirement in the initial version of the procedure that electors choose two candidates, at least one of whom could not be from their home state, was meant to keep states from supporting only "favorite sons."

Before the advent of strong political parties, the Constitution mandated that the runner-up would be vice president; a built-in incentive to political assassination if ever one existed.

Political Dispute and the Twelfth Amendment

Strong political parties had begun to emerge by the turn of the nineteenth century. The election of 1800 was bitterly contested, and—with the state legislatures in charge of choosing the method of picking electors—in several states votes by the state legislature replaced a popular vote for president. While there were some irregularities with the way the electors submitted the results of their votes, in the end, it was the two candidates from the Democratic-Republican Party that won the highest number of votes.

The tie between Jefferson and Burr meant that the House of Representatives, where each state would have just one vote, would decide who had won. The House was sitting in "lame duck" session—many of its Federalist members had been defeated, but were not due to leave office till the next year. Burr did not withdraw, and Alexander Hamilton (a Federalist who would later be killed by Burr in a duel that may have harked back to this electoral battle) campaigned for Jefferson, because Hamilton considered him less dangerous than Burr. The struggle in the House resulted in Jefferson's election on the thirty-sixth ballot.

Hard on the heels of this contested election came the Twelfth Amendment, passed in 1803 and ratified shortly before the next presidential election in 1804; it required each Elector to specify which of the two candidates they were choosing for president and which for vice president. The actual wording was:

> *The person having the greatest number of votes for President, shall be the President, if such number be a majority of the whole number of Electors appointed; and if no person have such majority, then from the persons having the highest numbers not exceeding three on the list of those voted for as President, the House of Representatives shall choose immediately, by ballot, the President. But in choosing the President, the votes shall be taken by states, the representation from each state having one vote . . . .*

There was similar wording concerning the election of the vice president.

Presidential Compensation

The Constitution mandates compensation paid by the federal treasury for those holding the office of president:

> *The President shall, at stated Times, receive for his Services, a Compensation, which shall neither be increased nor diminished during the Period for which he shall have been elected, and he shall not receive within that Period any other Emolument from the United States, or any of them.*

The Constitution keeps the president independent of Congress by forbidding Congress to increase or decrease a president's salary during that president's term of office. The cost of running and staffing the White House is paid by Congress pursuant to appropriations bills. Technically, the salary of the president falls under those appropriations as well, but that is the amount that can't be altered during the current president's current term. The president's other expenses may fall under different parts of the national budget, such as the Defense Department (military aides and certain flight crews), Department of the Interior (National Park Service), or even the Department of Homeland Security (Secret Service).

Removing a President from Office

The president serves for a defined term of office. Presidents are inaugurated at noon on the 20th day of January following their elections and leave office four years later, also at noon on January 20.

FACT

After George Washington was sworn in as the first president on April 30, 1789, subsequent inaugurations were set by Congress for March 4 (March 5 when the 4th fell on a Sunday). In 1933, the Twentieth Amendment mandated January 20 as the date for presidential inaugurations.

Although eight presidents have died in office, only one—Richard Nixon—has resigned before the end of his term. He was facing impeachment at the time.

Impeachment

Impeachment (the equivalent of an indictment) by the House of Representatives was, if followed by conviction after a trial in the Senate, the only process by which a president could be removed from office under the original version of the Constitution. Since then, a procedure for dealing with presidential disability has been added by amendment.

Impeachment can only be brought for treason, bribery, or other "high Crimes and Misdemeanors." That phrase had a long legal history in England, and had normally been used in instances of grave misconduct. Its use to bring charges against President Clinton in 1999 for ostensibly failing to be truthful about private acts (acts not unlike the kind in which many previous presidents had engaged) was a very partisan use of the process.

The only other president to be impeached was Andrew Johnson, in 1868. Johnson had succeeded to the presidency after Lincoln's assassination. When he failed to comply with a tenure act that he felt was unconstitutional— one that would not have allowed him to fire a holdover from Lincoln's cabinet, Secretary of War Edwin Stanton—Radical Republicans in Congress brought impeachment proceedings against him. The Constitution requires a two-thirds vote in the Senate for conviction, and in the case of Johnson, this failed by one vote. Subsequent court rulings, and the repeal of the act he was accused of violating, suggest that he may have been correct in his stance, although that didn't prevent him from being impeached and tried by a very partisan Congress.

The impeachment of Bill Clinton was equally partisan. The near-impeachment of Richard Nixon was not. Accused of using illegal contributions to pay off criminals for illegal acts, Nixon found himself facing impeachment proceedings supported by members of his own party as well as the opposition. When the House Judiciary Committee, voted to take the impeachment to the floor of that chamber, Nixon resigned.

Removal for Disability

The Constitution provides, in Section 1 of Article II, that the duties of the president devolve on the vice president in the case, among other things, of the president's "Inability to discharge the Powers and Duties of the said Office." No procedure for determining such inability was spelled out.

The health concerns of at least three presidents—the almost three months that James Garfield lingered in deteriorating health after he was shot by an assassin, the debilitating stroke that Woodrow Wilson suffered nearly a year and a half before leaving office, and Dwight Eisenhower's heart attack, stroke, and bowel surgery—prompted the passage in 1965 and the ratification in 1967 of the Twenty-Fifth Amendment, which provides for presidential succession in the event of disability as well as when a president leaves office. The fourteen months the country spent without a vice president after John F. Kennedy's 1963 assassination prompted that amendment. It contains provisions for replacing the vice president as well as for dealing with presidential disability. And the potential threat of nuclear annihilation prompted the portion of that amendment that allows Congress to provide for presidential succession in the event that both the vice president and the president are unable to continue serving.

FACT

"The curse of Tecumseh" is the myth that grew after every president who had been elected in a year ending in zero, starting with William Henry Harrison in 1840, ultimately died in office (although sometimes during a subsequent term). Besides Harrison, they included Lincoln (1860, assassinated 1865), Garfield (1880, assassinated 1881), McKinley (1896 and 1900, assassinated 1901), Harding (1920, died 1923), Franklin Roosevelt (1932, 1936, 1940, and 1944, died 1945) and John Kennedy (1960, assassinated 1963). A 1981 assassination attempt caused serious harm to Ronald Reagan, who had been elected in 1980, but the wound was treated with modern medical technique, and he survived. George W. Bush (2000) appeared to have finally evaded the "curse."

Other Processes

The Twenty-Fifth Amendment also provides for presidents to take what is in essence a temporary leave of absence (for such things as elective surgery or perhaps for personal emotional reasons). It also provides for the vice president and "the principal officers of the executive department or for such other body as Congress shall by law provide" to bring a petition for presidential disability before Congress. That "other body" could be a medical panel, although no provision for one was specifically made by the language of the amendment.

There is an inherent conflict of interest built into the terms of this amendment. It is the vice president, who would inherit the office were the president to be removed, who is charged with bringing such petitions. It is the Congress that weighs in on them, something that is antithetical to the separation of powers. And yet, it seems to be the best alternative, at least for now.

CHAPTER 5

The Legislative Branch

Although people today often think of the presidency as the most important of the three coequal branches of the U.S. government, the drafters of the Constitution began their document with a description of Congress because to them, a legislative body was the foundation of representative government. They had created this new *federal* government after operating under the Articles of Confederation (under which the government comprised *solely* a legislative body).

A Bicameral Legislature

Directly after the Preamble, the first article deals with the legislative branch of government. It begins with the statement of the existence of that branch:

All legislative Powers herein granted shall be vested in a Congress of the United States, which shall consist of a Senate and House of Representatives.

When the Articles of Confederation were created, the aim was to create an alliance of states working toward a common purpose: independence. By the time the Constitution was created, a country had begun to take shape, a country whose citizens began, in many ways, to think of themselves as being as important as the states they inhabited. In creating the legislative branch, the framers chose to establish a bicameral legislature, with one chamber—the Senate—representing the states, and the other—the House of Representatives—representing the people.

Here is how these two bodies are defined, first in Section 2 of Article I:

The House of Representatives shall be composed of Members chosen every second Year by the People of the several States, and the Electors in each State shall have the Qualifications requisite for Electors of the most numerous Branch of the State Legislature.

And then in Section 3:

The Senate of the United States shall be composed of two Senators from each State, chosen by the legislature thereof for six Years; and each Senator shall have one Vote.

Here the basic differences between the two houses are obvious. The voters (as defined by state law) would choose their representatives. The state legislatures, on behalf of their states, would choose the senators. (The manner of choosing senators would change in 1913 with the ratification of the Seventeenth Amendment, which provided for their direct election. The people now choose their representatives in both houses directly.)

The number of representatives in the two houses was designed be different as well. In the Senate, each state, no matter how large or small, no matter how wealthy or poor, has two senators (today, with fifty states, there are 100 senators). But in the House, though every state has at least one member, membership is apportioned according to each state's population.

A Numbers Game

In an attempt to keep the membership in the House to a reasonable number, it was decided, just before the Constitution was signed, that there would never be more than one member for every 30,000 people. Since, at the time, the population of the United States was fewer than 4 million people, that meant there would be no more than 130 members, and in fact, the Constitution actually provided a total of sixty-five until the first census could be taken.

ESSENTIAL

Article I, Section 2 of the Constitution initially grants the original thirteen states the following number of seats in the House: New Hampshire, three; Massachusetts, eight; Rhode Island, one; Connecticut, five; New York, six; New Jersey, four; Pennsylvania, eight; Delaware, one; Maryland, six; Virginia, ten; North Carolina, five; South Carolina, five; and Georgia, three.

Today, with a U.S. population of more than 300 million people, there are 435 members of the House. The current ratio is about one House member for every 700,000, except in more sparsely populated states. Alaska, Delaware, Montana, North Dakota, South Dakota, Vermont, and Wyoming each have only one member of the House, who serves the entire state, "at large." In the case of Wyoming, the least populous state, that means the at-large member of the House represents about 550,000 people, according to 2009 U.S. Census Bureau estimates. In the case of Montana, the at-large member represents a little over 900,000 people—not quite enough to warrant a second member, although this could change after adjustments are made for the 2010 census figures. Rhode Island, which has two seats in the House of Representatives, is the least populous state to do so, with a little over a million people.

States with more than one representative in the House are divided into districts roughly equal in population, each with its own representative. Redistricting takes place after the national census, and is the reason the Constitution requires that a census count be taken every ten years. Although the federal government decides, based on the census count, how many House members each state will get, it is up to the states themselves to decide what the boundaries of their districts will be. By law, they must be roughly equal in population, and contiguous, but beyond that, the requirements change according to federal and state law. And if it appears that districts are configured so that minorities are being systematically under-represented, the federal courts can, and do, step in to order the districts reconfigured.

ALERT

In addition to the 435 *voting* members who represent the people of the fifty states in the House, there are five *nonvoting* members, one for the District of Columbia, and one each from the territories or commonwealths of American Samoa, Guam, Puerto Rico, and the U.S. Virgin Islands.

Counting Slaves, Indentured Servants, and Women

Until the ratification of the Fourteenth Amendment in 1868, there was another kind of discrepancy in the calculation of House members. In their best euphemistic manner, the drafters of the Constitution, while avoiding any actual mention of slavery, mandated that the population base for calculating representatives "shall be determined by adding to the whole Number of free Persons, including those Bound to Service for a Term of Years, and excluding Indians not taxed, three fifths of all other persons."

FACT

Indentured servants—people who bound themselves to work off a debt over a certain period of time—were considered free persons, and were counted; slaves were counted as three-fifths of a person.

This boosted the population—and hence the representation—for slave states, but did not give them credit for a full count of this disenfranchised portion of the population. Without that compromise, a union between slave and free states probably would not have been possible. It would take until 1868 for Section 2 of the Fourteenth Amendment to eliminate that arithmetic fiction. The relevant part of the Fourteenth Amendment reads as follows:

Representatives shall be apportioned among the several States according to their respective numbers, counting the whole number of persons in each State, excluding Indians not taxed. But when the right to vote at any election for the choice of electors for President and Vice-President of the United States, Representatives in Congress, the Executive and Judicial officers of a State, or the members of the Legislature thereof, is denied to any of the male inhabitants of such State, being twenty-one years of age, and citizens of the United States, or in any way abridged, except for participation in rebellion, or other crime, the basis of representation therein shall be reduced in the proportion which the number of such male citizens shall bear to the whole number of male citizens twenty-one years of age in such State.

In other words, deny a male citizen over twenty-one the right to vote, and you can't count him in your population for the purpose of representation. At last the three-fifths rule had been laid to rest, and it had only taken a bloody war and a couple of constitutional amendments to do it. Where population was concerned, all men were finally deemed, as the Declaration of Independence declares, to have been created equal. It would take more than half a century longer for women to be included in the citizenry, even though the Fourteenth Amendment begins, "All *persons* born or naturalized in the United States, and subject to the jurisdiction thereof, are citizens of the United States and of the State wherein they reside." Women still were not "persons" under the law for voting purposes until the Nineteenth Amendment was ratified in 1920.

When Congress Meets

Because transportation took so long in the early days of the Republic, it was assumed that Congress would not meet in short sessions and go home for the weekend, as is often the case today. The Constitution mandates in Section 4 of Article 1, that "The Congress shall assemble at least once in every Year," and originally said that was to be "on the first Monday in December, unless they shall by Law appoint a different Day." It was changed to coincide with the election of new presidents, in March, which created a five-month lame-duck period.

As of 1933, the Twentieth Amendment moved the presidential inauguration to January 20, and also mandated that Congress meet annually on January 3, and that is when each new Congress is sworn in and takes office.

Powers of the Legislative Branch

When the framers hammered out the Constitution in less than three months during the hot summer of 1787, they did so without benefit of modern organizational tools. So what seems like an organized document sometimes has relevant portions hidden in odd places. The powers of Congress were set out, generally, in Article I, but certain other obligations and duties are found in other parts of the document.

Powers of Congress in General

Mainly, of course, Congress is charged with making laws. At the end of the long list of the powers of Congress set forth in Section 8 of Article I, there is this one, perhaps the most important: "To make all Laws which shall be necessary and proper for carrying into Execution the foregoing Powers, and all other Powers vested by this Constitution in the Government of the United States, or in any Department or Officer thereof."

Throughout the rest of the Constitution, there are references to Congress having power to draft laws concerning particular matters, to advise the president and consent to appointments he makes, to "declare the Punishment of Treason," and a whole slew of other specific rights and obligations that are part of the Congressional responsibilities. But in the end, it all boils down to Congress making laws.

Section 8 of Article I is a reminder of specific legislative actions Congress is charged with carrying out. First on this list is the "Power of the Purse":

The Congress shall have Power To lay and collect Taxes, Duties, Imposts and Excises, to pay the Debts and provide for the common Defence and general Welfare of the United States; but all Duties, Imposts and Excises shall be uniform throughout the United States;

and:

To Borrow Money on the credit of the United States;

and:

To coin Money, regulate Value thereof, and of foreign Coin, and fix the Standard of Weights and Measures;

and:

To provide for the Punishment of counterfeiting the Securities and current Coin of the United States;

and even:

To regulate Commerce with foreign Nations, and among the several States, and with the Indian Tribes; . . .

although the Commerce Department, which falls under the Executive Branch, is charged with enforcing such regulations. It was the lack of ability to regulate commerce that stymied the government under the Articles of Confederation.

FACT

The "power of the purse" is among the greatest powers the House possesses. No program can go forward unless the House of Representatives proposes an appropriation to cover it, although under most budgets, the president has some discretionary funds for unfunded emergencies, such as sending in the armed forces to cope with a natural disaster.

Congress is also specifically reminded in Section 8 of Article I to create laws in certain other areas:

- **"To raise and support Armies, but no Appropriation of Money to that Use shall be for a longer Term than two Years."** Appropriations for a standing army must be passed in every new Congress, which enforces civilian control over the army.
- **"To provide and maintain a Navy."**
- **"To make Rules for the Government and Regulation of Land and naval Forces."** It is under these rules that the president commands these forces. Together with the restrictions on appropriations, and naming the civilian leader in command of all military forces, having the civilian government make the rules for the armed forces enforces the idea of civilian control over the military. Consider this a "coup protector."
- **To call up the militias when needed and make rules by which militias operate when under the command of the United States.**
- **To create rules for naturalization and for bankruptcy.** Both of these areas of law promote commerce—naturalization by allowing immigrants to become full citizens, something that created the rich culture of the United States and provided the population to settle the west, and bankruptcy laws by allowing businesses and individuals to get out from under stagnating debt and make a fresh start. The founders believed in both, specifically noting them in the powers of Congress.
- **"To establish Post Offices and post Roads,"** thus fostering a way of connecting the country that would eventually reach across the continent.
- **To create copyright and patent laws.** By granting to authors and inventors the exclusive rights to their inventions and discoveries, this clause promotes creativity; by doing so for limited times, it allows others to build on that creativity.
- **To "define and punish" piracy and other crimes committed on the "high Seas" and against the "Law of Nations."** Such laws become more important in a world where enemies are not necessarily other nations, but often groups unaffiliated with a country.
- **To act as the governing body for the District of Columbia** (yet to be created when the Constitution was drafted) **and other territories of**

the United States (such as the frontier before states were created, the current territories, and forts and embassies of the United States).

The powers of Congress noted in other parts of the Constitution include:

- **To admit new states to the Union.**
- **To determine the time for choosing members of the Electoral College.**
- **To reinstate the rights of someone who has lost them by participating in a rebellion.**
- **To declare, within constitutional parameters** (which among other things prohibit Bills of Attainder and ex post facto laws), **the punishment for treason.**

In addition, only Congress has the power to declare war. That's why you see newsreel footage of President Franklin D. Roosevelt addressing a joint session of Congress the day after Pearl Harbor was attacked, asking Congress to declare war on the Japanese Empire (which was responsible for the attack) and its allies. The United States has formally gone to war, using a Congressional declaration, only five times: the War of 1812, the Mexican War (1846), the Spanish-American War (1898), World War I (1917), and World War II (1941).

During the drafting process, the wording regarding war was changed from "make war" to "declare war" so that a president, as commander in chief, could defend the country in emergencies without waiting for Congress to assemble and make a declaration. The country has also engaged in numerous military actions that were not actual declared wars. These include actions against the Barbary pirates, and against many of the Native American tribes, the Vietnam War, the Gulf War, and the Iraq and Afghan wars, as well as participation in United Nations actions in Korea, Lebanon, and Bosnia, among others.

Special Powers Granted to Each House

The legislative (or lawmaking) power vests in Congress as a whole, but each of the two houses has its own sphere of authority in some very specific areas.

The powers specifically granted to the House of Representatives are the right to originate "[a]ll Bills for raising Revenue" (although the Senate can modify them "with Amendments as on other Bills"). The House also possesses "the sole Power of Impeachment," which means that all such charges must originate in the House.

The Senate, too, has powers of its own—"the sole Power to *try* [author's emphasis] all Impeachments" once the House has brought charges, and the power to offer its "Advice and Consent" to the president on treaties (which require a two-thirds vote of the senators present for passage) and on the appointments of ambassadors, "other public Ministers and Consuls, Judges of the supreme Court, and all other Officers of the United States, whose Appointments are not herein otherwise provided for." Here the power lies in withholding that consent, and thus denying the appointment or the ratification of the treaty. Except on treaties, only a majority vote is required, but Senate rules can turn that into a so-called "supermajority" requirement by keeping a vote from occurring.

Delegating Congressional Power

As part of its lawmaking power, Congress can create "Tribunals inferior to the supreme Court." State Courts already existed, and the number of federal courts that might be needed wasn't known. This power allowed Congress to develop them as the need arose. Congress may also delegate some of its powers in other ways:

Congress may by Law vest the Appointment of such inferior Officers, as they think proper, in the President alone, in the Courts of Law, or in the Heads of Departments.

Congress has the power to propose amendments to the Constitution, which become part of it when ratified by three-quarters of the states. It has also picked up a few powers as a result of amendments that have become part of the Constitution, namely the power to assess income taxes, the power to confirm the appointment of a replacement vice president when the office becomes vacant, the power to create a hierarchy of those who will take over the presidency in the event of the death or disability of the officers prescribed by the Twenty-Fifth Amendment, and the right and obligation, under that same amendment, to weigh in on presidential disability.

Limits on Congressional Powers

Here are things Congress is or has been specifically prohibited from doing under the Constitution, mostly under Section 9 of Article I, but also found elsewhere and in some of the amendments:

- Prohibiting the import of slaves before 1808
- Suspending the writ of habeas corpus except during invasion or rebellion. The writ of habeas corpus allows someone who has been incarcerated to challenge that incarceration in court. President Lincoln suspended the writ during the early days of the Civil War, and then persuaded Congress—to whom the right of suspension belonged—to approve his action once it was in session.
- Creating bills of attainder (criminal laws applying to one specific person, naming that person as guilty without having held a trial) or ex post facto laws (laws declaring that acts which were legal when you did them are now retroactively declared to be crimes)
- Taxing commerce between states or charging duties for goods shipped between states
- Showing favoritism for one state or its ports over another
- Spending the country's money without an appropriation to do so
- Granting titles of nobility
- Making laws that restrict freedom of religion, of speech, of the press; and of the right to assemble peaceably and to petition the government

Congress had previously been prohibited from passing laws that allowed for direct taxation of individuals, but that was changed with the ratification of the Sixteenth Amendment, which allowed Congress to draft laws providing for an income tax starting in 1913.

Members of Congress

When the Constitution was drafted, communication was only as fast as a horse could travel on the roads of the day. No member of Congress who lived farther away than northern Virginia or southern Maryland could go home for the weekend, or poll the people in the district on a bill that was being considered. It fell to the voters to choose people whose judgment and opinions they respected to represent them, because there would be no checking back if a new measure came up that hadn't been discussed in the course of the election campaign or before it.

Because getting back home was so difficult, members of Congress often left their families behind when they did a stint in the House. And unless they were independently wealthy, they wound up sharing a room, or even a bed, in a Washington rooming house while doing a turn in the capital. Legendary frontiersman Davy Crockett, for example, served a couple of terms (not consecutive) in Congress, representing two different districts in his home state of Tennessee. Abraham Lincoln served one term in Congress, but did not run for re-election. Neither was independently wealthy; their families stayed home while they served their country in the capital.

There were, of course, some who became what today might be termed "career politicians," but even they did not hold a seat in either house in perpetuity. Henry Clay of Kentucky, for example, who eventually served as Speaker of the House, did several different stints in both the Senate and the House (from two different districts) during the first half of the nineteenth century. (He also served as secretary of state.)

John C. Calhoun of South Carolina served in both the Senate and the House, and also served as secretary of state, secretary of war, and vice president. Daniel Webster of Massachusetts had a similar career, serving in both houses of Congress and as Secretary of State twice (under a total of three presidents).

These men were the exceptions that proved the rule. Most people did not stick around more than a term or two, especially in the House.

Qualifications for Election

The Constitution says that to be a representative, you must be at least twenty-five years old, and you must have been a citizen of the United States for at least seven years. You also must, at the time of your election, be "an Inhabitant" of the state that has elected you (the rules of the legislatures, which govern this, often require residence in the district you represent). That's all—no education or training, not even a crime-free past. Of course, in the beginning, there was no need to mention that to be a citizen; you had to be free, white, twenty-one, and male. These things were assumed.

Initially, senators represented the state from which they came, rather than the people of that state. Unlike representatives, who are and always have been elected by direct vote, members of the Senate were selected by their state legislatures until the Seventeenth Amendment was ratified in 1913. (Since that time, senators have been elected directly by the voters). The Constitution specifies that a senator must be at least thirty years old and have been a citizen for nine years; those are the requirements for actually taking office. The requirement of residency—that you must be an inhabitant of the state from which you are elected—appears to apply as of the election day.

Getting Elected to Congress

The Constitution leaves up to the states who in those states gets to vote there, and under what circumstances, so long as no one is denied the right to vote as guaranteed by various amendments, but principally the Fifteenth and Nineteenth.

Originally the members of their state legislatures chose senators, while representatives were chosen for a shorter term directly by the people. When the Seventeenth Amendment, in 1913, provided for the direct election of senators as well, this also prompted a change in the way vacancies would be filled. Originally, the governor of the state that found itself down a senator could make a temporary appointment until the legislature chose a replacement to serve out the previous senator's term. For House members, vacancies were to be filled by special elections called by the governor of any state that had lost an elected member of the house. Because of the longer term served by senators, the Seventeenth Amendment gave states the choice of calling an election immediately, or having the governor appoint one and following that with a special election.

Because one-third of the Senate is elected in any given election year, some of those elected to the first session of Congress had to serve two- or four-year terms to establish the staggered terms. The Constitution established that with a provision that was used only once, "Immediately after they shall be assembled in Consequence of the first Election, they shall be divided as equally as may be into three Classes. The Seats of the Senators of the first Class shall be vacated at the Expiration of the second Year, of the second Class at the Expiration of the fourth Year, and of the third Class at the Expiration of the sixth Year, so that one third may be chosen every second Year." There is no direct provision for which class the senators of new states would be, nor is it mentioned here that no state should have senators from only one class. It has worked out that way, but it is one of those omissions that could have caused problems in a very partisan climate.

Congressional Salaries

Even though they represent their states, senators and representatives are paid, pursuant to Section 6 of Article I, by the United States, out of its treasury. They are essentially prevented by the Twenty-Seventh Amendment from voting their own pay increases. Any pay increase to which any sitting senator or representative might be entitled by virtue of a pay bill voted on during his or her term may not take effect until after an intervening election.

Freedom to Debate

One of the more important provisions of Section 6 of Article I grants members of both houses freedom from arrest (except in cases of "Treason, Felony and Breach of the Peace") while Congress is in session. This can be read—especially in the original document, with its absence of what would become the First Amendment—as a guarantee of freedom of speech and debate for those who served in Congress. Members of the legislative branch would be free to speak their minds on the subject of their debates without fear of arrest for saying what they believed.

Holding Office

Section 6 also spells out that "No Senator or Representative shall, during the Time for which he was elected, be appointed to any civil Office under the Authority of the United States, which shall have been created, or the Emoluments whereof shall have been encreased during such time;

and no Person holding any Office under the United States, shall be a Member of either House during his Continuance in Office." This has caused certain problems when a member of the Senate has been nominated for a cabinet post, and it has at times been read in such a way as to prevent a senator or representative from serving in the military or the reserves. There is no similar provision for members of the judiciary. However, Section 1 of Article II notes that, while in office, a president "shall not receive within that Period any other Emolument from the United States, or any of them."

Each Branch of Congress Makes Its Own Rules

Section 2 of Article I allows the House to "chuse their Speaker and other Officers." Section 3 decrees that the vice president is to be the president of the Senate, but can only vote to break a tie. Beyond that, the Senate also chooses a president pro tempore who presides when the vice president is absent, or when the vice president "shall exercise the Office of President of the United States."

Since there is no mention of parties in the Constitution, there is no mention of majority leader, minority leader, or any other political position. In both the Senate and the House, these offices fall under the "other officers" provisions.

Section 5 of Article I says that each house is to be the judge of the elections, returns, and qualifications of its own members. It specifies that a simple majority of the members of either house constitutes a quorum for conducting business, but a smaller number (not specified) may call the others to attend and assess penalties for failing to do so. This last is what is known as a "quorum call." Section 5 also notes, "Each House may determine the Rules of its Proceedings, punish its Members for disorderly Behaviour, and, with the Concurrence of two thirds, expel a Member."

It is under these rules (not the Constitution itself) that the need for a supermajority in the Senate has evolved. Although a simple majority should carry the day on any non-treaty bill, the complex procedural rules that have evolved have made votes far more complicated. For example:

- *Parties* are not mentioned in the Constitution. In the United States, a streak of independence in most senators and representatives meant that there was little party discipline. Individual senators would "vote their consciences," and compromises were reached so that laws could be passed with modifications. That happens much more infrequently nowadays.
- A *filibuster*, from a Spanish word for "freebooter" (pirate), is a debating tool, a way of capturing the floor and holding it for as long as any senator can stay standing and speaking. Senate rules formerly required that a senator who had the floor must speak, and those engaged in a filibuster have been known to read recipes, mail, and even the Constitution, to hold up proceedings and prevent a vote from occurring. A senator could "yield the floor" to a colleague for the purpose of taking a bathroom break, and the colleague could then yield it back. Sometimes a set of senators would tie up the floor with a group filibuster by yielding to each other over a long period of time. Nowadays, the mere threat of a filibuster is enough to keep something from going to the floor; no one is required to actually speak.
- *Cloture*, another Senate rule, is a means of cutting off debate. It can be used to silence a filibuster. Cloture requires a 60 percent vote—which, in a Senate of 100 people, means 60 senators. If a party has fewer than 60 votes it can count on, it cannot cut off a filibuster.
- *Committees* also are not mentioned in the Constitution. Much of the business of both houses of Congress begins in a committee, which can decide whether a proposed law or other action makes it "out of committee" and onto the floor. Depending on the size of the committee, a very small number of senators or representatives can keep something from being released for a full (floor) vote. Like filibuster, hanging something up in a committee is a way of keeping a bill or a nominee from reaching a vote on the floor.

Similarly, Congressional hearings and investigations are part of the rules and procedures that the two legislative chambers have developed for themselves. Hearings can take up so much of the time of members of both houses of Congress that nothing makes it to an actual vote.

Casework

Another thing the Constitution doesn't mention, but it is something that occupies most of a senator's or representative's time and staff, is casework. As the federal government has grown, people have developed the need for advocates in dealing with it. Many people rely on their senators and representatives for getting through to a federal agency that doesn't seem to be responding. Everything from needing a passport in a hurry to wanting extra tickets for a White House tour to obtaining disability benefits can be moved along faster if you can have your senator get behind it.

Very little of this is actually in the Constitution itself, although the basis for it may lurk in provisions for the way that Congress is meant to function. At bottom, the legislative branch of the government exists to make laws, and all the other rules and customs create the structure and system under which laws are made, and how far the Congress can or should go in making them.

How a Bill Becomes a Law

If there is one concept most people take away from their high school civics classes, it is this one: How the laws are made. Unfortunately, because Congress can make its own rules, the bare-bones outline of the process in the Constitution doesn't begin to describe how it is really done. There is, for example, sometimes an element of cooperation between the two houses: Often there will be a "companion bill" in the other house, so that passage in the two houses can be, under the best of conditions, simultaneous. There also is the element of "sponsorship," under which the author of a proposed law signs up as many members as possible from the chamber in which the bill is being introduced, to show that it has support and is likely to pass. Occasionally, cosponsors of a bill may change their minds and vote against their own bills.

This is sometimes due to the amendments others have tacked on to a bill. Sometimes these amendments are reasonable: A bill to divert water from farmlands to wetlands might need an amendment to define "farmlands" and "wetlands" so there is a clear understanding of what it covers.

But sometimes an amendment is only vaguely related, such as one to restrict the use of fertilizers containing certain heavy metals from areas containing wetlands. Such a bill would probably be better if standing on its own, but at least it bears some relationship to the subject matter of the bill.

And sometimes there will be an amendment tacked on that seems to bear no relationship to the subject matter at all, such as a bill to construct a highway in a specific district tacked on to a bill to fund a study of a new plane. Why such amendments find their way into bills has a lot to do with getting the number of members necessary for passage to vote for a bill; sometimes the only way they can be persuaded is if there is a bridge or a government office building in their district that will be constructed, a quid pro quo for a vote in favor of the whole bill. It becomes a matter of horse-trading, but the net result may be a multipage bill that no one has ever read all the way through.

ESSENTIAL

Sometimes people complain about the number of lawyers in Congress, but who better to draft a law than someone who has been trained in the legal consequences of word usage, or to understand when an inadvertent word substitution can change the meaning and use of a law? Training requirements for being a lawyer were very fluid in the eighteenth century, but still, as many as two-thirds of the delegates to the Constitutional Convention had either studied or practiced law.

This doesn't mean that large, even huge, bills aren't a good idea. The passage of the Copyright Reform Act of 1976, which went into effect in 1978, effectively reformed the entire U.S. Copyright Law, carefully defining every topic, working out how one use of a copyrighted work would interact with another, and how both authors and users of a work, and public entities such as libraries, would work out their differences.

It becomes easier to understand the process of creating a law if you first understand who is making those laws. For this reason, you need to understand the rights, duties, privileges, and obligations of members of Congress and of the president—and how they mesh and when they conflict. That makes the process much easier to understand.

The last paragraph of Section 8 of Article I of the Constitution reads that Congress has the power:

To make all Laws which shall be necessary and proper for carrying into Execution the foregoing Powers, and all other Powers vested by this Constitution in the Government of the United States, or in any Department or Officer thereof.

With that broad authority, Congress tends to make laws first and ask questions later.

Defining Law-Making Terms

A law begins as a *bill* that carries a number. A normal bill number begins by identifying its source: *HR* for the House of Representatives, or *S* for the Senate. Congress passes a large number of other things besides bills, such as resolutions in support of cancer research; these do not become laws, but are a way for Congress to acknowledge a constituency, like issuing a key to a city.

The Congress elected every two years has a new Congress number. The 2011–2012 Congress is the 112th Congress. A bill that has not passed in any Congress must be reintroduced in the next Congress in order to be considered. So a bill will bear the name of the Congress in which it was introduced, like "110th Congress," and an indication of its source, like "HR," and a bill number. Bill numbers are issued sequentially, beginning the day the new Congress convenes.

FACT

Although the Constitution is only 4,400 words long (8,500 including all of the amendments), the procedural rules Congress has adopted are much longer and far more complex. The Senate's rules can be found in *Riddick's Senate Procedure*, a book some 1,200 pages long, and that's without the rules for any Senate committees, which they make themselves. The House has its own separate procedural rules.

Once a bill has passed both houses, it is known as an *act*. If the president signs an act, or if a presidential veto is overridden by a two-thirds vote, it becomes a *law*, and is given the designation of *PL* (for Public Law) with a number.

A law that is enacted (passed and signed) is sent to the Office of the Federal Register, where it is assigned a Public Law Number, published first as a *slip law*, and then published as part of the United States Statutes at Large. It may be legally cited as a published slip law or from the printed (not electronically available) Statutes at Large. Often, however, what the law does is change elements of an existing law, so it will not be used by lawyers with its law number, but will change the way the existing law that it modifies or expands is read.

What the Constitution Says about How a Bill Becomes a Law

The rules for how a bill becomes a law are laid out in Section 7 of Article I of the Constitution.

Every Bill which shall have passed the House of Representatives and the Senate, shall, before it become a Law, be presented to the President of the United States: If he approve he shall sign it, but if not he shall return it, with his Objections to that House in which it shall have originated, who shall enter the Objections at large on their Journal, and proceed to reconsider it. If after such Reconsideration two thirds of that House shall agree to pass the Bill, it shall be sent, together with the Objections, to the other House, by which it shall likewise be reconsidered, and if approved by two thirds of that House, it shall become a Law. But in all such Cases the Votes of both Houses shall be determined by yeas and Nays, and the Names of the Persons voting for and against the Bill shall be entered on the Journal of each House respectively. If any Bill shall not be returned by the President within ten Days (Sundays excepted) after it shall have been presented to him, the Same shall be a Law, in like Manner as if he had signed it, unless the Congress by their Adjournment prevent its Return, in which Case it shall not be a Law.

Every Order, Resolution, or Vote to which the Concurrence of the Senate and House of Representatives may be necessary (except on a question of Adjournment) shall be presented to the President of the United States; and before the Same shall take Effect, shall be approved by him, or being disapproved by him, shall be repassed by two thirds of the Senate and House of Representatives, according to the Rules and Limitations prescribed in the Case of a Bill.

That's a lot of words that simply add up to this: A bill must pass both houses of Congress to be presented to the president, and all bills that pass both houses must be submitted to the president. If the president signs a bill, it becomes law. If the president vetoes a bill (the word "veto" is not in the Constitution; it is Latin for "I forbid"), it returns to Congress for reconsideration. If on reconsideration the bill gets a two-thirds vote in each house, the bill becomes a law even without the president's concurrence.

There are some time frames built into this process: The president gets ten days to sign or veto the bill. If a president fails to act within that time frame, the bill automatically becomes a law—unless Congress has adjourned within those ten days, in which case the president's failure to sign a bill becomes a "pocket veto" and the bill is considered dead.

This complex system is a great display of the checks and balances of the U.S. Constitution in action. It shows how Congress has the power to make laws, but the president has the power to stop them from being made—but then the Congress can, if it musters enough votes, stop the stoppage.

That's all there is to it, except for the rules of both chambers, because the rules allow bills to be hung up in committees that refuse to let them go to the floor of the House or the Senate, where they could actually be debated. Any single member of either chamber who can hold up a bill in committee comes to wield huge power.

The power of committees and the power of parties and the power of seniority all affect how a bill progresses from its initial introduction until it finally reaches the stage at which it can be debated, voted on, and sent to the president. None of those elements are in the Constitution, except where it gives each house the power to create its own rules.

CHAPTER 6

The Judicial Branch

Unless you are a lawyer, chances are the judicial branch of the government is a mystery to you. While the judiciary is the third leg of the stool on which the U.S. government is based, and without which it would collapse, most people can't fathom what those guys in the robes are doing (except when they're presiding over trials), or why they're doing it. The standard explanation—that the Congress makes the laws, the president enforces them, and the courts interpret them—leaves most people in the dark. But what the courts do, and why they do it, is a large part of why the Constitution actually functions!

Courts and the Constitution

The only court that the Constitution actually mandates is the Supreme Court, and it doesn't say much about it; not how many justices are to sit on the Court, not how they'll be chosen, not even what their qualifications should be. Article III, one of the shortest in the Constitution, does outline, in very broad terms, what those who hold the power of the judiciary are tasked with doing. Then it mentions that those charged with crimes are entitled to a jury trial, explains what will constitute treason, discusses the punishment for treason—and that's it.

> *The judicial Power of the United States shall be vested in one supreme Court, and in such inferior Courts as the Congress may from time to time ordain and establish. The Judges, both of the supreme and inferior Courts, shall hold their Offices during good Behaviour, and shall, at stated Times, receive for their Services a Compensation, which shall not be diminished during their Continuance in Office.*

This is an area where the framers just assumed—as they did when not specifying English as the country's official language—that anyone who read it would know what they meant. In "Federalist No. 2," John Jay said the United States was "one united people—a people descended from the same ancestors, speaking the same language. . . . " He also presumed that they would understand the traditions of English Common Law; after all, they had just fought a war to win themselves "the rights of Englishmen."

The Founders presumed the American people understood the system of precedents and written opinions that had grown out of English tradition. These presumptions were interwoven in the fabric of the Constitution. As a result of this reliance on written decisions and commentary, it could be said the Court created itself and the court system in which it operates, and in the course of doing that, created the way the country actually works.

What the Constitution Says about the Judicial Branch

The phrasing of the introduction suggests there is, or should be, a judicial power that exists, and the framers certainly didn't want to put that power into the hands of the executive, who could—given the power to judge as well as to prosecute—become a tyrant. Congress had enough to do, and if the president was not going to have this power, it had to go somewhere.

Courts already existed in the states, mostly municipal courts, and sometimes higher courts to which municipal rulings could be appealed. Courts were where juries sat, but juries were the principal decision-makers. The Constitution spelled out a number of matters the Supreme Court was to decide, but no one was sure while drafting the Constitution whether that caseload would be particularly burdensome; for example, whether lower federal courts would be needed, or how many there should be. Perhaps the Supreme Court could answer all federal questions that came up. If it couldn't, then Congress could create "such inferior Courts" as it found necessary.

Mysterious though the third branch was, the framers wanted it to be independent, a strong check to balance the other two branches. The judges would serve for as long as they conducted themselves with "good behaviour," and their salaries could not be reduced during their tenure on the court. Nothing was said about *increases* in compensation. Given the length of time many justices have served on the court—several in excess of three decades—failing to increase their salaries could be a cause of hardship that could affect a justice's independence.

FACT

> The two longest-tenured Chief Justices of the Supreme Court were John Marshall (1801 to 1835) and Roger B. Taney (1836 to 1864). The longest serving Associate Justice was William O. Douglas, who served on the Court from 1939 to 1975.

A judge or justice serves for "good behaviour," a term inherited from British law that amounts, in essence, to a lifetime appointment. (Specific acts of good behavior—or bad—have not been defined, but, as Justice Potter Stewart famously said about pornography, "I know it when I see it.") This lifetime tenure has contributed to a judiciary that is not only independent of Congress and the president, but also, over time, can become independent of politics. Because what judges do is weigh the law and write studied opinions based on what they come to believe the law actually means, many of them, even those who were not particularly learned at the time of their appointment, become scholars of the law. This is precisely what the framers intended, according to "Federalist No. 78." Furthermore, being removed from the political fray, many (though not all) of them become less didactic, modifying their views over time.

What the Constitution Says about Judges' Qualifications

There is nothing in the Constitution that requires a judge or a justice to be a lawyer, or even to have studied law—nothing, that is, but the requirement of confirmation by the Senate (which must "advise and consent" to judicial appointments made by the president). All who have served as justices of the Supreme Court have been trained in the law, but their prior experience has varied. Many have been judges, but that is not a prerequisite either. Earl Warren had been governor of California before being named Chief Justice. William Howard Taft had been president.

QUESTION

When was the first woman justice appointed to the Supreme Court? Although women won the right to vote with the Nineteenth Amendment in 1920, it took more than 60 years before the first woman justice, Sandra Day O'Connor, was appointed to the Court by Ronald Reagan in 1981. She was confirmed by the Senate with a vote of 99–0.

The process for choosing a Supreme Court Justice is contained in the Constitution, but not in the section that deals with the courts. In Section 2 of Article II, the Constitution grants the president the power, "by and with the Advice and Consent of the Senate," to appoint "Judges of the supreme Court" and such other "Officers of the United States, whose Appointments are not herein otherwise provided for, and which shall be established by Law." Section 8 of Article I gives Congress the specific power "To constitute Tribunals inferior to the supreme Court," which is where (along with Article III, Section 1) the authority to create lower courts comes from. And the only reference to a chief justice comes in Article I, Section 3, where it says that when a president who has been impeached is tried by the Senate, the chief justice is to preside (so clearly, there should be one!).

The Number of Justices

The Constitution also makes no reference to the number of justices that will comprise the Supreme Court; by its authority to "constitute tribunals," Congress has passed laws setting a different number of justices at different times. The first Congress, in passing the Judiciary Act of 1789, set the number of justices at five plus the chief justice. The act also created district courts (at least one for each state that had ratified the Constitution, with an extra district each for Massachusetts and Virginia, to cover the outlying areas of what would eventually become Maine and Kentucky).

The act also created the circuit courts. These heard appeals and also more serious cases and those involving larger amounts. The circuit courts got their name because two judges of the Supreme Court would "ride the circuit" of district courts, where they would sit as part of a panel with the local district judge.

Because each state had at least one district, the number of district courts increased as new states were added. The number of Supreme Court justices also increased as more circuits were added. At one point there were ten justices. Eventually, Congress set the current number, nine, including the chief justice.

At one point, because his New Deal legislation had been stymied by the "nine old men" on the Court, President Franklin Roosevelt proposed increasing the number of justices to as many as fifteen. This "court-packing plan" was never enacted. The number remains at nine.

Not every case is heard by the full Court. There may be fewer justices sitting because of temporary vacancies (usually due to the death of a justice, since retiring justices often time their retirement so no vacancy will occur). And sometimes justices (like judges in other courts) recuse themselves, withdrawing from a case in which they may have, or are perceived to have, a conflict of interest.

Federal Jurisdiction

The Constitution defines the power of the judicial branch in Section 2 of Article III. The first paragraph of this section of the Constitution creates what are known as federal questions—matters that must be heard in the federal courts, as opposed to the state courts:

The judicial Power shall extend to all Cases, in Law and Equity, arising under this Constitution, the Laws of the United States, and Treaties made, or which shall be made, under their Authority.

Where a case arises out of a violation of a federal law, whether that case is civil or criminal, it is normally heard in federal courts. When a case arises under a law passed by Congress under its powers listed in Section 8 of Article I, it is termed a "federal question." Copyrights and patents, immigration matters, and bankruptcies are some matters that are pre-empted; they must be brought into a federal court.

FACT

Cases in equity were an English tradition under which civil litigants could appeal a court decision to the king or his chancellor on "equity" or fairness. Legal remedies tend to be limited to monetary damages; equitable remedies can include injunctions (orders to stop doing something) or the return of an item. In most of the United States, courts of law and equity are now merged.

Cases involving federal crimes like counterfeiting are also tried in federal court. Section 2 of Article III enumerates a number of specific cases of federal question:

- All Cases affecting Ambassadors, other public Ministers and Consuls
- All Cases of admiralty and maritime Jurisdiction
- Controversies to which the United States shall be a Party
- Controversies between two or more States
- Between a State and Citizens of another State (This section was voided by the passage of the Eleventh Amendment.)

- Between Citizens of different States (This section has been modified over the years by requiring not only *diversity*—that no party on one side can be from the same state as any party on the other side—but also by requiring that the suit involve a substantial claim. Currently, unless a civil suit enters the federal courts because of its subject matter, the amount in controversy must be at least $75,000.)
- Between Citizens of the same State claiming Lands under Grants of different States
- Between a State, or the Citizens thereof, and foreign States, Citizens or Subjects

All of these matters except those between "citizens of different states" may be filed in a federal court as a matter of right without the threshold amount being reached.

Original Jurisdiction

When the types of cases mentioned in the previous list are filed in a federal court, the court in question is usually a district court (unless a special court exists to hear a particular kind of case). But the Constitution gives the Supreme Court "original jurisdiction" over certain very limited matters. "Original jurisdiction" means that by law, a case may be brought directly to the Supreme Court. All other cases that the Supreme Court hears get there on appeal; for them, the jurisdiction (right of the Court to hear a case) is termed "appellate jurisdiction."

The Supreme Court does not have to hear every case that is appealed to it. It can pick and choose those cases it feels have import or where a grave injustice appears to have been done. To get them to consider hearing your appeal, you must file for a writ of certiorari—literally an order to the lower court to send the case file up to them, but actually, the acceptance of the case for review. Only if they grant the writ will they hear the case.

Here is what Article III, Section 2 of the Constitution says about the Supreme Court's original jurisdiction:

In all Cases affecting Ambassadors, other public Ministers and Consuls, and those in which a State shall be Party, the supreme Court shall have original Jurisdiction. In all the other Cases before mentioned, the supreme Court shall have appellate Jurisdiction, both as to Law and Fact, with such Exceptions, and under such Regulations as the Congress shall make.

This has turned out to be one of the most important parts of the Constitution. It figures heavily in one of the most important Supreme Court opinions, *Marbury v. Madison*, in 1803.

The matters mentioned in Section 2 of Article III of the Constitution may be civil or criminal. But the Constitution has some very specific things to say about criminal proceedings.

ESSENTIAL

Civil and criminal cases exist in almost parallel universes within the court systems. Criminal matters involve breaking a law; the government prosecutes the accused; fines are paid to the government, and punishments, like incarceration, are imposed by the government. In civil matters, one person sues another, and a victory in court can result in substantial payment to the person who is suing. The rules and standards for the two kinds of cases can be very different.

Because the enforcement of justice could be arbitrary in England, the framers of the Constitution were determined to make sure that in American criminal law, there would always be protections for individuals.

Criminal Cases

The portions of the Constitution that deal with Congress and the president set forth the way in which *impeachments* are to be handled. *This* section deals not with reasons for removing someone from office, but with persons accused of crimes.

The Trial of all Crimes, except in Cases of Impeachment, shall be by Jury; and such Trial shall be held in the State where the said Crimes shall have been committed; but when not committed within any State, the Trial shall be at such Place or Places as the Congress may by Law have directed.

What is a crime? Before there can be a crime, there must be a law that defines an act as being criminal, or a duty as being mandatory. For example, a law may state that it is illegal to steal from someone; stealing is therefore an example of a criminal act. The requirement to file tax returns and pay your taxes when they are due is an example of a duty that, if you fail to perform it, can be another kind of criminal act.

Unless there is some constitutional authority for Congress to pass a law defining a crime, *state* law defines various crimes. And if a criminal act happens within a single state, and does not violate a federal law, it will be prosecuted in the courts of that state. But the Constitution is the "supreme law of the land," and certain rights are guaranteed to criminals throughout the country by the Constitution.

For example, Americans are guaranteed a right to trial by jury in all criminal matters. In a civil case, the right to trial by jury depends on whether it is a federal case (in which the Seventh Amendment gives you that right) or a state case. If it's a state case, the right to a jury in a civil matter is determined by the law in each state. The right to a trial by jury can be waived by both parties in a civil case, or by the defendant in a criminal case; just because you have a right does not mean you must exercise it.

Americans are also guaranteed the right to be tried for any crime in the state where it was committed. This was a grievance the colonists had against the British; sometimes people accused of a crime in the colonies were taken to London for prosecution. Away from a familiar support system, if becomes more difficult to mount a defense. Despite this right to be tried where the crime occurred, a defendant may ask the court to remove the case to another locale, especially if there appears to have been excessive local publicity about it, which could prejudice a jury and preclude a fair trial.

The Heritage of English Common Law

American law is based on English law, and the English had a common law system. Rulings became precedents, and people came to rely on them. When courts were established in the British colonies in North America, these same precedents were incorporated into American law. (These precedents tended to move westward according to latitude. Thus the legal traditions of New York found their way into Michigan and Wisconsin law, while the common law and other legal traditions of Virginia found their way to Kentucky and Arkansas.)

In some countries, like France, every little detail appears in the code books. The United States and most states follow English common law in this respect; however, Louisiana, as a former French colony, bases its law on the Code Napoleon, but with the same constitutional guarantees as the rest of the country nonetheless.

The Only Defined Crime: Treason

Although it was dubbed "the Age of Reason," the eighteenth century was not that far removed from the excesses of the fifteenth and sixteenth centuries, and the way kings got what they wanted by arbitrarily accusing those in their way of treason. The founders were determined to make sure this never made its way into their new nation.

Treason is the only crime defined in the Constitution, and it is found in the section on the Judiciary. Here is what it says in Section 3 of Article III:

Treason against the United States, shall consist only in levying War against them, or in adhering to their Enemies, giving them Aid and Comfort. No Person shall be convicted of Treason unless on the Testimony of two Witnesses to the same overt Act, or on Confession in open Court.

While the phrase "giving them Aid and Comfort" broadens the definition somewhat, the constitutional definition remains quite narrow. You can't be accused of treason for insulting the president, for example, or for burning the flag, a protection that was also guaranteed by the First Amendment. And you can't be proven guilty of treason unless there are two witnesses to the same overt act; later decisions noted that plotting treason would not qualify unless you attempted to carry it out. You can also be convicted of treason based on your confession, but other parts of the Constitution guarantee that the confession cannot be coerced.

The Constitution also says that the punishment for treason cannot extend to a person's family: "but no Attainder of Treason shall work Corruption of Blood, or Forfeiture except during the Life of the Person attainted." The actual penalties for treason are not set forth; the Constitution gives Congress the right to set punishment for treason, but pursuant to the Eighth Amendment, that punishment cannot be "cruel and unusual." And the prohibition against ex post facto laws further prevents Congress from creating a crime out of an act which, when performed, was not illegal. This can make it difficult to punish someone who publishes purloined government documents, but it is really there to protect the average acts of the average citizen from being made illegal after the fact.

Chief Justice John Marshall

In 1801, John Marshall, who had been secretary of state under President John Adams, became the fourth chief justice of the United States. He would become the longest-serving chief justice, remaining on the bench until his death in 1835. During that time, the Court's decisions, many of them written by him, would shape the course of the Court and of the country. These cases established the precedents under which the United States has operated ever since, and the earliest ones established the precedent of their authority.

FACT

In 1776, John Marshall joined the Continental Army where he served under his father's old classmate, George Washington. Marshall was involved in fighting in New Jersey, New York, and Pennsylvania and was also present during the brutal winter of 1777–1778 that the army spent at Valley Forge.

Marbury v. Madison (1803)

In 1801, just as President John Adams was about to leave office, he appointed forty-two justices of the peace who were confirmed by a lame duck Senate. Although their commissions were signed, some were not delivered before the new president, James Madison, was sworn in. He refused to have them delivered.

William Marbury was one of the men who did not receive his commission. He sued in the Supreme Court, under original jurisdiction granted to it by the Judiciary Act of 1789. Justice Marshall wrote the opinion for the Court, saying that Marbury did have a right to his commission, but that the case could not be brought directly to the Supreme Court, because the Constitution established when the Supreme Court should have original jurisdiction, and the Congress could not change that.

Marshall reasoned that because the Constitution was the "supreme law of the land," what it said could overrule any law Congress made that did not conform to the Constitution—and the original jurisdiction of the Court was limited by the Constitution, although Congress had the right to expand the Court's appellate jurisdiction.

But most important, he ruled that when the Constitution says, "The judicial Power shall extend to all Cases, in Law and Equity, arising under this Constitution, the Laws of the United States, and Treaties made," it meant that "it is emphatically the province and duty of the judicial department to say what the law is." This established the precedent of judicial review of laws passed by the Congress.

Martin v. Hunter's Lessee (1816)

This case, involving the inheritance of some land in Virginia, and its subsequent sale and lease, dragged on for decades, complicated by the fact that the land had been left to a British citizen (Martin). Since Justice Marshall had purchased part of the vast tract of land in question, he recused himself, declining to participate because of his conflict of interest. Associate Justice Joseph Story, therefore, wrote the opinion.

The Court had sent the case back to a Virginia court to decide, directing them to act in compliance with a 1796 treaty. When the Virginia court refused, Justice Story wrote, for the court, that according to the Constitution, the ratified treaty was a part of the "supreme law of the land." The ultimate conclusion of this complex case was that where state and federal laws were in conflict, the states were subservient to the federal law and decisions, because of the Constitution's supremacy. And the Supreme Court had the authority to overrule state courts because there had to be a national authority to determine what the federal law was for the whole country.

McCulloch v. Maryland (1819)

This case involved the second Bank of the United States' refusal to pay a tax that was enacted on its banknotes by the state of Maryland. McCulloch was the bank's cashier, which is how his name got onto the case.

Justice Marshall wrote the opinion, stating that the last clause in Section 8 of Article I, which gives Congress its powers, allows Congress to make all laws "necessary and proper" to carry out the other powers. Because the Constitution is superior, as are the laws created under its specific authority, no state can interfere with them, and taxing the banknotes of a bank that had been chartered by Congress was interfering.

Writing for the Court in *McCulloch*, Marshall gave broad scope to what Congress could do under the "necessary and proper" clause, thus expanding the authority of Congress just as he had expanded the authority of the Court in *Marbury*. In this way, one case at a time, the Supreme Court created the nation that has evolved over 200 years.

Federal Jurisdiction and State Jurisdiction

Although the Constitution is the "supreme Law of the Land" under Article VI of the Constitution, the Tenth Amendment modifies this when it says, "The powers not delegated to the United States by the Constitution, nor prohibited by it to the States, are reserved to the States respectively, or to the people." There are vast areas of the law that the federal government does not deal with, everything from regulating the shores of inland lakes to sweeping the streets to determining the nature of marriage and the age of consent. These powers are reserved to the states, and when a case involves them—such as a case in trespass, or a divorce, or a crime (such as burglary), that takes place totally within a single state—these cases must be brought in state courts.

Each state's courts are run according to that state's laws, subject only to the rights guaranteed to people by the Constitution and its amendments. Each state's courts have their own appeals route. You can get into the federal court system with a state court matter, but it needs to have "exhausted all state remedies"—that is, have appealed as far as possible within the state court system—or it needs to pose a federal question. If, for example, on a state criminal matter, the defendant's right to a jury has been denied, an appeal can be made to federal court on a constitutional (civil rights) basis. A person who has been incarcerated without being told why the arrest was made can appeal to the federal courts for a habeas corpus writ, demanding to be released. Or if the case somehow falls under the Supreme Court's original jurisdiction, an appeal can be made directly, straight to the Supreme Court.

How the Federal Courts Are Organized

Under the Constitution, only one court is mandated: the Supreme Court. But Congress is empowered to create "inferior courts" as it deems necessary. These are called "Article III courts" because of the section of the Constitution that authorizes them. Congress has been creating inferior courts since the Judiciary Act of 1789. Currently, these courts consist of district courts and circuit courts of appeals, as well as the U.S. Court of Federal Claims and the U.S. Court of International Trade.

There are also "Article I courts." These are tribunals created by Congress as part of other agencies (including, sometimes, the courts). They include military courts martial, administrative judges who determine things like eligibility for disability payments under Social Security, and even federal magistrate courts (who take minor administrative hearings off the desks of district court judges) and bankruptcy courts. The judges in these courts do not serve for life but for limited terms; in addition, their salaries can be reduced. Magistrate judges and bankruptcy judges are appointed by the judges on the court of appeals under which they serve, and they have limited jurisdiction.

Court decisions have ruled that Article I judges can't deprive anyone of life, liberty, or property, but must stick to minor administrative matters. As a rule, what this means is that their decisions can be appealed to the district court under which they serve, although usually a court trial is a much less efficient process than an administrative hearing, and reversal is generally unlikely.

There are also Article IV courts, created under the power of Congress in Section 3 of that article, for administering territories outside of the fifty states.

District Courts

There are ninety-four federal district courts. Every state has at least one judicial district; there is also one for the District of Columbia and one for the Commonwealth of Puerto Rico. In addition, there is a special U.S. Court of Federal Claims that hears claims against the U.S. government.

More populous states may have several districts, usually designated by their territory, such as the Southern District of New York (SDNY) or the Eastern District of Wisconsin (EDWI). The term "district court" refers to the class of court; each district court may have more than one judge. Each judge has a courtroom and staff; cases are assigned to different district judges on a random basis.

Although one of the judges in a district may be designated "chief judge" for administrative purposes, the judges have coequal power and occasionally make decisions that conflict as to principles of law. An appeal to the circuit court of appeals in which the district court sits may result in a ruling that will bind all district courts for that circuit, but not those of other circuits.

Circuit Courts

There are a dozen circuit courts of appeals, so named because originally, justices of the Supreme Court "rode the circuit" to hear appeals from various district courts. There may be a number of judges on any circuit court of appeals, but they usually appear in panels of three judges, although on some cases they are empowered to sit *en banc*, meaning all of the judges for that circuit hear the trial together. This may happen when different courts in the same circuit have issued conflicting rulings, in order to resolve the inconsistencies.

Courts in different circuits have co-equal power and do not have to follow the decisions of courts in other circuits, although they may choose to do so. Often, cases are appealed to the Supreme Court to resolve differences between the rule in one circuit and that of another. Decisions made by a circuit court of appeals bind only the district courts in that circuit, not in other circuits.

There is also a U.S. Court of Appeals for the Federal Circuit. This court hears appeals from all district courts in patent matters and also hears appeals from the U.S. Court of Federal Claims.

Magistrates

Federal magistrate judges are Article I judges who assist district court judges by hearing motions or holding preliminary hearings and scheduling hearings, in order to free up the district courts for trials. The magistrates may also hear prisoner appeals, like habeas corpus hearings.

Bankruptcy Courts

Bankruptcy judges are Article I judges, appointed by the circuit court of appeals in whose territory they serve. Cases are "referred" to them by the district court under which they serve, and their decisions are considered decisions of that court, but may be appealed to that court—or, if there is a bankruptcy appellate panel in that circuit, they may be appealed to that panel. Only five of the circuits have such panels. They are made up of bankruptcy judges from their circuit serving in groups of three. Bankruptcy judges are appointed for fourteen-year terms.

The Federal Appeals Process

The normal route to an appeal in the federal courts is up the chain of command, but you do not have to wait until a trial is finished before you can appeal. Often, there will be an appeal from a decision on a motion. A "motion" is a legal petition to the court to do something that will affect a trial, such as compel testimony of a witness, or freeze assets pending the resolution of a trial. You can also move to disallow certain evidence, that is, to keep it from presentation at trial. After the appellate court makes a ruling on this procedural matter, the trial resumes.

Matters from bankruptcy courts and magistrate courts are normally appealed to the district court in whose district the Article I court hears cases. Cases from district courts are generally appealed to circuit courts of appeals.

These appeals are generally considered "of right"—the courts to which you've appealed will have to hear your case. Not so with the Supreme Court. If you want to appeal a case to the Supreme Court, unless it comes under the Supreme Court's original jurisdiction, you petition for certiorari. The Supreme Court chooses which cases it will hear, and turns down most of them.

It is also possible to appeal a matter from a state court to the Supreme Court. The first time that occurred was in *Fletcher v. Peck*, in 1810. The current rule is that you must exhaust your state remedies before you can appeal to the Supreme Court of the United States. This usually means that you have appealed to, or been denied an appeal by, the highest court in your state.

There are occasions when a matter may be removed to a federal district court; for example, when a matter brought in a state court turns out to be something pre-empted by federal law, which should be in the federal system. This would involve matters such as copyright disputes or bankruptcy hearings, or a federal habeas corpus hearing. On rare occasions, there may be a direct appeal to the Supreme Court, bypassing the court of appeals. This might happen when a law affecting the entire country, such as the military draft, is ruled unconstitutional by a district court. As in other certiorari cases, the Supreme Court is not obligated to accept the case, and may issue a decision saying it is not "ripe." But if the case really is of national import, it may take it so a decision can issue sooner.

When a Court Must Defer to Another Court

Rulings of the Supreme Court must be followed by all lower courts (unless the opinion says this is a unique matter and need not be followed, something very rare). Generally, courts are not bound by the decisions of other courts at their level, although they may take notice of a decision and incorporate it into their decision-making process. In other instances, they may take notice of it to specifically disagree with it.

When the superior court agrees with the lower court's ruling, it will usually *affirm*; when it disagrees, it will *reverse*. If it wants further information than the trial court provided, it may reverse and *remand*. A remand amounts to an order to do it over the right way. Sometimes it will issue a hybrid ruling, reversing in part and affirming in part.

The Supreme Court's holdings are seldom unanimous. Sometimes there is not even a full majority behind the written opinion "for the Court." There may be additional justices who concur, so that the decision carries the day, but for different reasons. Justices who disagree usually write a dissent, or dissenting opinion.

What the justices say "for the court" is the law of the land until and unless the Court reverses itself—and the Court may do that, although it usually tries to adhere to *stare decisis* (the standing decision). Perhaps the most famous example of a reversal was when *Brown v. Board of Education of Topeka, Kansas* (1955) reversed *Plessy v. Ferguson* (1896), ruling that racially segregated public schools could never be equal.

ALERT

Some Southern states defied the ruling of *Brown v. Board of Education of Topeka, Kansas*. In 1957, President Eisenhower used federal troops to protect African-American students attempting to attend a previously all-white public high school in Little Rock, Arkansas.

Hidden in what the justices say in an opinion may be *dicta*, or statements of opinion that have no real bearing on a case, and therefore do not have to be followed. But if they are commentary on something that has no other statements about it whatsoever in the annals of the court, they may sometimes be cited by lawyers in an attempt to create a basis for putting forth an argument.

The Need for Case or Controversy

In Section 2 of Article III, the Constitution lists all the matters that may be brought before the judicial branch of the government. All of them are cases or controversies; in other words, when the Supreme Court undertakes to weigh a matter, it must affect an individual or an entity (like a corporation or school board). The courts do not issue rulings in a vacuum, just because a law strikes them as wrong.

Someone must have been arrested, or injured, or damaged, or been threatened, by someone or something else, in order for the matter to get into court. Congress can pass a law saying the moon is made of green cheese, but unless you are a manufacturer of green cheese whose business has been hurt by the assertion, there is no case, and nothing for the court to rule on.

All opinions involve parties. The court rules for one side or the other, based on facts in evidence, and then explains why it came to that conclusion. Without the case or controversy, it cannot rule.

CHAPTER 7

The Bill of Rights: How the Constitution Affects People

Although the Constitution begins with the words "We the People," there is not very much about the people of the United States in the seven articles that make up the Constitution proper. This was a sticking point for a number of the Founding Fathers, so much so that some, like George Mason of Virginia, refused to sign the Constitution because it did not contain a bill of rights. The Federalists insisted that ratification by the states had to be on the Constitution as a whole, with no changes. But discomfort with a potentially strong central government without a bill of rights led to rancorous debates on the state level. In 1788, Massachusetts, in what became known as the "Massachusetts Compromise," ratified the Constitution, but included a recommendation for a bill of rights in its ratification document. A number of the other states, including New York and Virginia, made similar recommendations.

The Anti-Federalists

A group of the founders known as the "Anti-Federalists" were concerned that the strong central government, with a president at its helm, would run roughshod over the rights of individuals, and the president would soon take on the trappings of a monarch. These men, who included Patrick Henry, Samuel Adams, future president James Monroe, and George Mason, were especially vocal about the need for a bill of rights for individuals.

After all, the Articles of Confederation had consisted mainly of a bill of rights for the *states* that had joined together to form the union. The Constitution created a central government and attempted to define its rights and the way it would function. In fact, at the Constitutional Convention in the summer of 1787, there had been a great deal of debate as to whether it should contain a statement of the rights of individuals; the Constitution was only signed after there was an agreement that a bill of rights would be added by amendment.

Who Were "the People"?

Despite the fact that they were very conscious of their own liberties, the Founding Fathers took a narrow view of whom they meant by "We the People." Most of them were of Anglo-Saxon stock. All of them spoke English. All of them were white. And all of them were male.

Indeed, at various times, various states had even restricted the right to vote to those who not only met all those criteria, but also owned land.

ESSENTIAL

Congresswoman Barbara Jordan, who was both black and female, noted in 1974: "'We, the people.' It's a very eloquent beginning. But when that document was completed on the seventeenth of September in 1787, I was not included in that 'We, the people.' I felt somehow for many years that George Washington and Alexander Hamilton just left me out by mistake. But through the process of amendment, interpretation, and court decision, I have finally been included in 'We, the people.'"

Abigail Adams, writing to her husband when he was a delegate to the Continental Congress that drafted the Declaration of Independence in 1776, asked him to "remember the ladies." That wouldn't happen until 1920, with the ratification of the Nineteenth Amendment.

Congress Passes Twelve Amendments

The first U.S. government under the Constitution was eligible to take office on March 4, 1789. Due to problems with roads and with weather, George Washington was not sworn in as president until April 30 of that year; the House did not achieve a quorum until April 1, and the Senate did not achieve one until April 6.

However, once it got started, the First Federal Congress engaged in a flurry of activity. Among other things, it passed America's first copyright law and first patent law (these are two separate laws, but both are authorized by Article I, Section 8.) It created the Department of Foreign Affairs (now called the State Department), the Department of War (now called the Defense Department), and the Department of the Treasury. It passed the Judiciary Act of 1789, establishing the number of justices on the Supreme Court (six, including the chief justice, whose existence is referenced in Article I, Section 3) and creating the federal district and circuit courts and the office of attorney general. It also passed a naturalization act.

FACT

It takes approval of three-fourths of the states for an amendment to be ratified. When the Bill of Rights was proposed, ten states would have been enough. But ratification took two years, and in the interim, Vermont was admitted as a state, so the number of states required for ratification rose to eleven. Virginia was the eleventh state to ratify amendments three through twelve. By the time the second of the proposed amendments was ratified, in 1992, it required the approval of thirty-eight states.

And on September 25, 1789, it passed twelve amendments and sent them to the states for ratification. The third through the twelfth of these, which would become known as the Bill of Rights, were ratified by the requisite three-fourths of the states as of December 15, 1791, and became Amendments One through Ten. Appended to the end of the original document, they were incorporated into the Constitution and became part of the "supreme Law of the Land."

The first of the twelve proposed amendments, having to do with the number of constituents per House member, was never ratified, but the second (which did not have a time limit built into it, as most proposed amendments have had since the early twentieth century) was ratified in 1992 and became the Twenty-Seventh Amendment (dealing with Congressional pay).

The Bill of Rights

The first ten amendments to the Constitution restrain the federal government from imposing on certain rights granted to individuals. However, for the first seventy-seven years after ratification, these amendments applied only to the federal government, not to the states. The Fourteenth Amendment, ratified in 1868, in the wake of the Civil War, extended them to the state governments as well, but it would be at least three decades before the Supreme Court began to clarify that with its decisions.

ALERT

Most people do not know that the Bill of Rights has a preamble, just like the Constitution, because the preamble was not submitted for ratification and is not a part of the Constitution. However, it is an explanation of why these amendments were proposed, because "The Conventions of a number of the States, having at the time of their adopting the Constitution, expressed a desire" to prevent the federal government from abusing its power over the people.

There had originally been some discussion in Congress about how an amendment would be incorporated into the constitution. One alternative considered was adding the new language within the Constitution. However, it was decided that the original document should remain exactly as it was when ratified, and the amendments should be added to the end. This means that there is some language within the Constitution, when you read it, that is no longer valid, having been annulled or modified by amendments.

These are the ten amendments that make up the Bill of Rights:

- The First Amendment deals with freedom of religion, speech, the press, assembly, and the right to petition the government.
- The Second Amendment deals with the right of citizens to bear arms.
- The Third Amendment deals with quartering soldiers in private homes.
- The Fourth Amendment deals with unreasonable searches and seizures.
- The Fifth Amendment deals with the rights of those accused of crimes.
- The Sixth Amendment deals further with the rights of those accused of crimes.
- The Seventh Amendment deals with civil lawsuits.
- The Eighth Amendment deals with bail, fines, and punishment for crimes.
- The Ninth Amendment states that the list of rights in the Bill of Rights is not exclusive; there are others that are not listed.
- The Tenth Amendment says that if the Constitution hasn't given a right to the federal government, that right belongs to the states or to the people.

Most of the rights set forth in the Bill of Rights have been more finely defined in rulings the Supreme Court has issued over the past two centuries. How do you define "reasonable" or "unreasonable"? You do it by looking at examples where the Court has said, "This goes too far," or "This doesn't go far enough."

The First Amendment

The first thing you need to notice about the First Amendment is that it begins "Congress shall make no law. . . . "

Congress shall make no law respecting an establishment of religion, or prohibiting the free exercise thereof; or abridging the freedom of speech, or of the press; or the right of the people peaceably to assemble, and to petition the Government for a redress of grievances.

This did not originally mean that the *states* could not make laws that did what the amendment forbade. Until the Fourteenth Amendment was ratified, there were states, such as Massachusetts, that favored a particular church (in the case of Massachusetts, the Congregational Church) or limited freedom of speech or of the press. It wasn't until the early twentieth century that the Supreme Court began to apply these restrictions to the states by using the "incorporation doctrine," based on the words of the Fourteenth Amendment that promise no one should be deprived of life, liberty, or property without "due process of law."

Freedom of Religion

The religion clause has two parts: first, that the government (today this means all parts of the government in the United States, including state and municipal governments) may not establish a state religion (or favor one religion over the rest); and second, that it may not impede the right of people to practice the religion of their choice.

This can create an inherent conflict, because sometimes the free exercise of your religion may impinge upon someone else's right to exercise her beliefs. If you erect a cross in front of the courthouse on public land in your hometown, does this make it appear that your town is supporting Christianity to the detriment of non-Christian religions? If all of the children in the local primary school have a Christmas party where they eat cookies and sing Christmas carols (religious ones as well as secular ones), are the students who are intimidated into singing those carols, or who want to attend the party and therefore feel they must participate in a religious tradition that is alien to them, being inhibited from the free exercise of their own religion?

Do you get around this by having a joint Christmas and Chanukah party, with a Christmas tree and a menorah? What then of the students who are Muslim or Sikh, or atheist? Each of them is equally entitled to the free exercise of her religion.

FACT

The 1961 case *Torcaso v. Watkins* challenged the question of required religious tests. Roy Torasco was appointed a notary public in Maryland, and as an atheist, he refused to recite a statement declaring a belief in the existence of God. The Supreme Court reaffirmed that the Constitution forbids state and federal governments from requiring religious tests for those running for public office.

And what if your religion conflicts with what the public believes is the good of society? What if you do not believe in immunization in the midst of an epidemic? Or wish to practice polygamy? Or believe in female sexual mutilation? All of these situations may give rise to a limitation on the free exercise of religion, especially where it collides with the general welfare.

There is, in addition to the provisions of the First Amendment, one—just one—other place in the Constitution where religion is mentioned. It occurs in Article VI, where it says, "no religious Test shall ever be required as a Qualification to any Office or public Trust under the United States." So even before the passage of the First Amendment, the Constitution rejected what had been a fairly common practice in England and even in America. In view of the fact that a number of the original colonies were founded by particular religious groups, such as the Quakers in Pennsylvania and Catholics in Maryland, the abolition of religious tests is a testimonial to the belief—even before they said so in the First Amendment—that religious tests were incompatible with American ideals. Your right to hold public office in the United States would not be restricted by your religion once the Constitution was ratified.

Freedom of Speech and the Press

These two freedoms go hand in hand: the ability to speak freely, to say what you believe, and the freedom to commit your ideas and beliefs to print and to disseminate what you've printed. Nowadays, as the electronic frontier grows, there is a certain amount of blurring between spoken and written speech.

It is also considerably easier today to publish your ideas yourself, whether as a blog or as an e-book, or even as a self-published book. Disseminating your thoughts to people around the world has never been easier. With that ease, however, must come a certain amount of self-restraint, because as always with constitutional rights, these, too, are not absolute. Like everything in the Constitution, freedom of expression is part of a balancing act.

QUESTION

Is burning the flag a form of free speech?
The Supreme Court has not conclusively ruled on whether nonverbal acts such as wearing armbands can be construed as "speech." However, it has invalidated laws, both state and federal, that banned private owners from burning their flags, seeing this as an exercise in free speech.

Restraints and Defamation

With every right comes a certain amount of responsibility. There are three basic restraints on the freedom to express yourself. The first of these is social responsibility. This was perhaps best summed up by Justice Oliver Wendell Holmes, Jr., in 1919. In the case of *Schenck v. United States*, "The most stringent protection of free speech would not protect a man falsely shouting fire in a theater and causing a panic." Clearly, when the exercise of your freedom of speech causes harm—and does so for no good reason—then the needs of society as a whole may require a curtailment on that free speech.

There is also the problem of defamation. Defamation is a civil wrong, committed against another person or group, rather than against society as a whole. If you publish something false about another person, and the defamation causes that person harm or economic loss, you can be made to compensate the person you have defamed. This may be a kind of curtailment of free speech, but it is a variation on that balancing act: Your right to swing your arm ends where your fist collides with another person's nose.

Copyright

A third restriction on freedom of speech lies in one of the other areas of Congressional power: copyright. The first U.S. copyright law was passed by the First Federal Congress, in 1789. The United States is signatory to the Berne Convention for the Protection of Literary and Artistic Works, a multinational treaty that, because it was ratified by the Senate in 1989, is now part of U.S. law. Indeed, pursuant to Article VI of the Constitution, which says, "This Constitution . . . and all Treaties made . . . under the Authority of the United States, shall be the supreme Law of the Land," the Berne Convention, too, is part of the supreme law of the United States. And as a consequence of U.S. copyright law and U.S. membership in the Berne Convention, you cannot reproduce a copyrighted work (whether photograph, music, audiovisual work, text, or a combination of those) owned by another person without that person's permission. If you do so, you can suffer both civil and criminal penalties.

Freedom to Peaceably Assemble

Gathering in support or in protest is one of the basic freedoms Americans think of as fundamental. Over the years, however, such actions have met with police restriction (from the Haymarket riot in 1886 to the gathering outside the 1968 Democratic National Convention in Chicago to the Kent State shootings in 1970) that has led to bloodshed. One of the ways the right to assemble was curtailed back in the 1960s and 1970s was to require a parade permit for any gathering, and then make the permit difficult to obtain. The key word here is "peaceably." Throwing rocks or Molotov cocktails doesn't qualify; the government has a right and a duty to quell a riot. (And the key word here is "riot." Mere shouting, or trying to escape from tear gas used as a weapon against a crowd, rather than a means of dispersing it, does not necessarily qualify as a riot.) The courts may eventually invalidate arrests made under such circumstances.

The Second Amendment

The juxtaposition of the two parts of the Second Amendment has driven people crazy for years.

> *A well regulated Militia, being necessary to the security of a free State, the right of the people to keep and bear Arms, shall not be infringed.*

Does it mean that everyone in the United States is entitled to own a gun? Does it mean that the Constitution favors the establishment and maintenance of a band of citizen soldiers and that owning guns is part of their requisite equipment? Are, perhaps, the two parts not related at all? Are they just two unrelated statements—that militias are a good thing, and so is owning a weapon (if you want to do so)?

The meaning of the "right to keep and bear arms" in 1789 meant a flintlock rifle, not an Uzi. The word in the Constitution is "arms." Could this mean a Taser, or a blowgun? Or perhaps a lightsaber?

In 2008, in *District of Columbia v. Heller*, the Supreme Court struck down an ordinance that restricted gun ownership by individuals. The Court held that under the Second Amendment, individuals, even those not affiliated with a militia, can own guns for hunting and self-defense in a federal enclave.

However, the Court indicated that it did not mean that the government could not impose some restrictions on gun ownership—for example, the right of convicted felons and the mentally ill to possess guns. It also did not ban the prohibition of guns in schools and other public buildings, nor did it mean to ban the kinds of guns not normally used for self-defense (such as automatic or semi-automatic weapons). Additionally, because this case struck down a District of Columbia (federal) rule, the Court did not decide whether the Second Amendment is, by virtue of the incorporation or other doctrine, applicable to state law concerning gun control as well.

The Third Amendment

The fourteenth grievance that the Americans set forth in the Declaration of Independence against King George was "For Quartering large bodies of armed troops among us." The king and Parliament had sent large numbers of troops to keep the peace in the colonies, which had been growing more and more unruly. The Americans had further been ordered to provide lodging for these troops. Bristling from this insult, the Americans banned their own country from quartering troops in their homes without their consent, and without a set legal framework for doing so.

No Soldier shall, in time of peace be quartered in any house, without the consent of the Owner, nor in time of war, but in a manner to be prescribed by law.

Since such quartering was never done (except on occasion in the aftermath of battle during the Civil War), cases have not come up. It is not even certain whether this law also applies to the states under the incorporation doctrine, although the statement "but in a manner to be prescribed by law" might imply a requirement of due process. This amendment has simply not been tested in the courts.

The Fourth Amendment

If you watch police procedural shows on television, like *Law & Order*, you are familiar with the workings of the Fourth Amendment, although you may not realize it.

The right of the people to be secure in their persons, houses, papers, and effects, against unreasonable searches and seizures, shall not be violated, and no Warrants shall issue, but upon probable cause, supported by Oath or affirmation, and particularly describing the place to be searched, and the persons or things to be seized.

This is the amendment that requires police to get a warrant before they can enter a private home or office and search it. This amendment has been applied to state as well as federal matters using the incorporation doctrine of the Fourteenth Amendment.

Basically, if evidence is obtained illegally, it is inadmissible at trial. Police need a warrant for a legal search. To get a warrant, they need probable cause. "Probable cause" is in itself an ambiguous term; it is based on a reasonable presumption that a crime has been committed and that a reasonable person would infer from the information publicly available that the person or place to be searched has something relevant to do with it. Words like "probable" and "reasonable" abound; their definition is somewhat elastic, but if they are stretched too thin, and information is obtained on a warrant that was not reasonably issued, that evidence cannot be used at a trial.

This is known as the "exclusionary rule." Moreover, if the search uncovers other evidence that leads to the discovery of still more evidence, that final proof may be excluded as "fruit of the poisonous tree" (evidence that was obtained illegally). In other words, if the original search was tainted, so will be all evidence that it turns up, and all evidence that *that* evidence leads to.

There are some exceptions to this need for a warrant. If the officer is a witness to the crime, or if, after pulling someone over for a reasonable search—for example, if a car is stopped for a broken taillight or an expired license plate—contraband, such as an assault rifle or drug equipment is visible in plain sight (i.e., through the window of the car), the officer may have probable cause to make an arrest and conduct a search on the spot.

The Fifth Amendment

The Fifth Amendment is probably, along with the First Amendment, the most well-known article of the Bill of Rights. It contains a number of protections that safeguard people from such things as double jeopardy and self-incrimination, terms most Americans know, even if they don't know the source.

> *No person shall be held to answer for a capital, or otherwise infamous crime, unless on a presentment or indictment of a Grand Jury, except in cases arising in the land or naval forces, or in the Militia, when in actual service in time of War or public danger; nor shall any person be subject for the same offence to be twice put in jeopardy of life or limb; nor shall be compelled in any criminal case to be a witness against himself, nor be deprived of life, liberty, or property, without due process of law; nor shall private property be taken for public use, without just compensation.*

Although originally applied only to federal court matters, most of the Fifth Amendment has been expanded to cover state procedure as well, under the incorporation doctrine of the Fourteenth Amendment. (The requirement for an indictment by a grand jury is not always used in the states, although "informations" or "complaints" issued by prosecutors, along with probable cause hearings, usually fill the gap.)

The parts of the Fifth Amendment bear looking at individually in order to understand this important rule.

Indictment by a Grand Jury

Most other common law countries have abandoned the grand jury but the entity persists in the United States, probably because of this constitutional provision. The grand jury is part of the system of checks and balances; it forces a prosecutor to make a case for probable cause before issuing an indictment—an accusation or charge—against someone, who will then be tried for the charges set forth in the indictment.

Grand jury proceedings are secret, and the defendant does not have the opportunity to cross-examine witnesses, since the only reason these proceedings exist is to find out whether the available testimony and evidence add up to enough to bring an accused to trial. If a grand jury does not find there is probable cause (in some jurisdictions, there is a probable cause hearing before a judge to determine this, instead of a grand jury), then no indictment is issued.

Grand juries have the power to subpoena reluctant witnesses, which is one of the reasons prosecutors like to use them. The kind of jury that you usually serve on when you have jury duty is properly termed a "petit jury." Generally in the United States, a petit jury consists of twelve people, but there can be fewer if local laws permit it.

Cases Arising in the Land or Naval Forces

The military exception to the grand jury rule exists because cases arising under military justice systems—either within the military or in territories that are under "martial law" in times of war or insurrection—are tried in courts martial, with different rules.

The debate about where to try those being held at Guantanamo Naval Base under accusations of terrorism is really about whether they can, or should, be tried in civilian courts, with all the protections of the American legal system, or in military courts, under the rules for such courts, or in specially constituted courts created for the purpose. Since Congress has the power both "to constitute Tribunals inferior to the supreme Court" and "to define and punish . . . Offences against the Law of Nations" under Article I,

Section 8 of the Constitution, there are legal arguments that can be made for any of the three courses of action.

QUESTION

Have military tribunals/commissions been used before in United States history?
Yes. Military tribunals have been used to bring enemy forces to trial in our history by General George Washington during the American Revolution, President Lincoln during the Civil War, and President Franklin D. Roosevelt during World War II.

Twice Put in Jeopardy of Life and Limb

This is the famous prohibition against "double jeopardy." You can only be tried once for any crime, and if you are acquitted, you are free, even if evidence or a witness turns up later that could prove your guilt.

In actual practice, there are certain circumstances that look like they are exceptions to the rule of double jeopardy, but they are not. For example, if something you did constitutes both a state offense and a federal crime, you can be tried in state court for the state offense and in federal court for the federal offense. And sometimes, the same act gives rise to a wholly different federal offense; for example, theft or fraud at the state level, and conspiracy to commit fraud at the federal level. These are actually different crimes.

In addition, the victim or victims of your criminal acts can bring a civil suit against you to recover damages. When a criminal case is brought, the government prosecutes you and, if you are found guilty, it imposes punishment, such as incarceration or fines. It can sometimes require that you pay restitution to your victims for their losses, but because the actual victims can be hard to ascertain, it may not do so. On the other hand, a civil case is brought by an aggrieved party, the victim of a crime or the survivor of a victim. If you lose in a civil case, you may be ordered to "make your victim whole"—pay enough money to make up for the damage you did. No jail time is involved unless you refuse to pay, in which case you could be held in contempt of court.

A person can be subject to both civil and criminal penalties for the same act. Since the standards are different, it is possible to be found not guilty of a crime that was not proved beyond a reasonable doubt (the criminal standard), but liable in civil court, where the standard is proof by a preponderance of the evidence. The O. J. Simpson murder and civil trials are an example of this.

Nor Compelled to Be a Witness Against Himself

The Fifth Amendment says that no one "shall be compelled in any criminal case to be a witness against himself." When you are under oath in a criminal matter, you are required "to tell the truth, the whole truth, and nothing but the truth," but what if the truth would implicate you in wrongdoing? Without the protections that the Fifth Amendment affords, your only alternative would be to lie under oath, which, if found out, would mean compounding the crime by committing perjury, another criminal act.

The Fifth Amendment allows you to say, "I refuse to testify on grounds that I might incriminate myself." Known as "pleading the Fifth" or "taking the Fifth," it is a privilege everyone has under the Constitution. Should you worry that making that statement could make you appear to be hiding something? The jury is normally given a specific instruction that they may not take your refusal to answer as anything but that—a refusal to say anything lest your words be twisted or misinterpreted, a refusal that is within your rights as an American.

Because not everyone realizes that this right is available, the "Miranda warning" has been given to all persons arrested since 1966. That was the year the Supreme Court, in *Miranda v. Arizona,* overturned the conviction of Ernesto Miranda, who had confessed to a crime, not realizing that he had the right to remain silent, and that if he chose to speak, everything he said could be used against him.

ESSENTIAL

The standard Miranda warning reads as follows: "You have the right to remain silent. Anything you say can and will be used against you in a court of law. You have the right to speak to an attorney, and to have an attorney present during any questioning. If you cannot afford a lawyer, one will be provided for you at government expense."

Without Due Process of Law

Taking someone's life, liberty, or property without "due process of law" is flatly prohibited by the Fifth Amendment. But what is meant by "due process"? The traditional view meant that all the appropriate documents had been served, and all proper procedures followed. In the United States, this is what would normally be called "procedural due process." There is also another kind of due process, known as "substantive due process." This is a rather complex concept that may give the Supreme Court a reason to invalidate a law because it denies not just the litigant, but all people of a certain category, or perhaps even all citizens, a fundamental right. Based ultimately on a theory of "natural law," fundamental rights are spelled out in the Declaration of Independence as "life, liberty and the pursuit of happiness" and in the Fifth Amendment as "life, liberty, or property." When a law deprives some or all of the people of the United States of these rights, it may be declared unconstitutional, because its effect is to deny people substantive due process.

The "Takings" Clause

Under a theory of "eminent domain," the government has always been able to take private property for public uses such as bridges, dams, and roads. But the final clause in the Fifth Amendment stressed the idea that this should not be done without appropriate payment. The clause reads, "nor shall private property be taken for public use, without just compensation."

This section of the Fifth Amendment has been expanded to include the states as well as the federal government under the incorporation doctrine since the passage of the Fourteenth Amendment. But if the law is to be read literally, property that is taken, even when the state is willing to pay for it, must be taken for "public use." This was construed to mean to eliminate a public nuisance, to create a public use (such as a park or housing project) or because of public need (for example, so a road could be widened).

The Court has ruled, over the last hundred years or so, that property may also be taken for a public "purpose" as well as a public "use." The 2005 case of *Kelo v. New London* took it a step further: the Supreme Court ruled that a government may take private property (with just compensation, but whether the owner wanted to sell it or not), and may then transfer it to another private party, if the purpose of that transfer appears to have some legitimate public value. (In this case, the city condemned some older waterfront homes so that they could transfer the land to a private company, the Pfizer Corporation, which intended to develop a plant, an office park, and some high-end housing. The city hoped to create jobs and enrich its property tax base by enabling the company to do so.)

The Court's majority held that this kind of taking was permissible, but invited state legislatures to redefine the purposes of eminent domain more narrowly if they disagreed, and many states did so in the wake of this decision. But it was too late for the homeowners who lost their property—and in the end, after the economic downturn, Pfizer abandoned the project.

The Court was divided five to four in this case, and Justice Sandra Day O'Connor's dissenting opinion noted that the decision would allow any property to be taken "for the benefit of another private party" and that the "beneficiaries are likely to be those citizens with disproportionate influence and power in the political process." Justice Clarence Thomas dissented even more strongly, saying that the Court had turned around the framers' intent, "against all common sense." It remains to be seen if the new laws created in the wake of this decision will narrow the scope of the government's ability to take properties in this manner.

The Sixth Amendment

Together with the Fifth Amendment's protections against self-incrimination and double jeopardy, the Sixth Amendment forms the basis for all American criminal procedure.

> In all criminal prosecutions, the accused shall enjoy the right to a speedy and public trial, by an impartial jury of the State and district wherein the crime shall have been committed, which district shall have been previously ascertained by law, and to be informed of the nature and cause of the accusation; to be confronted with the witnesses against him; to have compulsory process for obtaining witnesses in his favor, and to have the Assistance of Counsel for his defence.

Here are the rights to a speedy, public trial, to counsel, to an impartial jury, to confront your accusers, and to subpoena witnesses in your defense, all in a single paragraph. This was the rejection of the secret trials of the Star Chamber in England, and of the Crown's tendency to ship those accused of a crime in America all the way back to England for trial. It was also an affirmation of the rights that had been developing in both English and American law to protect the rights of those accused of crimes. It is worth exploring this powerful amendment phrase by important phrase, in the order that an arrest and trial would take.

All Criminal Prosecutions

This does not mean just federal crimes, but any criminal prosecution— *all* criminal prosecutions. Bear in mind that criminal and civil matters are not alike. These rules apply to the procedure in criminal cases.

Being Informed of the Nature of the Accusation

Unless you are informed of the nature of the accusations against you, there is no way to defend yourself from them. In England—indeed, in much of the rest of the world—arbitrary arrests were the norm, and you could sit in a cell for days, weeks, or months without knowing why. This still happens in some parts of the world.

To Confront the Witnesses

Part of the right to be confronted with the witnesses against you is the right to question them and, if you can, to challenge their testimony.

The Assistance of Counsel

As the law has evolved, it not only allows you to retain counsel, but convictions have been reversed when your lawyer has been found to be less than competent. Moreover, as the Miranda warning suggests, "If you cannot afford an attorney, one will be appointed for you."

Trial Venue

You have the right to be tried in the state and district where the crime was committed. This makes it easier for you to find witnesses, and if it is a district in which you reside, to have the assistance of friends and associates to help you.

Subpoena Power

You have the right to a "compulsory process for obtaining witnesses" in your favor. This can be helpful where defense witnesses are reluctant to come forward. If they are at your trial under subpoena—a court order to appear—not only will they be more likely to show up, but if they need an excuse for coming forward, the subpoena may get them off the hook with their associates who would rather they kept a lower profile.

A Speedy and Public Trial

Both of these factors are important. As William Gladstone, a nineteenth-century prime minister of England, noted, "Justice delayed is justice denied." While it is true that if you are found guilty, pretrial time served will often be deducted from your sentence, if you are acquitted (found innocent), any time you spend in pretrial custody or in trial preparation is time that is gone forever. Unlike people who are wrongfully convicted and who can often collect sums of money from the state, people who are wrongfully accused get no compensation if they are acquitted, only the right to go free.

The idea behind a public trial is that the prosecution is less likely to produce trumped-up evidence or shady witnesses. In the secret trials of England's Court of the Star Chamber, you could be railroaded—indeed, it was possible no one would know what had happened to you.

FACT

The Court of the Star Chamber was originally established to ensure the enforcement of laws against prominent people that would normally escape punishment from ordinary courts. Eventually, the court was used as a weapon against any citizens, and became a symbol of an abuse of power by the monarchy.

Trial By Jury

You have the right to be tried by an impartial jury from the area where the crime was committed. If this is your home district, you will be tried by people who know the area even if they don't know you. And they *shouldn't* know you. During the *voire dire*, the questioning session when the jury is chosen, members of the panel are specifically asked, "Do you know the accused?" or the victim, or the lawyers, and are rejected if they do.

Over the past two hundred years, the idea of what makes up an impartial jury has changed. The Court has ruled that not having any minority members on the panel from which the jury is chosen (especially if you are a member of a minority) can be a reason for reversing a verdict. (If the panel has enough of a variety of citizens on it, it may not matter if that variety is on the actual jury. But the possibility must exist.) By the same token, the panel should contain a mix of old and young, male and female.

Panels are usually chosen from the lists of registered voters. As a result, they will not normally include people who have former convictions themselves. (Some states allow those who have served their time for a crime to regain their right to vote; others do not.) But the broader the panel, the more likely the actual jury that is picked will have a varied background, and the more likely it is to be impartial.

The Seventh Amendment

The point of the Seventh Amendment was to keep appeals courts from overturning the verdicts juries had decided on the facts. Although the incorporation doctrine has not been applied to this amendment, and state courts in civil matters can therefore follow their own rules, it has become established law that appeals are made on the *law* and not on the *facts* of a case.

> *In Suits at common law, where the value in controversy shall exceed twenty dollars, the right of trial by jury shall be preserved, and no fact tried by a jury, shall be otherwise re-examined in any Court of the United States, than according to the rules of the common law.*

Only the jury (and this amendment guarantees the right to a jury in civil matters of consequence) has seen the witnesses and heard their testimony and examined the exhibits. Only the jury (or if a jury is waived, the trial court) can assess the facts.

Appeals are made on the law alone—they can be made if some procedural issue is amiss, if certain evidence was not allowed in, or if improper testimony was allowed. These are the "rules of the common law" on which the appeals court rules, and it rules on the law alone. If there is a matter of fact that was not allowed in but should have been, the appeals court can send the case back for retrial. But it cannot re-judge the facts itself.

The Eighth Amendment

This is the third of the amendments in the Bill of Rights that form the basis for American criminal law system. There are three parts to this amendment, and all of them are important, but the third is the one that is perhaps the most far-reaching: the prohibition against cruel and unusual punishment.

Excessive bail shall not be required, nor excessive fines imposed, nor cruel and unusual punishments inflicted.

This amendment, with minor grammatical differences, is virtually identical to one of the articles in the Virginia Declaration of Rights, passed a dozen years earlier. Its adjectives are subject to interpretation: "excessive," "cruel," "unusual." They have made for many a court case, and a sense of what they mean has emerged over the past two centuries.

The reason for the prohibition against excessive bail goes to the reason bail exists: so that the accused will not be incarcerated for an excessive time before trial. The point of bail is twofold: low enough to allow the accused to be released so that he can work on his defense, but high enough to make sure he shows up for trial, rather than forfeiting the money.

Alternatives to cash bail exist: You can purchase a bond, paying a percentage of the full bail amount, if a bondsman is willing to take the risk. If you show up for trial, the money you've paid for the bond is spent; if you don't show up, the bondsman pays the court, and then comes after you (and anyone who may have cosigned the bond) for repayment. Sometimes you'd rather deal with the courts! In the alternative, the bondsman may take a piece of property as security; if you fail to show up, he gets the property.

But in all instances, the idea behind bail is to find an amount that will cause you to think twice before you forfeit it, but that is small enough so that you can actually afford it, winning release until the trial date.

The prohibition against excessive fines is one with the prohibition against cruel and unusual punishment. This was part of the revulsion of the Americans at some of the punishments meted out in England and the rest of Europe: the rack, the wheel, burning at the stake, drawing and quartering— not to mention simple methods of execution like hanging and beheading. (Hanging survived in the United States as an appropriate death penalty. The others did not.)

This is not to say that some cruel and unusual punishments didn't make it to the American shores. The Salem witch trials are proof of that, and happened only a hundred years before the rational Founding Fathers created their enlightened new government. Furthermore, slaves, being regarded as property rather than people, could be whipped, branded, or otherwise mutilated, raped, and killed with impunity; the only thing stopping a slave owner was the idea of damaging his investment.

Recent cases have argued that the very existence of the death penalty is cruel and unusual punishment. Others have argued against certain methods, like lethal injection, based on the suffering it is alleged to cause. At this point, both the death penalty and that particular method are still considered legal, though interpretations may change with the times.

The Ninth Amendment

The language of the Ninth Amendment is not nearly as clear as the rest of the Constitution, but what it means is that the list of rights guaranteed to the people in the Bill of Rights (and the rest of the Constitution) is not exclusive or conclusive; there are many more rights out there, rights that haven't been mentioned or even alluded to, and they belong to the people.

The enumeration in the Constitution, of certain rights, shall not be construed to deny or disparage others retained by the people.

These are what are known as "unenumerated rights." How basic they are to those living under the Constitution probably depends on when they surface and how important they are to people after they do so. Among the unenumerated rights most often mentioned is the right to privacy. But they might include the right to health care at a reasonable cost. And who knows if they might not someday include the right of access to the Internet or the right to die. For now, they remain, for the most part, unmentioned.

The Tenth Amendment

The Tenth Amendment is a catchall, not unrelated to the Ninth Amendment. Where the Ninth maintains that there are rights out there that aren't mentioned, haven't been defined, and shouldn't be claimed by anyone but the people, the Tenth says flat out that any rights (known or unknown) that aren't granted to the federal government by the Constitution, and aren't forbidden to the states, belong to the people and the states.

> *The powers not delegated to the United States by the Constitution, nor prohibited by it to the States, are reserved to the States respectively, or to the people.*

The federal government is only claiming the powers spelled out in and granted to it by the Constitution. Whether the last eight words of this amendment have set up a future battle between the states and the people of the United States is anybody's guess.

CHAPTER 8

The Expansion of Individual Rights

Considering the fact that the United States was created with the assertion that "all men are created equal" (according to the Declaration of Independence), the Americans who drafted that declaration, most of whom had descended from European stock, had developed a deep sense of "otherness" where people of different races were concerned. The treatment of Native Americans by all of the European invaders was appalling; the treatment of imported African slaves no less so.

Demographics Influence the Attitude of "Otherness"

Unlike settlers in the Spanish and Portuguese colonies of South and Central America, the settlers of North America, who came from Protestant countries, tended to arrive in family units, seeking a new life of religious or political freedom. They coalesced into cities with diverse urban industries, to which additional laborers from Europe migrated.

In the South, the plantation system that developed imported Africans to work crops that were alien to northern Europeans. But perhaps because the Europeans in the English colonies often brought their families with them, they developed an attitude of "otherness" where the people of other races were concerned. This attitude was so ingrained that the drafters of the Constitution saw no contradiction in, for example, declaring that the official populations of the states would exclude "Indians not taxed" or would—in the great euphemisms of Article I ("other persons" than "free Persons, including those bound to Service for a Term of Years") and Article IV (a "Person held to Service or Labour")—count only three-fifths of the slaves. In America, slaves would only be persons of at least some African ancestry.

The rights declared in the Declaration of Independence and the Bill of Rights were those of free men. They might sometimes belong to *freed* men, but—except for the criminal regulations—they did not belong to any women.

The Slavery Issue

To persuade the southern states, whose economies were largely tied to slave labor, to ratify the Constitution, Article I denied Congress any power to limit the "Migration or Importation of such Persons as any of the States now existing shall think proper to admit" before 1808. If you didn't know that this referred to slaves, you might almost think, from the wording, that it was meant to encourage immigration.

Although Congress couldn't ban the importation of slaves for the first two decades of the country's existence, this section did not prevent the states from enacting legislation concerning slavery. The same year the Constitution was signed, New Jersey and Rhode Island banned the slave trade, and other northern states soon followed suit. By the time the prohibition expired, only South Carolina was still allowing the importation of slaves.

In 1807, Congress passed (and President Thomas Jefferson, himself a slave owner, signed) a law abolishing the importation of slaves as of January 1, 1808, the earliest possible date allowed by the Constitution. This law banned only the international slave trade; it did not ban slavery.

The Abolition Movement

Many throughout the United States and throughout the world had begun to find the practice of owning slaves to be morally repugnant. Slavery was abolished in Great Britain in 1833. But in the American South, where so much of the economy was tied to slave labor, people found all kinds of excuses for maintaining the institution. Not the least among them was that belief in the "otherness" of the slaves—usually incorporating the belief that slaves were, being of another race, inferior, either morally or intellectually, or that they were descended from Noah's son Ham and were thus being appropriately punished for his sins.

Using the Ohio River as a boundary, the Northwest Ordinance of 1787 prohibited slavery in the Northwest Territory and in the states that would be carved out of that territory. Those states, Ohio, Indiana, Illinois, Michigan, Wisconsin, and part of Minnesota, were "free states" in which slavery was prohibited. But even in free states, citizens of other states were free to travel and bring their property with them—and slaves were property.

The Missouri Compromise

Throughout the first half of the nineteenth century, the people of the United States became increasingly polarized over the issue of slavery. Interwoven with that was a polarization over the rights of the states to make their own decisions about things not prohibited to them by the Constitution. While the states were evolving from regarding themselves as sovereign nations, they still held on to varying degrees of independence from the central government and jealously guarded the right to pass laws in areas that were not reserved to the federal government.

The states were also extremely aware of which states were aligned with them when it came to the issue of slavery. The admission of Alabama in 1820 as a slave state made the number of slave states and the number of free states equal. There was southern opposition to the admission of Maine as a free state unless Missouri could be admitted as a slave state. A compromise was finally reached allowing the admission of both states (in separate bills) and prohibiting slavery in the states formed out of the Louisiana Purchase territory above the latitude of 36°30' north, except for the state of Missouri.

ESSENTIAL

Until the incorporation doctrine of the Fourteenth Amendment expanded the reach of the Bill of Rights, many of its guarantees applied only to the *federal* government, and states did not always see fit to apply these limitations on their own powers where only *state* laws were involved.

The Kansas-Nebraska Act of 1854 repealed (for future states) the Missouri Compromise, and allowed the people of the territories, through their legislatures, to decide if a territory would or would not permit slavery. This led to the bloody internal strife that took over what became known as "Bloody Kansas" and was the occasion for the Lincoln–Douglas debates (in which Abraham Lincoln earned the reputation that launched him to the White House). It also pushed the country closer to civil war.

The *Dred Scott* Decision

An inflammatory decision by the Supreme Court in 1857 contributed to the volatility that led to the Civil War. The history of this decision is convoluted. Dred Scott was a slave purchased in Missouri by a soldier, John Emerson, whose assignments led him to reside at different times in various free states as well as slave states. After Emerson's death, Scott attempted to purchase his freedom, and that of his wife and children, from Emerson's widow. She refused his attempts to do so.

After wending its way through the courts, some of which held for Scott and some of which held for Mrs. Emerson, the case found its way to the Supreme Court, where it was docketed as *Dred Scott v. Sandford* (John Sandford was Mrs. Emerson's brother and the administrator of her husband's estate). There, seven out of the nine members of the court held that Scott was not a citizen and thus did not have a constitutional right to sue, but the court then went on to decide the case anyway, with far-reaching effect. What the court decided was that the Fifth Amendment barred Scott's owner from being deprived of property (Scott) just by bringing that property into a free territory. The Court then went on to say (although it was not an issue before the Court) that Congress did not have the right to pass the Missouri Compromise prohibiting slavery in a state, nor did the territorial legislatures have the right to ban slavery, because such action was reserved to the state legislatures by the Constitution. It therefore negated the Missouri Compromise.

The Civil War

Volumes have been written about the American Civil War, also known (primarily in the South) as the War Between the States. All that need be noted here is the constitutional argument made by the secessionist states that they had voluntarily entered the Union and could leave unilaterally. In February 1861, the legislatures of seven states (South Carolina, Mississippi, Florida, Alabama, Georgia, Louisiana, and Texas) voted to secede, or withdraw from the Union, and in April of that year, South Carolina forces fired on Fort Sumter, an American fort located on an island off of Charleston, South Carolina.

FACT

The delegates of the Confederacy's provisional congress constructed and ratified their "nation's" constitution in a matter of weeks. It had taken the U.S. Continental Congress two years from draft to ratification (1787–1789) to achieve a similar feat. Of course, the U.S. Continental Congress started from scratch, whereas the Confederacy provisional congress at least had a template from which to work.

Though called a "war," the action that took place from 1861 to 1865 was technically a "rebellion." War was not declared, and the United States took the position that no separate country existed. The seven states that seceded called themselves the Confederate States of America, and they were shortly joined by Arkansas, North Carolina, Tennessee, and Virginia; but all of those states were held by the United States to be in rebellion, and that rebellion was quelled.

There is no legal basis in the Constitution for secession; the Constitution discusses, in Article IV, the admission of new states, but nowhere does it mention the withdrawal of any states. Indeed, if the Constitution is legally just a "revision" of the Articles of Confederation by which the United States was governed until the Constitution was ratified—as the Continental Congress authorized—then what the states joined was a *perpetual* union. There is no legal decision that says whether secession is legal or illegal. The United States took the position that it was putting down a civil disturbance, and after four bloody years the rebellion ended. The Thirteenth, Fourteenth and Fifteenth amendments to the Constitution were passed shortly after the hostilities ended, to eliminate the rebellion's most egregious cause, slavery, and expand the legal rights of those who had previously been slaves.

The Emancipation Proclamation

On January 1, 1863, President Abraham Lincoln signed and issued an executive order known as the Emancipation Proclamation. It freed the slaves in the territories in rebellion; the army enforced it in those where the United States had put down the rebellion. It did not—because a president single-handedly could not—free the slaves in the slave states that had not seceded (Maryland, Missouri, Delaware, and Kentucky). Nor could it remedy the situation caused by the Supreme Court's decision in the Dred Scott case, which held that slaves who were brought to the free states by their masters to remain slaves.

Congress quickly remedied the gaps left by the Emancipation Proclamation with the passage of the Thirteenth Amendment on January 31, 1865, before Lee's surrender—more proof that the government of the United States continued to function even as the rebellion raged on around it.

Section 1.

Neither slavery nor involuntary servitude, except as a punishment for crime whereof the party shall have been duly convicted, shall exist within the United States, or any place subject to their jurisdiction.

Section 2.

Congress shall have power to enforce this article by appropriate legislation.

This amendment was ratified by the requisite three-quarters of all the states as of December 6, 1865, including the states of Virginia, Louisiana, Tennessee, Arkansas, South Carolina, Alabama, North Carolina, and Georgia. The remainder of the thirty-six states that then formed the Union ratified it shortly afterward. The swift ratification was accomplished because those who had participated in the rebellion had been stripped of their civil rights and could not vote for or serve in the legislatures that ratified this amendment.

FACT

In addition to the two Doric columns that frame the entrance of the Lincoln Memorial in Washington, D.C., the monument is encircled by a row of thirty-six Doric columns, one for each of the thirty-six states in the Union that Lincoln's leadership preserved.

The Thirteenth Amendment voided the third paragraph of Section 2 of Article IV, which allowed for the return of fugitive slaves to their masters.

It should be noted, however, that the Thirteenth Amendment allows for involuntary servitude by people convicted of crimes, providing a legal basis for chain gangs and similar labor on the part of prisoners.

The Fourteenth Amendment

The Fourteenth Amendment of the Constitution changed the way the Constitution operated. After the Civil War it—among other things—eliminated the three-fifths rule for counting slaves in the U.S. census.

This Amendment was passed in 1866 and ratified by 1868, although some of its import wasn't fully understood until the turn of the twentieth century.

Section 1

Section 1 of the Fourteenth Amendment deals with citizenship.

All persons born or naturalized in the United States, and subject to the jurisdiction thereof, are citizens of the United States and of the State wherein they reside. No State shall make or enforce any law which shall abridge the privileges or immunities of citizens of the United States; nor shall any State deprive any person of life, liberty, or property, without due process of law; nor deny to any person within its jurisdiction the equal protection of the laws.

This is the paragraph that requires the states, as well as the federal government, to abide by the Bill of Rights. It guarantees all persons the "equal protection of the laws" and requires "due process of law" before any abridgement of any "rights, privileges, and immunities."

Meant to provide full citizenship for freed slaves, this section also grants citizenship to anyone born in the United States, including those in the United States under petitions for asylum, those who are permanent residents, and illegal aliens. If a child is born in the United States, he is a citizen of the United States.

Section 2

Section 2 of the law says that a State's representation in the House of Representatives, and in choosing members of the Electoral College, will be reduced by the number of male citizens over the age of twenty-one who have been denied their rights and privileges as citizens by that state. An exception is made for criminals and those participating in rebellion. This last was meant as a punishment for those who fought for the Confederacy or participated in its government.

Representatives shall be apportioned among the several States according to their respective numbers, counting the whole number of persons in each State, excluding Indians not taxed. But when the right to vote at any election for the choice of electors for President and Vice President of the United States, Representatives in Congress, the Executive and Judicial officers of a State, or the members of the Legislature thereof, is denied to any of the male inhabitants of such State, and citizens of the United States, or in any way abridged, except for participation in rebellion, or other crime, the basis of representation therein shall be reduced in the proportion which the number of such male citizens shall bear to the whole number of male citizens twenty-one years of age in such State.

This section was modified by the Nineteenth Amendment, granting women the vote, and the Twenty-Sixth, which lowered the voting age to eighteen.

Section 3

Section 3 of the Fourteenth Amendment was also directed at those who had supported the Confederacy.

No person shall be a Senator or Representative in Congress, or elector of President and Vice President, or hold any office, civil or military, under the United States, or under any State, who, having previously taken an oath, as a member of Congress, or as an officer of the United States, or as a member of any State legislature, or as an executive or judicial officer of any State, to support the Constitution of the United States, shall have engaged in insurrection or rebellion against the same, or given aid or comfort to the enemies thereof. But Congress may by a vote of two-thirds of each House, remove such disability.

Section VI of the Constitution requires all who hold federal or state offices to swear to uphold the Constitution of the United States. This section of the Fourteenth Amendment says that anyone who took that oath, and later participated in a rebellion—or anyone who gave "aid and comfort" to the enemies of the United States, which pretty much included all Confederate soldiers and most civilians—may not hold federal or state office again unless Congress removes that disability by a two-thirds vote of both houses.

This brought about a shift of power in the South, because anyone who had supported the Confederacy could not hold public office, while those who had not served—mainly former slaves and so-called "carpetbaggers" from the North—were the only people eligible to do so.

Section 4

Section 4 is purely economic. It affirms any debts the Union incurred to put down any rebellion (not just the Civil War), denies any liability for the debts of those in rebellion, and denies any liability for compensation to former slave owners for the loss of their property:

The validity of the public debt of the United States, authorized by law, including debts incurred for payment of pensions and bounties for services in suppressing insurrection or rebellion, shall not be questioned. But neither the United States nor any State shall assume or pay any debt or obligation incurred in aid of insurrection or rebellion against the United States, or any claim for the loss or emancipation of any slave; but all such debts, obligations and claims shall be held illegal and void.

Section 5

Section 5 of the Fourteenth Amendment gave Congress broad power to enforce this amendment, which it did with laws that imposed conditions for readmission for the states that had seceded and others that granted civil rights to freed slaves, although much of this legislation was later invalidated as unconstitutional by the Supreme Court:

The Congress shall have the power to enforce, by appropriate legislation, the provisions of this article.

The Women's Suffrage Movement

As early as 1776, Abigail Adams had asked her husband, John, in a letter, to "remember the ladies" in creating the Declaration of Independence. The idea of nonsexist language did not exist in the eighteenth century, and the Declaration had used the words "All men are created equal."

Although there were incidents of women owning property and even, in New Jersey between 1790 and 1807, of women being allowed to vote, for the most part women were denied that right.

In 1848, a year of revolution throughout the world, a group of feminists, both male and female, gathered in Seneca Falls, New York, in support of the establishment, throughout the country, of the right of women to vote. It would take more than seventy years for this to finally become law in the form of the Nineteenth Amendment.

Women's rights, not only to vote, but also to own property, to keep their earnings, and to obtain divorces, were achieved only slowly, with progress being made in some categories but not in others, and achieved at different rates in different parts of the country. Holding elective office was something even more rare. Jeannette Rankin of Montana became the first woman to serve in Congress, three years before women throughout the United States were granted the vote by the Nineteenth Amendment.

FACT

Jeannette Rankin, who was a peace activist as well as a feminist, served twice in Congress, her terms separated by two decades, and ironically both times was called upon to vote on a declaration of war pursuant to Article I, Section 8, of the Constitution. In both instances she voted against the declaration. In voting against the U.S. entry into World War II, she noted that since, as a woman, she could not serve, she felt she could not send anyone else to war.

Women would gain the right to vote in 1920, but equal rights in other areas were slower in coming. The inclusion of women among those protected by the Civil Rights Act of 1964 was meant to embarrass supporters of the law into dropping their support. Most of the rights that women have gained in the years since that law went into effect have been because of this inclusion. The Nineteenth Amendment reads:

The right of citizens of the United States to vote shall not be denied or abridged by the United States or by any State on account of sex.

Congress shall have power to enforce this article by appropriate legislation.

With these simple words, suffragettes who had chained themselves to the White House fence, endured being force-fed during hunger strikes, and being ridiculed, denounced, and abased, finally achieved the right to vote throughout the country, and with it the right to hold office throughout the country as well. Passed by Congress in 1919, the Nineteenth Amendment was ratified slightly more than a year later, in time for women to vote in the presidential election of 1920 that November.

Other Voting Rights

Americans like to think that voting is a right that is theirs simply because they are citizens of the United States, but this hasn't always been the case. Early laws in the colonies and the original states often required voters to be not only citizens, but also landowners—or to at least possess a certain minimum amount of money. Color and sex were barriers to the right to vote, but so, too, was national origin.

Not everyone who immigrated to America was entitled to become a citizen. Japanese immigrants were denied that right under a 1922 Supreme Court case, *Ozawa v. United States.* The Court held that the law in effect since 1906 provided for the naturalization of "free white persons" and "persons of African nativity and . . . descent" but not Asians. (When the United States went to war with Japan in 1942, many long-time U.S. residents of Japanese descent, ineligible for naturalization, thus became classified as "enemy aliens.")

Age was another barrier that would be dropped as a result of a constitutional amendment. And case law concerning the fairness of redistricting tried to accomplish what amendments had not: the equal representation championed by the slogan, "One man, one vote"—or, in the nonsexist language that developed after the 1960s, "One person, one vote."

ALERT

During the early months of 1942, more than 100,000 Japanese Americans living on the west coast (many of whom were American-born U.S. citizens) were ordered into "relocation camps" in the interior of the country. A set of four Supreme Court cases ultimately held that though this kind of evacuation might be justified in time of war, those relocated could use the writ of habeas corpus to compel their release. By the time these cases were decided, the U.S. was winning the war. The camps were closed, but the damage was done, and in 1988, the government authorized reparations for evacuees.

The Fifteenth Amendment was the third of the post–Civil War amendments, passed in February of 1869 and ratified almost precisely a year later.

The right of citizens of the United States to vote shall not be denied or abridged by the United States or by any State on account of race, color, or previous condition of servitude.

Although the Fourteenth Amendment threatens states with a reduction in their representation for denying all citizens the right to vote (and disenfranchised many of those who had participated in the rebellion), it is this amendment that flatly states that every citizen of the United States is entitled to vote, no matter what race or color, or if that person had previously been a slave. Unfortunately, for the purpose of voting, "citizens" did not appear to include women until the Nineteenth Amendment was passed.

The Twenty-Fourth Amendment

Despite the clear language of the Fifteenth Amendment, creative legislators throughout the South came up with ways to deny the vote to black citizens, through poll taxes, literacy tests, and out-and-out intimidation, among other methods. Congress would remedy this with the Twenty-Fourth Amendment, ratified in 1964.

A second clause in this Amendment, which gives Congress "power to enforce this article by appropriate legislation," forms part of the basis for the landmark Civil Rights Act passed later that same year.

The right of citizens of the United States to vote in any primary or other election for President or Vice President, for electors for President or Vice President, or for Senator or Representative in Congress, shall not be denied or abridged by the United States or any State by reason of failure to pay poll tax or other tax.

One of the means the southern states employed to prevent blacks from voting was to impose a poll tax, a fee that had to be paid before a person could vote. Because blacks were more likely to be economically disadvantaged, and because wealthier whites might even pay poll taxes of their economically disadvantaged white neighbors, blacks were systematically prevented from voting. This amendment was meant to ensure that the poorest citizen could always cast a ballot.

This amendment was one of the results of the civil rights movement of the 1960s. Passed in 1962 and ratified in 1964, it guarantees the right to vote in federal elections—for Congress and the president—but the Supreme Court used the equal protection clause of the Fourteenth Amendment to extend the right to state elections as well.

The Twenty-Sixth Amendment

Two things coalesced in the early 1970s to bring about a downward shift from the traditional voting age of twenty-one. The first was that the first members of the "baby boom" generation born after World War II came of voting age and began to exercise the muscle that their numbers gave them. The second was the military draft, which subjected this generation to involuntary military service for the unpopular Vietnam War. If taxation without representation was anathema to the Founding Fathers, how much more so was the idea that one could die in a war that one had not had the opportunity to vote against (or rather, vote to elect representatives who would vote against it).

The right of citizens of the United States, who are eighteen years of age or older, to vote shall not be denied or abridged by the United States or by any State on account of age.

This amendment was passed and ratified in a space of little more than three months in 1971. Around the same time, the drinking age was also lowered to eighteen in most states, using a similar argument: How could you be old enough to die for your country but not old enough to drink alcohol?

When the voting age was lowered, the age of majority was lowered as well (although the amendment did not actually say this). People who reached the age of eighteen could legally sign contracts and leases, take out loans, and serve on juries. They were also classified as adults for the purposes of the criminal laws.

Ironically, in the following decade, when it was discovered that a disproportionate number of young people between the ages of eighteen and twenty-one were dying in alcohol-related traffic accidents, the states were coerced into raising the drinking age back to twenty-one by the federal government's withholding of highway subsidies from states that did not do so.

CHAPTER 9

Fine-Tuning the Law of the Land

When a newspaper makes an error, it prints a retraction or correction in the next edition. When Congress discovers an accidental discrepancy in a bill it has already passed, it often passes a "technical corrections" bill to fix the errors. This can happen when there is a term in the law that is not defined, or when there is a contradiction between different parts of a law. But the Constitution is meant to be a more permanent document, the "supreme Law of the Land." Creating a government from scratch was a great experiment, and once the Constitution went into operation, problems surfaced. That was why the framers included an amendment process, and why they made it fairly difficult, so that there wouldn't be frequent amendments that could change their basic idea of how the U.S. government should work.

The Amendment Process

Article V provides the process for *proposing* an amendment (by a two-thirds vote in both houses of Congress or in a convention called for by two-thirds of the state legislatures) and for *ratifying* one (by three-quarters of the state legislatures or by conventions called for that purpose in three-quarters of the states). There have been twenty-seven amendments over two and a quarter centuries, and the first ten of them make up the Bill of Rights, a basic list that many of the drafters felt should have been included in the Constitution in the first place.

Remember, the Constitution creates a system for operating the governement. For handling everyday matters that reflect the changing needs of operating the country, laws are drafted by Congress and signed by the president. These are more easily passed or corrected than constitutional amendments would be, and as directed by Article VI, are incorporated into the supreme law of the land (although when they conflict with the Constitution, the Constitution wins).

FACT

> Often, the Senate version of a bill is slightly different from the House version. An *"ad hoc"* (meaning *"for this* purpose") conference committee with members from both houses will then work out the differences so that the bill presented to the president for signing reflects the will of both houses.

What kinds of errors should be remedied by amendments, which are an actual change in the fabric of the Constitution? They tend to fall into two categories. The first is the correction of an operational error. The Twelfth Amendment is a perfect example of this—problems with presidential election surfaced once two active political parties formed.

The second is the need to correct for eighteenth-century sensibilities as times change. The Thirteenth Amendment, abolishing slavery, is an example of this. So is the Nineteenth Amendment, extending voting rights to women. When an error surfaces in either of these categories, sometimes an amendment is the best way to remedy it.

The Eleventh Amendment

The Eleventh Amendment was the result of the states demanding sovereign immunity after a 1793 Supreme Court case appeared to deny it to them. Among the powers that belong to the Supreme Court under Section 2 of Article III is to hear "Controversies . . . between a State and Citizens of another State." That looks good on paper as a reasonable power for a court to have; what it meant was that by implication, states had lost their sovereign immunity.

The concept of sovereign immunity is an English tradition that means, essentially, that you can't sue the king unless he allows you to sue him. Because even kings make mistakes, a monarch—or a representative government—can waive its sovereign immunity. But the states did not like the idea that it had been waived for them. What brought this to the amendment stage was the 1793 decision of the Supreme Court, in the case of *Chisholm v. Georgia.*

The suit was brought by Alexander Chisholm, the executor of the estate of Robert Farquhar of South Carolina, who had sold supplies to the state of Georgia during the Revolutionary War. Chisholm sought payment for the goods Farquhar had supplied to Georgia. The Court heard the case under the list of its powers in Article III, but Georgia contended that the Court did not have jurisdiction over a sovereign state and refused to appear. The court entered a default judgment for Chisholm.

The states were up in arms. They did not believe that a branch of the federal government should be able to rule on their obligations. Congress almost immediately (in 1794) proposed the Eleventh Amendment, and it passed less than a year later:

The Judicial power of the United States shall not be construed to extend to any suit in law or equity, commenced or prosecuted against one of the United States by Citizens of another State, or by Citizens or Subjects of any Foreign State.

The Eleventh Amendment bars lawsuits by an individual against a state unless the state consents. It does not bar a suit by a state against an individual, and of course, once in court, that individual can countersue.

A state can expressly waive its right to sovereign immunity and allow a suit to go forward. And a state can allow a suit to go forward in its own court system rather than in the federal system. But the Supreme Court has also ruled that where a state has a constitutional obligation, such as an equal rights matter under the Fourteenth Amendment, the federal government can sue the state, and this suit will be in the federal courts. In other words, a state can be sued to enforce a federal law!

The Twelfth Amendment

The Twelfth Amendment came about as a direct result of a piece of the original Constitution that didn't really work. The Constitution originally laid out the way a president would be elected—by electors chosen in the states to form an Electoral College—in Section 1 of Article II. The electors were to vote for two persons, and that section noted specifically that "The Person having the greatest Number of Votes shall be the President, if such Number be a Majority . . . [and] after the Choice of the President, the Person having the greatest Number of Votes of the Electors shall be the Vice President." If there was a tie between the presidential candidates, the House of Representatives was to decide who should be the president.

ESSENTIAL

A system of two principal political parties has existed almost from the start, although there is no provision in the Constitution for parties. Though there are usually two major parties, these have not always been the *same* two parties. Historically, when a new party gains ground, it will usually either replace one of the existing major parties or be absorbed into it.

The Founders hadn't considered that a party system might evolve (although perhaps they should have; they had aligned themselves into Federalist and Anti-Federalist groups at the Convention). By the election of 1800, the party then known as the Republicans, or Democratic-Republicans, or Jeffersonians (not the Republican Party of today, but the Democratic Party, although party goals and ideals may have shifted over the years) had produced a ticket, or slate, to put before the electors. The party had meant to nominate Thomas Jefferson for president, and Aaron Burr to be vice president, but they had neglected to tell one of the electors to hold back a vote for Burr, so that he would be the runner-up.

Without someone holding back that one vote, the election was a tie, which threw it into the House—a lame-duck House ruled by Federalists (the other party at the time). John Adams, the incumbent president, was a Federalist, and had been a candidate for re-election. Party politics were just as nasty then as they would be 200 years later, when a fight over voting rights and "hanging chads" resulted in the involvement of the Supreme Court to decide the results of presidential balloting in Florida (and, as a result, the presidential election of 2000 itself). Eventually, Jefferson was elected to the presidency, but not without a lot of political intrigue.

FACT

There were many who were nervous at the thought of Jefferson as president. His actions during the Adams administration suggested that Jefferson rejected the very powers of the executive branch that he now swore to uphold. The Federalists wondered how Jefferson would "preserve, protect and defend" the government that on occasion he had sworn to dismantle. However, in his inaugural address, Jefferson struck a note of conciliation as he stated, "We are all republicans—we are all federalists."

Clearly, this flaw in the Constitution had to be remedied before the next election. In 1803, Congress passed the Twelfth Amendment to clarify the election process. It was ratified by the states by June of 1804, in advance of the next presidential election. Electoral ballots would now designate which candidate was to be president and which was to be vice president.

The Sixteenth Amendment

The Sixteenth Amendment passed in 1909 and was ratified in 1913, and the first income tax went into effect that year. The income tax produces most of the money to fund the federal government.

The Congress shall have power to lay and collect taxes on incomes, from whatever source derived, without apportionment among the several States, and without regard to any census or enumeration.

Before this amendment passed, Congress was limited by Article I, Section 9, to taxing the states in proportion to their populations, rather than taxing individuals (although excise taxes were another source of revenue). Attempts at taxing individuals were ruled unconstitutional by the Supreme Court in 1895, and this amendment was a reaction to that ruling.

This amendment does not discuss the rate of taxation, or whether it should be a flat tax or a progressive tax, but progressive taxes have been the rule in the century since the income tax was authorized. A progressive tax is one that taxes incomes at progressively higher rates as they grow larger.

It works like this: Everyone is allowed a certain amount of money that is not taxed at all. This is equal to your personal exemptions. Then a ceiling is set—let's say $50,000—and on that you pay a low rate. On the next amount over that—let's say another $100,000—you owe a slightly higher rate. And above that, you owe the highest rate. A progressive tax gets progressively higher as your income gets larger.

Progressive taxes are believed by many to be more fair than collecting the same amount from everyone, including those who barely make enough for basic food, clothing, and shelter.

The power to assess and collect taxes belongs to Congress. But within the power to tax is the power to create the society you want. Want more people to get married, rather than living together? Give them a lower tax rate if they marry and file jointly. Want people to have more children? Give them much larger tax deductions for each child. Want them to get an education or buy a house? Let them deduct the expenses for those things from the taxes they would otherwise owe.

Taxation can also discourage certain behaviors. For example, if you want people to stop smoking, you can raise the taxes on cigarettes. Want them to buy more fuel-efficient cars? Give them a tax credit for trading in their "clunkers." (Sound familiar?)

According to the Constitution, though, all tax policy originates with the House of Representatives, and the Senate must concur in order to send an appropriations bill to the president for signing. The most a president can do is *ask* Congress to pass certain tax legislation, or veto what they send him. Congress can delegate some of the details of tax policy to federal agencies, like the IRS. But the overall responsibility rests with the legislative branch.

The Seventeenth Amendment

Until 1913, when this amendment was ratified, senators were elected by state legislatures, not directly by the people. In theory, senators represented the states, while the House represented the people of the states.

The Seventeenth Amendment was one of a number of progressive reforms. It provided for the direct election of senators by the people, rather than the legislatures, in all future elections:

The Senate of the United States shall be composed of two Senators from each State, elected by the people thereof, for six years; and each Senator shall have one vote. The electors in each State shall have the qualifications requisite for electors of the most numerous branch of the State legislatures.

In addition to direct election, this amendment also deals with how Senate vacancies are to be filled when they occur. Essentially, when a senator resigns or dies, the governor of a state that senator represented is empowered to make an appointment. The state legislature can decide if that appointment will be temporary—until an interim election can be held—or for the rest of the term.

The Twentieth Amendment

Traditionally, the new Congress and each new president, took office the first week in March. This was necessary when the Constitution first took effect, because transportation was so slow. Indeed, George Washington had so much trouble getting to Washington that his inauguration took place in April!

However, with the advent of railroads, and then of cars and planes, the long wait between the November election and the time Congress and the president would take office became unnecessary. The built-in delay held up the start of the new government and left lame ducks in power for five months. This amendment was passed in 1932 and ratified the following year. It moved presidential inaugurations to January 20 and the first session of a new Congress to January 3.

FACT

Members of Congress are not always sowrn in on the prescribed date. In 1963, Gaylord Nelson became the least senior member of his class in the Senate because he was sworn in five days later than the other new senators. Even days count where seniority (which is not mentioned in the Constitution) is concerned.

Other provisions of the Twentieth Amendment attempt to deal with some problems of mortality that the Constitution didn't address. It provides that if a president-elect dies before he can be sworn in, the vice-president elect shall become president on inauguration day. It addresses exigencies that may have appeared far-fetched at the time, but the Twenty-Fifth Amendment, passed in the aftermath of the Kennedy assassination, goes even farther.

Here are the relevant sections of the Twentieth Amendment:

Section 3.
If, at the time fixed for the beginning of the term of the President, the President elect shall have died, the Vice President elect shall become President. If a President shall not have been chosen before the time fixed for the beginning of his term, or if the President elect shall have failed to qualify, then the Vice President elect shall act as President until a President shall have qualified; and the Congress may by law provide for the case wherein neither a President elect nor a Vice President shall have qualified, declaring who shall then act as President, or the manner in which one who is to act shall be selected, and such person shall act accordingly until a President or Vice President shall have qualified.

Section 4.

The Congress may by law provide for the case of the death of any of the persons from whom the House of Representatives may choose a President whenever the right of choice shall have devolved upon them, and for the case of the death of any of the persons from whom the Senate may choose a Vice President whenever the right of choice shall have devolved upon them.

This fills some of the gaps, but didn't address many things that would later be addressed in the Twenty-Fifth Amendment.

The Twentieth Amendment contained an expiration date. The amendment declared that it "shall be inoperative" if not ratified by the requisite three-fourths of the states within seven years of passage. In fact, it was ratified in less than a year.

FACT

Limiting the time for ratification was first applied to the Eighteenth Amendment. The Twentieth, Twenty-First, and Twenty-Second Amendments contain a similar requirement. So did the proposed Equal Rights Amendment and the District of Columbia Voting Rights Amendment, both of which failed to achieve ratification by the requisite number of states within their time limits. Time limits have not been required for other amendments.

The Twenty-Second Amendment

Passed in 1947 and ratified in 1951, the Twenty-Second Amendment formalized the two-term maximum that had been in effect until Franklin Roosevelt was elected to four terms, starting in 1932. (His death in office, in 1945, meant he did not actually serve out all four terms.) Two previous presidents, Theodore Roosevelt and Ulysses Grant, had sought, but not been elected to, third terms.

No person shall be elected to the office of the President more than twice, and no person who has held the office of President, or acted as President, for more than two years of a term to which some other person was elected President shall be elected to the office of President more than once. But this Article shall not apply to any person holding the office of President when this Article was proposed by Congress, and shall not prevent any person who may be holding the office of President, or acting as President, during the term within which this Article becomes operative from holding the office of President or acting as President during the remainder of such term.

If you look carefully at the wording in the amendment, it does not limit a president to precisely two terms. A president may be elected to two terms in his own right if he has served fewer than two years of a previous president's term, so ten years is actually the maximum term anyone can be president.

The Twenty-Third Amendment

Congress was authorized to form what would become the District of Columbia by Article I, Section 8 of the Constitution, with this reference within the powers granted to Congress: "To exercise exclusive Legislation in all Cases whatsoever, over such District (not exceeding ten Miles square) as may, by Cession of particular States, and the Acceptance of Congress, become the Seat of the Government of the United States." The idea was that this seat of government would not be part of any state, so no state could claim the favoritism of being home to the central government.

Section 1 reads as follows:

The District constituting the seat of Government of the United States shall appoint in such manner as Congress may direct:

A number of electors of President and Vice President equal to the whole number of Senators and Representatives in Congress to which the District would be entitled if it were a State, but in no event more than the least populous State; they shall be in addition to those appointed by the States, but they shall be considered, for the purposes of the election of President and Vice President, to be electors appointed by a State; and they shall meet in the District and perform such duties as provided by the twelfth article of amendment.

The District occupies former swampland along the Potomac River between Virginia and Maryland. But the provision in Article I that keeps it from being part of any state had the unfortunate effect of disenfranchising its residents. Because they did not live in any state, they could not vote for president and were not represented in Congress.

Various bills had been put forth over the years to make the District the equivalent of a state or otherwise grant its residents the right to vote, but none came to fruition until this one, which was passed in 1960 and ratified in 1961. It gives Congress, which makes the laws for the district anyway, the power to "enforce this article by appropriate legislation." And the amendment itself gives the district the right to vote for president, but with no more electors than the least populous state. Additionally, since 1971, the District of Columbia has been represented by a nonvoting delegate in the House of Representatives.

The Twenty-Fifth Amendment

This was an amendment that was ratified in the nick of time, considering what happened in the seven years following its ratification. The motivation for its passage was John F. Kennedy's assassination. Lyndon Johnson, who succeeded Kennedy, served as president for fourteen months without a vice president. Barely two decades earlier, Harry S. Truman had served without a vice president from April of 1945 until January of 1949. Remembering President Dwight D. Eisenhower's temporary incapacitation due to a stroke and a heart attack, and aware that a nuclear attack could wipe out virtually all the senior government officials at once, Congress came up with an emergency succession plan.

This plan addresses several areas that had been problematic for the entire existence of the country:

In case of the removal of the President from office or of his death or resignation, the Vice President shall become President.

ALERT

Hours after President Kennedy was assassinated, Dallas police arrested the suspect Lee Harvey Oswald, an employee in a warehouse building along the motorcade route. Oswald himself was killed two days later and so was never tried for this crime. Chief Justice Earl Warren headed a special commission to investigate Kennedy's death and other investigations have followed. Without the closure of a trial, the Kennedy assassination is the subject of much debate.

It had never been legally clear whether the vice president *became* president or just *acted* in that capacity. Vice presidents had been sworn in when a president died, but the Constitution was silent on this point. This amendment cleared that up.

Whenever there is a vacancy in the office of the Vice President, the President shall nominate a Vice President who shall take office upon confirmation by a majority vote of both Houses of Congress.

This section of the law provided for filling a vice presidential vacancy when one occurred (usually because the vice president had become president, but also on the death or resignation of the vice president). Within barely more than half a dozen years of the ratification of this amendment, Spiro Agnew resigned as vice president, Richard Nixon appointed Gerald Ford to fill the post, and then Nixon resigned, leaving Ford to succeed to the presidency and appoint a new vice president himself.

That took care of the vacancy problem, but what hadn't been addressed yet was presidential disability. Whose finger would be on the nuclear retaliation button if the president was undergoing surgery? What were the provisions if a president was incapacitated—as had been Woodrow Wilson—for as much as a year?

Congress answered those questions with this amendment, too:

Whenever the President transmits to the President pro tempore of the Senate and the Speaker of the House of Representatives his written declaration that he is unable to discharge the powers and duties of his office, and until he transmits to them a written declaration to the contrary, such powers and duties shall be discharged by the Vice President as Acting President.

But what about involuntary circumstances? What if the president were in no manner capable of declaring he was incapacitated? That was handled in the next section:

Whenever the Vice President and a majority of either the principal officers of the executive departments or of such other body as Congress may by law provide, transmit to the President pro tempore of the Senate and the Speaker of the House of Representatives their written declaration that the President is unable to discharge the powers and duties of his office, the Vice President shall immediately assume the powers and duties of the office as Acting President.

Well, that took care of a president in a coma, or kidnapped, or otherwise incapacitated—but how could there be an orderly transition once he woke up, or was freed? There remained a need for some method by which the president could take back his office after his disability had ended. And there was now the possibility that in the guise of solicitousness, some government members might use the disability provision to stage a coup. The president needed a way to take back the office—and the next paragraph of the Twenty-Fifth Amendment provided it:

Thereafter, when the President transmits to the President pro tempore of the Senate and the Speaker of the House of Representatives his written declaration that no inability exists, he shall resume the powers and duties of his office unless the Vice President and a majority of either the principal officers of the executive department or of such other body as Congress may by law provide, transmit within four days to the President pro tempore of the Senate and the Speaker of the House of Representatives their written declaration that the President is unable to discharge the powers and duties of his office. Thereupon Congress shall decide the issue, assembling within forty-eight hours for that purpose if not in session. If the Congress, within twenty-one days after receipt of the latter written declaration, or, if Congress is not in session, within twenty-one days after Congress is required to assemble, determines by two-thirds vote of both Houses that the President is unable to discharge the powers and duties of his office, the Vice President shall continue to discharge the same as Acting President; otherwise, the President shall resume the powers and duties of his office.

This sets the way for an orderly transfer of power—and, probably, a media circus.

There still remains the problem that might be caused by a major catastrophe that wipes out most of those in line for the presidency. The Presidential Succession Act of 1947, as amended, spells out who will be in charge.

FACT

President Woodrow Wilson suffered a stroke on October 2, 1919, with seventeen months left in his term. His wife Edith and his personal physician, Dr. Cary Grayson, kept the extent of his disability a secret; all communication between the president's sickbed and the outside world was through Mrs. Wilson. The extent to which the president was disabled during this period may never be fully known.

Currently, the order of succession goes from the president to the vice president, the Speaker of the House, the president pro tempore of the Senate, and then to the secretary of state. Beyond that, it runs through the various cabinet officers in a set order. Some of those people may not be constitutionally qualified to become president—they may not be natural born citizens, or thirty-five years of age, or they might be former presidents who had reached their term limits. (The Twenty-Second Amendment doesn't seem to have anticipated someone coming into the presidency after having served as president, rather than before.)

The Twenty-Seventh Amendment

This amendment, exquisite in its simplicity, was one of the twelve proposed amendments sent by Congress to the states in 1789 as part of the prospective Bill of Rights. The compensation of the other branches of the federal government is discussed in the Constitution, but not that of Congress, which, holding the "power of the purse" and being in charge of the authorization of money, is probably the branch most in need of constitutional controls.

No law, varying the compensation for the services of the Senators and Representatives, shall take effect, until an election of representatives shall have intervened.

Article II, section I, says, "The President shall, at stated Times, receive for his Services, a Compensation, which shall neither be increased nor diminished during the Period for which he shall have been elected, and he shall not receive within that Period any other Emolument from the United States, or any of them." In other words, the president's salary can neither be increased or reduced during his time in office.

FACT

The Congressional Quarterly's *Guide to the Presidency* reports that in 1789, the president of the United States earned $25,000 ($585,000 adjusted for inflation). Today, the president earns $400,000 annually (with many benefits, including a house).

Article III says of the judges that they "shall, at stated Times, receive for their Services a Compensation, which shall not be diminished during their Continuance in Office." Their salaries may not be reduced during their time on the bench; the Constitution doesn't say they can't be increased.

But as for Congress, where spending bills originate, nothing is said about increases or decreases, just: "The Senators and Representatives shall receive a Compensation for their Services, to be ascertained by Law, and paid out of the Treasury of the United States."

It was an omission that probably should have been addressed early on—and indeed, that was attempted in 1789, but it wasn't approved by the requisite three-quarters of the states. Over the centuries, of course, the number of states required for ratification went up as the number of states increased.

In the 1980s, as the public became more aware of the income the members of Congress had voted themselves, people began to propose the limitations similar to those that Amendment XXVII contains. When voters discovered they already had a pending amendment, and that it didn't have a ratification time limit on it, they resurrected it. Two hundred and three years after it was first proposed, it was finally ratified and became the Twenty-Seventh Amendment.

CHAPTER 10

The Great Mistake

What the drafters of the Constitution feared most, in creating a stronger government than they had had under the Articles of Confederation, was that the government might develop into a monarchy, or be so strong that it would curtail the rights of the people. As a result, they used the Constitution to define the limitations of the government, not the limitations of the people. Only one crime is defined in the Constitution (the crime of treason), and it must be proven by confession of the person accused, or by two corroborating witnesses to an overt act. The Bill of Rights noted that its listed rights did not mean that the rights of Americans were limited to *just* those rights. The remaining amendments expanded freedoms, extending them gradually to others who had been left out. No amendment ever restricted the freedom of individual Americans until the Eighteenth Amendment, which was also the only amendment ever to have been repealed.

Drinking in Early America

The people of the American colonies, like their compatriots in England, consumed alcoholic beverages to an extent that would have scandalized modern Americans. Drinks like hard cider, beer, wine, and rum were served at almost every meal, including breakfast. This had been a custom as long ago as the Anglo-Saxon period, when mead, beer, and wine were typical accompaniments for meals, and between meals as well.

FACT

Many of the beverages readily available today were not available to colonists. Coffee and tea first appeared in Europe in the seventeenth century; citrus fruits grew in southern Europe but had to be imported to England and were beyond the means of most people. There was no refrigeration for milk, and carbonated drinks did not exist.

Alcoholic beverages were believed to have medicinal value and were less likely to carry diseases than water from streams and lakes into which animal and human wastes flowed freely. The Founding Fathers believed in the benefits of alcoholic beverages: John Adams was given to starting the day with a glass of hard cider, and both George Washington and Thomas Jefferson kept extensive wine cellars.

At the time the Constitution was written, coffee houses could be found in larger metropolitan areas, but taverns were also plentiful and were the more likely gathering places in rural areas. The amount of alcohol consumed by the average citizen was prodigious by modern standards, and the resulting impairment of the work force, together with the irresponsible behavior of those with a constant buzz on, led to the rise of the temperance movement.

The Temperance Movement

An anti-alcohol campaign developed among many fundamentalist Christian church groups in the first half of the nineteenth century, often tied to the abolitionist movement. It died out during the Civil War, but was revived shortly thereafter, often supported by feminist activists as well as religious groups.

Manufacturers also supported it in the hope of improving the productivity of workers. And anti-immigration groups tended to support it because they believed that drinking was a flaw to be found among the newer groups of immigrants.

FACT

Doctor Benjamin Rush, a signer of the Declaration of Independence, was known for his belief that drinking alcohol to excess was a disease that could be cured by abstinence, but that didn't stop him from including "medicinal alcohol" in the first aid kits he prescribed for the members of the Lewis and Clark expedition.

The Women's Christian Temperance Union, also known as the WCTU, was founded in 1874, and the Anti-Saloon League in 1895. Many activists from the women's suffrage movement, like Frances Willard and Susan B. Anthony, were active in the temperance movement as well. And Carry Nation became famous for invading saloons with a Bible in one hand and, in the other, an ax that she used to destroy the bottles she found there.

The Eighteenth Amendment

By the early twentieth century, the temperance movement encompassed all segments of society. The Progressives supported it as part of their social welfare programs. Many states had gone "dry" independently, although that just meant that people seeking to drink could slip across state lines.

The Eighteenth Amendment was passed in 1917 and ratified in 1919, which meant that, by its terms, it took effect a year later, in 1920. The substantive portion of it read:

After one year from the ratification of this article the manufacture, sale, or transportation of intoxicating liquors within, the importation thereof into, or the exportation thereof from the United States and all territory subject to the jurisdiction thereof for beverage purposes is hereby prohibited.

The proposed amendment passed by an overwhelming majority in both houses, voted for even by those senators and members of Congress who were personally opposed to it, but feared they would not be re-elected if they failed to support this popular legislation. For the first time, they built in a time limitation—seven years—for ratification, in the hope that the states would not ratify it in that limited period. But the state legislatures, bowing to popular sentiment, passed it within thirteen months.

This was not the first time the country would attempt to legislate morality, but it was the first time it would take this legislation to the constitutional level.

The amendment authorized both the federal government and the states to pass laws to implement it. A bill to do so was introduced in Congress by Congressman Andrew Volstead of Minnesota within six months of ratification. The bill, which would become known as the Volstead Act, prohibited the sale and manufacture of all beverages containing more than .05 percent alcohol, including beer and wine.

This came as a surprise to many, who had thought the bill would apply only to hard liquor. Only liquor for "non beverage purposes" and sacramental wine were exempt, as was a limited amount of alcohol for medicinal purposes, and alcohol used for scientific purposes or for use as fuel was intentionally poisoned (denatured) so that it could not be consumed. The act did not forbid the *drinking* of alcohol, however, just its manufacture, sale, and importation. It even allowed individuals to produce limited amounts of alcoholic beverages for their own consumption and that of their family and "bona fide guests," and no search warrants were to issue except if someone was suspected of *selling* alcoholic beverages.

President Woodrow Wilson vetoed the Volstead Act but Congress overrode the veto within twenty-four hours. On January 16, 1920, the Eighteenth Amendment and this enabling legislation took effect.

Social and Economic Effects of Prohibition

While the net result of prohibition was to reduce the average annual amount of alcohol consumed by Americans (today it is less than half of what it was before passage of the amendment), the Eighteenth Amendment produced profound social and economic changes in the United States. Among other things, prohibition resulted in:

- Loss of legitimate income from breweries, distilleries, and taverns while illegitimate businesses like moonshiners, organized crime (which took over importation and distribution), and "speakeasies" (illegal establishments that sold alcohol and provided entertainment) thrived
- Loss of tax revenue on legitimate sales of alcohol
- General disrespect for and flouting of the law

An interesting side effect was the growth of jazz in America, as black entertainers in many of the speakeasies moved over from brothels and similar illegal businesses in which they had worked.

FACT

In the South, many makers of illegal "moonshine" (so-called because it was brewed by the light of the moon) "souped up" their vehicles to avoid being caught by pursuing government agents. Developing these cars led, eventually, to what would become NASCAR racing.

Many breweries and a nascent wine industry in the United States went out of business because of Prohibition, but some survived by switching to other products. The Uihlein family, who owned the Schlitz brewery, for example, switched to the manufacture of Eline (the pronunciation of their name) chocolates. The Miller brewery sold malt syrup.

Repeal

Eventually, it became apparent that this attempt at legislating morality was not working, much as the war on drugs doesn't seem to be (drug restrictions, however, are governed by laws, rather than by a change in the Constitution). Although President Herbert Hoover thought of Prohibition as a "noble experiment," the beginning of the Great Depression created a need for the government to gain the lost revenue that taxes on alcoholic beverages had provided, and a very real need for legitimate jobs. President Franklin Delano Roosevelt included in his platform a pledge to make drinking legal again. Shortly after he took office in 1933, Congress passed a law legalizing 3.2 percent, or "near" beer, and in 1933 passed the Twenty-First Amendment, an amendment so popular it was ratified in less than nine months, despite the cumbersome ratification process built into it (conventions called for the purpose rather than voting by the legislatures of the states.)

The Twenty-First Amendment is unique for a number of reasons. First of all, it is the only amendment to have repealed another amendment. In very simple language, it states, "The eighteenth article of amendment to the Constitution of the United States is hereby repealed."

FACT

According to *Time* magazine, The first legal bottle of beer produced by Washington's Abner Drury Brewery was delivered to President Roosevelt at the White House shortly after midnight on April 14, 1933 and stored in the president's pantry because he was still asleep.

Further, it allowed states and territories that wished to remain "dry" to maintain their own prohibitions of alcohol. The second section of the law states, "The transportation or importation into any State, Territory, or Possession of the United States for delivery or use therein of intoxicating liquors, in violation of the laws thereof, is hereby prohibited." A number of states, and even some counties and municipalities, have remained "dry" after the repeal of Prohibition; the state of Missouri did so until 1966. And the state of Kansas banned public bars until 1987.

Ratification

The ratification process for the Twenty-First Amendment was also unusual. Not only did it build in a seven-year limitation for ratification (which, as mentioned earlier, didn't take anywhere near that long), but it also included the following language: "This article shall be inoperative unless it shall have been ratified as an amendment to the Constitution by conventions in the several States, as provided in the Constitution." This was a direct legacy of a case in which the Supreme Court ruled, in 1920, that a referendum held in Ohio the year before could not rescind the ratification of the Eighteenth Amendment by the Ohio legislature the year before.

Mindful of the fact that members of the legislature could fall prey to special interests and ignore the will of the population on such a hot button issue, this amendment specified the use of the alternative procedure provided for in Article V of the Constitution, which calls for ratification by state legislatures "or by Conventions in three fourths thereof, as one or the other Mode of Ratification may be proposed by the Congress."

The Eighteenth Amendment had specified ratification *by the state legislatures* within seven years. Except for the twelve amendments that were originally submitted as the Bill of Rights, which specifically called for ratification by the state legislatures in its preamble, no previous amendment had specified which method should be used for ratification. The Twenty-First has been the only one to use the convention process.

The Legacy of Prohibition

The Eighteenth Amendment was the only amendment ever to restrict the rights of the people. Laws have done so, and many have proven ineffective. The so-called "war on drugs," which also attempts to regulate behavior that might be better regulated by making the prohibited drugs legal but regulated (and taxed), is made up of laws, rather than an attempt to change the Constitution.

QUESTION

What do prohibition and proposed amendments to prohibit flag burning or same-sex marriage have in common?
These proposed laws restrict the rights of people, and run contrary to constitutional tradition. The primary purpose of amendments to the Constitution, except those that have cured later-discovered glitches in the system of government, has been to expand the rights of the people.

The Eighteenth Amendment was flawed in another way: It effectively adds that specific prohibition to what is essentially an operating system.

The Constitution is an outline for the way the government should operate, and a mandate to the government to protect the people's freedoms. Prohibition ran counter to that basic premise and probably should never have been passed on that basis alone. Its repeal restored those freedoms.

CHAPTER 11

Clearing Up Some Misconceptions about the Constitution

Many people think that all the rules of everyday life are contained in the Constitution. They are not. The genius of the Constitution is that it makes rules for the government so that the government can make laws that affect the people it governs as well as the states that comprise the country.

The Composition of the United States Government

At every level, the Constitution creates a balancing act between rights and responsibilities, between privileges and duties. The government of the United States can be looked at in different ways. First, it can be looked at according to whom it represents:

- The United States is a nation made up of fifty independent states. Each of those states has the right to govern itself according to its own rules, so long as they don't conflict with certain basic rules defined in the Constitution. Ultimately, the Constitution guarantees each state a "republican form of government," so the state must represent its people. So long as it does that, and plays by the rules in the Constitution, it has broad latitude to make its own laws within the state.
- The government of the United States represents the people of the whole United States according to powers granted to it by "the people" in the Constitution.
- The Constitution gives the federal government certain responsibilities, such as keeping the peace between the states and dealing with foreign nations. It is also the guardian of the basic rights of the people of the United States.

Another way of looking at the government is by its division of powers. According to the Constitution, the country is divided into three branches: the legislative, executive, and judicial branches. Every part of the government falls under one of these branches. The Library of Congress and the Copyright Office fall under the legislative branch. The military, the Treasury Department, and the Department of the Interior, to name just a few, fall under the executive branch. All of the federal courts fall under the judicial branch (except for Article I courts which are part of the various agencies they serve).

Why There Is a Constitution

The Constitution defines the government—the *federal* government. It creates the basic working system for the federal government and defines its relationship with the states.

However, it says clearly in the Tenth Amendment that powers not granted to the federal government and not forbidden to the states by the Constitution are reserved to the states and the people. The Ninth Amendment makes it clear that the list of rights that belong to the people is not an exclusive one, and is not meant to preclude the existence of other rights.

FACT

In 1987, a public opinion poll was conducted to commemorate the 200th anniversary of the Constitution. The poll found that 26 percent of Americans believed that the purpose of the Constitution was to declare independence from England.

When in doubt, the Constitution gets the last word; it is the "supreme Law of the Land." When the original states ratified it, they affirmed that. When other states joined the Union, they agreed to that.

Powers of the Federal Government

One of the most important powers the federal government has is that it can regulate commerce with foreign countries and among the states. Historically, Congress has broadly interpreted this power, and the courts have backed that up. It has used this grant of power to create interstate roads (even the portion of those roads that lies within a single state), to establish trademarks for businesses that deal in interstate matters, and to regulate the interstate shipment of food; it uses the commerce power to create and enforce consumer protection laws, workplace protection laws, airline safety rules, and environmental protection laws.

The federal government has the power to create and regulate the country's money and punish counterfeiters; it can borrow money and levy taxes to pay for the cost of government. It also can declare war and maintain the military forces of the United States (although the states can maintain militias, but the president is commander in chief of the militias as well as the U.S. military forces). Anything that concerns the country *as a whole* generally falls under the purview of the federal government.

QUESTION

Why does Congress protect trademarks?
Unlike patents and copyrights, trademarks (the names businesses use to identify their products and services), are not mentioned in the Constitution. So Congress can only regulate trademarks that are used in interstate commerce—those goods shipped or advertised to other states. Trademarks protect a company's "goodwill," but they also protect consumers by verifying the source of a product.

Powers of the States

So what powers are reserved to the states? Basically, the states hold every power that the federal government hasn't claimed for itself, unless it infringes on the rights of the people of the state. So a state government cannot—at least since the passage of the Fourteenth Amendment—curtail your right to practice your religion (unless that religion includes harming someone else, like making human sacrifices). But it can govern the hours you can keep your restaurant open.

A restaurant is a good place to look at the interaction of federal, state, and local laws. Federal law protects the right of every American to eat in a restaurant that is open to the public. It also protects the quality of food that is shipped in interstate commerce, but not locally grown food. However, the state and local government can make rules that require a local restaurant to get a license and open its kitchen to inspectors. Federal trademark laws protect the name of a restaurant doing business in interstate commerce, so you can't use the name "McDonald's" on your restaurant, because that name is trademarked. Federal minimum-wage laws require you to pay your employees at least what those laws specify; your state may require you to pay a higher minimum wage, but not a lower one. But federal law requires you to deduct Social Security and Medicare contributions from every check you pay your employees, and then forward that money to the federal government at regular intervals.

States and Crimes

Some crimes are a matter of federal law, such as committing mail fraud, or counterfeiting, since only the federal government has the right to regulate money and punish people who print their own. These cases are prosecuted in federal court. The U.S. district attorney appointed by the president (and confirmed by the Senate) prosecutes these cases in the local federal district court.

Some crimes are a matter of state or local law, such as opening a restaurant without a license, driving the wrong way on a one-way street, snatching a purse, or committing murder. These crimes will be prosecuted by local district attorneys or even town or village attorneys, and will be brought in state or local courts.

FACT

Although murder generally falls within the jurisdiction of state laws, if the victim is a federal official, or if the crime is committed on federal land (like a national park), it may constitute a federal crime.

And some crimes have concurrent jurisdiction, which means that they can be prosecuted in either the federal or state courts, or sometimes different elements of the same crime can be prosecuted in both kinds of courts. For example, beating up a person who is a member of a minority may be the crime of "battery" under state and local laws. But if you chose your victim because of his race or her religion, the federal government might be able to prosecute you for depriving your victim of civil rights, which would be a federal crime.

Remember, many crimes may also have a *civil* aspect. If you beat up someone, the state may prosecute you for the crime, but your victim may also sue you for civil damages—his hospital bill and lost wages and pain and suffering as a result of the beating. If your crime has a federal aspect—if, for example, you infringed a person's copyright—that suit would be brought in a federal court rather than a state one. And sometimes you have a choice; if you run over a person from another state, and cause her more than $75,000 in damages, she may have the choice of bringing suit in the courts of the state where the accident happened or in federal court under "diversity jurisdiction," which covers suits between citizens of different states that meet the minimum dollar amount set by federal law.

When Federal Law Trumps Local Laws

When the rights guaranteed to all persons in the United States are violated by state laws or local ordinances, or by state or local enforcement officials, you have both state and federal recourse. For example, you (or your attorney) can move to dismiss a case brought in state court if your arrest was the result of an unreasonable search and seizure (something the Constitution protects you from). But if it is not dismissed, you can appeal the matter to federal court or even bring a separate federal lawsuit against those you believe may have violated your civil rights.

For the most part, state law enforcement officers have learned to obey the rules, like using the Miranda warning, that are the result of constitutional guarantees. When they don't, or when there is a technical question about when or to what extent they must do something, the matter may be appealed to the federal courts, even the Supreme Court, for direction.

The Federal Government and Immigration Matters

There are two places in the Constitution that deal specifically with immigration matters. Section 8 of Article I gives Congress the power "To establish an uniform Rule of Naturalization." Under this power, Congress can decide who can become a naturalized American citizen, and under what circumstances. The Fourteenth Amendment—possibly subject to the "law of unintended consequences," because it was meant to grant citizenship to former slaves—says, "All persons born or naturalized in the United States . . . are citizens." It is doubtful that the drafters of that amendment had any idea that illegal aliens would slip across the border so that their children could be born in the United States. But perhaps they should have seen it coming: Living in America has long been the dream of people from all over the world, who came to the United States in waves and were incorporated into American society.

Congress also has the power to create all laws "necessary and proper" to maintain its other powers and the powers granted to the government by the Constitution. As a result, Congress can and does make immigration policy.

English Only?

The founders did not anticipate that anyone would ever challenge the use of English as their national language, so they never thought to include a provision to that effect. At various times there have been proposals for an amendment proposing that English be the official language of the United States, and also federal laws that would say this.

FACT

The idea of an amendment to make English the official language of the United States, possibly through a constitutional amendment, has been circulating since the 1970s. Two proponents of this idea have been S.I. (Samuel Ichiye) Hayakawa, a U.S. senator from California from 1977 to 1983, and Senator Lamar Alexander of Tennessee.

First Amendment Rights

There is no law that prevents a person from speaking any other language nor, under the First Amendment, should there be. But there is a vast difference between speaking a language at home, or even in the workplace (unless that use is detrimental to the business conducted there), and using it for official purposes. There is also a difference between requiring the ability to speak English in order to be hired for a particular job, and forbidding the use of another language while on the job. Suits have actually been brought under the 1964 Civil Rights Act on this subject.

Conflicts and Historical Relevance

To a certain extent, this kind of conflict is actually promoted by lawmakers who don't consider the far-reaching ramifications of a ruling. For example, it may not be unreasonable to require a working knowledge of English in order to become a citizen. If that is the case, and if only *citizens* can vote, then having ballots available in other languages may be unnecessary. Generations of immigrants—from French speakers who came under American rule after the Louisiana Purchase to Spanish speakers in California, as well as the immigrants from Germany, Russia, Italy, China, and many other countries who came to the United States in the nineteenth and early twentieth centuries—learned to speak English in their public schools, no matter what language they spoke at home. The English language has been a unifying factor in a country made up of immigrants, and it could be argued that the "greatest generation" who won World War II, most of whom were of varied immigrant stock, were only able to work together toward victory because they spoke a common language.

FACT

The United States federal government does not specify an official language. However, all official U.S. documents are written in English, though some are also published in other languages. A majority of the states recognize English as their official language.

Case Law Expands the Meaning of the Constitution

The United States comes from a common-law tradition. As such, it is a country where the written opinions of judges expand and explain the meaning of the Constitution and of the laws made pursuant to it. The requirement that there be a particular "case or controversy" to get into court means that the opinion of the court deals with a law's application under a specific fact situation: One person did something to another person, and the result was a circumstance that needs to be addressed. Case law could be interpreted as not unlike parables in the Bible: Court opinions explain how a rule works under specific circumstances.

When you read a law created under the authority of the Constitution, or the Constitution itself, and find that there are sentences whose meaning is confusing, you may need to look to the common law (case law) to understand what the official meaning is. The Constitution cannot be understood without an understanding of how it has been interpreted.

Conflicts Were Built Into the Constitution

When the drafters of the Constitution assembled in Philadelphia in the summer of 1787, the United States had been functioning as a country for a little over a decade. Since the summer of 1776, when the Declaration of Independence was signed, the people of the thirteen colonies had died together in battle, managed to live together as civilians, and even managed to coexist as a country. They had had a decade to function as a loose alliance under the Articles of Confederation, and a large number of them had come to believe that for the new country to function and hold its own among the nations of Europe, it would have to develop a more cohesive central government.

The maxim that "a camel is a horse that was put together by a committee" is a twentieth-century joke, but the Americans of the 1780s had discovered that governing the country by committee—by a legislative body alone—was not conducive to dealing successfully with the domestic or international problems that arose. Various patches were suggested for the Articles of Confederation, but some of those involved in the government (the Federalists in particular) believed that only a country with a stronger central government would succeed.

But even though the United States had come to see itself as a country, the individual states still zealously guarded their sovereignty and their independence from each other. While proclaiming that Americans were principally of one heritage, with the same underlying traditions, they recognized that there were inherent differences between the agrarian southern states and the industrial northern ones. When different factions came together to draft the Constitution, certain conflicts were built in, which remain to this day.

Conflict Between States and a Strong Central Government

While not proclaiming the rights of the states quite as vociferously as did the Articles of Confederation, the Constitution supports both those rights and those of a strong central government. This creates a tension that nearly snapped the country in two just shy of a century after it was founded: the Civil War.

Certainly a lot of that war was about slavery, but much had to do with the rights of the states as opposed to those of the federal government. This is one of the basic conflicts built into the Constitution. Clearly, the more power the federal government has, the less the states will have. The Constitution fosters that conflict by guaranteeing certain powers to the states, just as it guarantees certain other powers to the central government.

The federal government is charged with, among other things, regulating commerce and conflicts among the states, maintaining an army and a navy, coining money, establishing weights and measures—in other words, it has all of the powers that are given to Congress, to the president, and to the Supreme Court. In some cases, when a power of the central government is stated in one part of the Constitution, it is a power that is denied the states in another section, as though to emphasize where that power actually resides.

For example, in Article I, Congress is given the power to declare war; in Article II, the president is given the power to make treaties (with the advice and consent of the Senate). In case any of the states missed that, Section 10 of Article I reminds them that "No State shall enter into any Treaty, Alliance, or Confederation."

Section 10 re-lists many of the things Congress can do, and specifically forbids the states from doing them:

No State shall enter into any Treaty, Alliance, or Confederation; grant Letters of Marque and Reprisal; coin Money; emit Bills of Credit; make any Thing but gold and silver Coin a Tender in Payment of Debts; pass any Bill of Attainder, ex post facto Law, or Law impairing the Obligation of Contracts, or grant any Title of Nobility.

No State shall, without the Consent of the Congress, lay any Imposts or Duties on Imports or Exports, except what may be absolutely necessary for executing its inspection Laws: and the net Produce of all Duties and Imposts, laid by any State on Imports or Exports, shall be for the Use of the Treasury of the United States; and all such Laws shall be subject to the Revision and Controul of the Congress.

No State shall, without the Consent of Congress, lay any Duty of Tonnage, keep Troops, or Ships of War in time of Peace, enter into any Agreement or Compact with another State, or with a foreign Power, or engage in War, unless actually invaded, or in such imminent Danger as will not admit of delay.

Rights That Cannot Be Denied to the States

Similarly, certain rights are guaranteed to the states, both by the text of the Constitution (which guarantees them, among other things, a "Republican Form of Government") and by the Tenth Amendment, which notes that, "The powers not delegated to the United States by the Constitution, nor prohibited by it to the States, are reserved to the States respectively, or to the people."

Conflict Among the States

While some parts of the Constitution were clearly meant to keep relations between the states amicable, such as the one that mandates all states must grant "Full Faith and Credit" to the laws of other states, others lay the seeds for strife; and indeed, the Constitution even makes provisions for one state to sue another, if it comes to that.

The compromise that allowed the southern states to continue to keep slaves, while most people in the northern states believed slavery to be barbaric, was such an inherent conflict. So was counting a slave as three-fifths of a person for voting purposes.

Rights That Belong to the People

A republican form of government, which the Constitution guarantees to each of the states, still needs to keep order while it provides people with basic rights. The Constitution provides for states to maintain militias, for the federal government to call out those militias, and for whatever else it needs to do to maintain order. It also states, in the Bill of Rights, that people have a right to free speech, a free press, freedom of religion, and the right to assemble and petition their government. But where does freedom to assemble begin and keeping the peace end?

Some of the conflicts that have developed in this era have dealt with the fine line where the rights of the people and the need of the government to maintain order have intersected. Nowhere is this more obvious than with the implementation of the Patriot Act and dealings with enemy combatants after the attacks of September 11, 2001.

The Wikileaks circumstances are a further example. The Constitution defines treason narrowly because English kings historically used that charge broadly, in order to get rid of their enemies. To commit treason, one must levy war against the United States, or "adhere" to the country's enemies, "giving them aid and comfort." Did the Wikileaks publication of government documents constitute adhering to America's enemies? Or was it an exercise in generic freedom of expression? The Espionage Act of 1917 (and the related sedition acts which followed it over the next four years) could not anticipate the possibility of Internet publication, and the constitutional prohibition against ex post facto laws makes it impossible to criminalize the act after the fact.

The Three Branches Struggle with Each Other

The system of checks and balances that keeps one branch of the government from dominating the other two forces them to work together to accomplish anything, but the independence of each branch makes them more likely to do battle with each other than to cooperate. This builds gridlock into the system, and the party system only compounds it.

But one can't be sure that this wasn't intentional on the part of the framers. A government that stymies itself will have difficulty oppressing its citizenry. The framers were certainly aware of that.

ESSENTIAL

The concept of separation of powers dates back as far as ancient Greece. Aristotle favored a mixed government composed of monarchy, aristocracy, and democracy. He believed that none of the three were perfect, but that a government should combine the best aspects of each.

A Bicameral Congress Pits One House Against the Other

Because of the initial purpose of the two houses—one representing the states and the other the people—and because of their different terms of office, there is a conflict built into the way they handle the legislative function. The staggered six-year terms of the Senate make a swift political turnover of that chamber less likely. This timing contributes to the odds that a party may predominate in one of the houses while another party predominates in the other. A partisan effort to counter the votes of the other house is thus built into the Constitution. In other words, gridlock was intentional, and may actually be a good thing!

The People Versus the State

Inequitable representation is built into the way Congress is elected. Even without the infamous three-fifths person clause, the fact that every state, regardless of size or wealth, gets two senators, and every state, no matter how small its population, gets at least one representative, is contradictory to the idea of "one-man-one-vote." Even the House (although it ostensibly represents the people on a population basis), can never represent all of the people equally, when allocations of representation are by population divisions within states, as opposed to a portion of the population as a whole.

Civilian Checks on Military Power

The fact that the president, a civilian, is commander in chief of the armed forces keeps the military from asserting its power to stage a coup. The fact that Congress controls the army's appropriations, and must renew them every two years, also keeps the military in check. So does the fact that Congress is responsible for the rules that govern the armed forces.

Fair Trial and Free Press

The fact that the First Amendment of the Constitution guarantees freedom of the press has long created a situation that is problematic not only for those parts of the government that need to operate in secret for public safety purposes, like diplomacy and defense, but also the prosecution of criminals. This has only been aggravated since the advent of the Internet. Where traditional newspapers and magazines employed professional journalists who usually verified their stories, as well as editors who called upon them to provide a factual basis for what they'd written, anyone with a blog can post anything, whether it has been verified or not. Half-truths and outright lies can go viral, as can facts that would not be admissible in court.

ESSENTIAL

The original version of the Freedom of Information Act (FOIA) went into effect in 1967. (It has been amended several times since then.) With exceptions that protect national security, it allows people to see and correct records the government has kept about them, and—so long as doing so doesn't violate national security or the privacy of individuals—allows the press access to information about the activities and practices of the government.

Anonymous posts can negate the right of an accused to face the person who has brought accusations. Publication of unverified facts can contaminate the jury pool so that it is impossible for an accused to get a trial by an unbiased jury.

This kind of publicity can affect elections as well as trials. Once something is out on the web, it is virtually impossible to get it back. While this can lead to more open government, it can also, in the hands of skilled manipulators, lead to a misinformed electorate or a biased jury. Again, this conflict is inherent in the structure of the American government.

CHAPTER 12

Preserving the System: Changes That Didn't Make It

Sometimes, change is *not* good. Changing the Constitution, the system for running the government, is not necessary when passing an ordinary law will do. Luckily for the Constitution and the people governed by it (since it is the supreme law of the land), most attempts to amend it have failed. Indeed, most proposed amendments should have been proposed laws (at most), because laws are easier to pass, to amend, and to annul.

Remembering What the Constitution Is

The Constitution is a legal document that dictates how the government will be shaped, and how it should function. Once established as prescribed in the Constitution, the Congress makes laws. And since those laws, once passed, become part of the supreme law of the land, it usually isn't really necessary that they have the force and permanence of amendments.

After all, it is easier to pass a law. Article I of the Constitution sets forth how a law is created: The process requires passage by both houses and the signature of the president or the override of a presidential veto. And Article VI makes clear that "This Constitution, *and the Laws of the United States which shall be made in Pursuance thereof* . . . shall be the supreme Law of the Land." The italics aren't in the Constitution itself, but the phrase is.

What the Constitution was designed to do is create a government. It is a *limited* government by virtue of the Tenth Amendment, which says "The powers not delegated to the United States by the Constitution, nor prohibited by it to the States, are reserved to the States respectively, or to the people," and the Ninth, which makes it clear that the Bill of Rights *includes, but is not limited to*, the rights it lists.

And because the Constitution was carefully designed to work as a system, the process for amending the Constitution was made more difficult than the passage of a law so that the system wouldn't grind to a halt.

The Amendments That Have Been Ratified

With the exception of the failed and repealed Eighteenth Amendment, all of the amendments to the Constitution have accomplished one of two things (or sometimes both): They have fixed a glitch in the way the system worked (such as the method for electing a president, which failed to anticipate the establishment of political parties) or they have *expanded* the rights of the people under the Constitution.

Many of the proposed amendments that did not pass, would have, like the Eighteenth, *contracted* those rights. The Twenty-First Amendment, which repealed the Eighteenth, could be said to have fixed a glitch that was put into the system when the Eighteenth Amendment was ratified.

The Amendment Process

Article V of the Constitution describes how to amend the Constitution. It starts out either of two ways: Either both houses of Congress must pass the Amendment (with the same wording; if the wording is different, they have to compromise their differences), or the legislatures of at least two-thirds of the states can call for a constitutional convention for proposing amendments.

Once an amendment is passed, it is sent to the states, where it must be ratified by three-fourths of the legislatures, or by conventions held in three-fourths of the states, before it becomes part of the Constitution. Congress can specify which method of ratification should be used.

ESSENTIAL

Amending the Articles of Confederation required unanimous consent of all the states. The "more perfect Union" created by the Constitution allowed for ratification of proposed amendments by three-fourths of the states, increasing the possibility that amending could actually be accomplished.

In the Constitution, there is no limit on the amount of time that an amendment can wait for the required number of states to ratify it, but the Supreme Court has ruled that once a state has ratified an amendment, it cannot rescind its ratification. Since the Eighteenth Amendment, many pending amendments have had a "sunset" provision built into them: They must be ratified by the required number of states within a limited time, or they lapse.

FACT

Only one amendment has required the ratification by conventions, the Twenty-First, which repealed Prohibition.

However, some amendments that were passed long ago are still technically waiting for the requisite number of states to ratify them (although, as the number of states increases, so does the number required for ratification, since approval by three-fourths of the existing states is required). The

Twenty-Seventh Amendment, restricting congressional pay raises, was proposed in 1789 as part of the original Bill of Rights, but was not ratified until 1992.

Amendments That Passed but Were Not Ratified

Six proposed amendments were actually passed by Congress but have failed to achieve ratification. Two of them, the Equal Rights Amendment (ERA) and the District of Columbia Voting Rights Amendment, are dead, because they failed to receive ratification by the states within the required seven-year period. The other four are technically still eligible for ratification:

- The 1789 amendment dealing with voter apportionment was submitted with the ten amendments that make up the Bill of Rights and the one that is now the Twenty-Seventh Amendment. This amendment, actually the first of the twelve submitted in 1789, proposed specific numbers of representatives as the population of the United States increased, ultimately resulting in one for every 50,000 people. At that rate, the House of Representatives would today consist of over 6,000 members instead of the current 435. Over the years, it has been more practical to change the actual numbers by law, according to the principles outlined in Article I of the Constitution. This amendment is unlikely to ever be ratified.
- With the War of 1812 brewing, the Eleventh Congress passed a proposed amendment saying that any American who accepted a title of nobility or a pension or grant from any monarch would be stripped of American citizenship. There already was a provision in Section 9 of Article I stating that no one holding office in the United States could accept a title or any payment from any monarch without the consent of Congress, and that Congress would never grant any titles of nobility, but this proposed amendment went even farther. It never passed, but is ripe for passage. Americans today are more likely to be amused by the grant of a title than to fear it, but at the time, there was real fear that it could undermine the Republic.

- A pro-slavery amendment was passed by a lame-duck Congress two days before President Abraham Lincoln took office. This proposed amendment forbade any amendment that would interfere with slavery. The outgoing president, James Buchanan, signed it, although the Constitution does not require a presidential signature on proposed amendments. It is the only proposed amendment that has ever been signed by a president, and it is still technically available for ratification, although its passage would conflict with the already ratified Thirteenth Amendment (and possibly the Fourteenth, since this proposed amendment forbids amendments that will interfere with a state's "domestic institutions"). The wording of this proposed amendment would have forbidden any future amendments that might interfere with state law, especially where it concerned the institution of slavery. This runs counter to the Constitution's precedence over state law as the supreme law of the land. It also would have added another prohibition against amendment to the only two contained in the Constitution (in Article V). One of these also deals with slavery: The importation of slaves could not be curtailed before 1808. The other says that no state can be deprived of its representation in the Senate without its consent.
- The Child Labor Amendment, passed in 1926 and ratified, so far, by twenty-eight states, gave Congress the "power to limit, regulate, and prohibit the labor of persons under eighteen years of age." Such laws could override state laws addressing child labor where there was a conflict, but did not forbid the states from passing their own more expansive child labor laws. Today, the Department of Labor regulates child (and other) labor practices, under, among other things, the Commerce Clause (in Article I), which empowers Congress to regulate interstate commerce, and has been interpreted very broadly.

The two amendments that expired before ratification, the Equal Rights Amendment and the District of Columbia Voting Rights Amendment, caused furious public debate before their time ran out. As with the proposed Child Labor Amendment, other means have been found to achieve the goals of these proposed amendments.

The Equal Rights Amendment

The proposed Equal Rights Amendment (ERA) was part of the second feminist movement, which arose in the late 1960s and early 1970s as an outgrowth of the civil rights movement. Although women had had the vote since 1920, and had been an important part of the homefront effort during World War II, they were restricted by many laws on the books in many states, and by custom and practice as well.

Discrimination Against Women

Women's advancement in the military and in many types of employment was limited, and they were often subjected to sexual harassment on the job, for which they had no recourse. Family laws (such as divorce and adoption) were often skewed against them. They were often denied the right to be hired in traditionally male occupations, and when hired, were often paid less than their male counterparts for the same job. They could be denied employment if they became pregnant, and indeed, were often asked by prospective employers if they intended to become pregnant. Colleges and universities were allowed to spend vast amounts on athletic programs for male students without spending anything on programs for female students. In some states, banks denied women the right to equal credit, meaning that they could not buy property because they could not, by virtue of their gender, qualify for mortgages.

The Fight for Equal Treatment

As the injustices of race discrimination were aired during the civil rights movement, women began to air their own complaints about unequal treatment, and this awareness led to mounting anger. The result was a trend toward nonsexist language ("chair" or "chairperson" instead of "chairman," for example), first in the public press and then in the wording of laws, and in the passage by the House in 1971 and by the Senate in 1972 of the ERA.

Its text was simple: "Equality of rights under the law shall not be denied or abridged by the United States or by any State on account of sex," but the passions it aroused were profound.

Among the arguments against passage were that women would be subject to the draft (which became moot when the draft was eliminated and an all-volunteer army initiated); that women might be required to serve in combat; that public bathrooms would have to be unisex (apparently these people had never set foot on an airplane). It was argued that women would lose certain protections they already had as the "more delicate" sex.

Gradual Change

The ERA was given seven years for ratification, and when it hadn't been ratified in that amount of time, the term was extended for another three years (although there was some doubt as to whether that extension was constitutional). It eventually failed, but in the meantime, women had discovered that they had been included in the landmark 1964 Civil Rights Act and began to bring suits under that law. They ran for office, and began to win. They applied to professional schools and were no longer told they were "taking a man's place," or that after they had their degrees, they were "taking a job away from a man."

FACT

Only a lawyer could love the arguments against the extension of the time for ratification, among them that extending the time for ratification meant that states ratifying after the extension were presented with a proposed amendment that was technically different—because of the extended time for ratification—from the one earlier states had ratified, even though the substantive portion was identical.

The Equal Rights Amendment failed, but while it was pending, the arguments for and against it came out into the open. Women were admitted to the military academies, graduated, and served with distinction—often in combat. Although not protected by an actual amendment, the goals of the amendment appear to have been largely accomplished by legislation and by evolving custom.

The District of Columbia Voting Rights Amendment

The District of Columbia was created by Congress under the authority of Article I, Section 8, Clause 17, which gave Congress the power "To exercise exclusive Legislation in all Cases whatsoever, over such District (not exceeding ten Miles square) as may, by Cession of particular States, and the Acceptance of Congress, become the Seat of the Government of the United States." The District of Columbia would not be part of any state, and thus no state would be shown favoritism by containing the seat of the federal government. The site of the district was approximately central in a collection of states clustered along the Atlantic coast.

As the seat of government, the district would contain people who would be there only temporarily while they were serving in the government. Somehow, the Founding Fathers didn't think it through that people might work permanently in government jobs, or might choose to live in the capital in order to provide services to those who were serving in the government. As in any metropolitan area, the district needed barbers, laundresses, deliverymen, and hotels and boarding houses. It needed grocers and a fire department and a police department. All of those people would come to live in the district; and by virtue of its being federal territory, they were disenfranchised.

And a large proportion of these citizens were black—something that didn't escape the attention of those involved in the civil rights movement, or those who opposed it. In 1961, with the Twenty-Third Amendment, residents of the district had been given the right to choose electors and thus vote for president. But although they paid taxes, they did not have a representative in Congress, and it was Congress that passed the laws governing the district. In 1978, Congress passed a proposed amendment that was an outgrowth of the civil rights movement. It would have rescinded the Twenty-Third Amendment and substituted an amendment that read, "For purposes of representation in the Congress, election of the President and Vice President, and article V of this Constitution, the District constituting the seat of government of the United States shall be treated as though it were a State." This would have given the district two senators, and a voting member of the House.

The Amendment was opposed in the South, and failed to gain sufficient traction in the North. It did not achieve ratification by three-fourths of the states within seven years, and died.

Congress did, in the meantime, authorize the district to elect a nonvoting member of the House, who can speak to debate on the floor, and intercede for constituents much as any other member of Congress can. But the district has no representation in the Senate, although it still votes for presidential electors under the Twenty-Third Amendment.

Amendments Proposed but Not Passed

Members of Congress who don't understand the difference between a law and a constitutional amendment, or who feel so strongly about the rightness of their point of view that they think what they want to pass should be part of the Constitution, both for the import and so that it is harder to repeal, have proposed a large number of amendments. These come up in every Congress. Here are some that have been introduced in the twenty-first century but were never passed:

- To make the filibuster (a Senate procedural rule) part of the Constitution
- To require a balanced budget (which could be a serious problem in the event of a war, natural disaster, or other emergency)
- To allow a naturalized person to become president after twenty years as a U.S. citizen
- To declare that life begins at conception
- To restrict marriages in all states to one man and one woman (like Prohibition, this would contract, rather than expand, individual rights—and deny the states the right to decide this issue for themselves)
- To give the president a line-item veto (upsetting the careful checks and balances the Constitution contains)

Do these belong in the Constitution? Bear in mind that as recently as 1967, when the Supreme Court overruled the law in *Loving v. Virginia*, it was illegal in that state (and some others) for people of different races to marry. Times change and beliefs change. The Constitution endures because it expands rights, rather than contracting them, and because in the end, it is just an outline for a system of government. People's pet peeves do not belong in the Constitution any more than Prohibition did.

CHAPTER 13

The Controversial Constitution

From the start, the U.S. Constitution has sparked controversy. Created by a committee that had been charged with revising and amending the Articles of Confederation that then governed the nascent United States of America, it instead provided a wholly new document that totally replaced the Articles, although without specifically saying so.

The Battle Over Ratification

Although amendments to the Articles of Confederation required unanimous approval, the Constitution, presented as a single document, required only the ratification by nine states—but it specified conventions in those states, rather than ratification by the legislatures. Conventions were duly called, and the debate about ratification began.

There were arguments that the Constitution went too far, and that the new federal government would be too powerful, with a strong central government that would overpower the individual states. There were arguments that the Constitution did not go far enough because it did not guarantee individual rights to the people.

ALERT

One of the arguments against including a bill of rights in the original Constitution was that listing specific rights might be regarded as limiting citizens to those rights. The Ninth Amendment—incorporated into the Constitution in 1791 as part of the Bill of Rights—specifically states that the list is not meant to preclude other rights retained "by the people."

The campaign to ratify the Constitution put men at odds who had been on the same side a dozen years earlier in declaring the independence of the United States. Among those opposed to ratification were champions of independence Patrick Henry and Samuel Adams, along with George Mason (who had attended the Constitutional Convention but had refused to sign the Constitution because it did not contain a bill of rights at the time).

Among those championing the ratification were men who would later become bitter political enemies, James Madison and Alexander Hamilton. Madison and Hamilton, together with John Jay (who would later become the first Chief Justice of the United States Supreme Court, once the Constitution had been ratified), wrote the Federalist Papers, under the joint pen name "Publius," to explain the ideas behind the way the Constitution had been drafted, and to advocate its ratification by New York.

Checks and Balances and the Power of the Judiciary

In "Federalist No. 51," James Madison—who was the primary drafter of the actual wording of the Constitution—argues that the new government will be based on a system of checks and balances, creating "rival interests" so that no one branch can dominate. He makes an argument that federal judges should have "permanent tenure" so as to "destroy all sense of dependence" on the president who had appointed them or the Senate that had confirmed them.

Hamilton reiterates this idea in "Federalist No. 78," in which he discusses the judiciary branch. He says that "the complete independence of the courts of justice is peculiarly essential in a limited Constitution," because it is their duty "to declare all acts contrary to the manifest tenor of the Constitution void."

The basis for some of the more recent controversies about the Constitution can be found in those words: What is the *manifest tenor* of the Constitution? Do the words mean what they meant when it was drafted, or when it was ratified, or what they mean today? Is there an implication in the Constitution, perhaps set forth in the Preamble, which lists its purpose, that isn't clear in the document?

In "Federalist No. 78," Hamilton notes that when there is a conflict, it is the last act of a legislature that has traditionally governed over the earlier ones. Yet in recent years, there has been a discussion that one should go back to the "original meaning," or the "original intent" in order to interpret what a constitutional phrase might mean, and whether the government—or which part of it—has the right to create laws that expand on that original meaning.

What Is Constitutional Law?

As recently as the 1980s, when you took Constitutional Law in law school (and it is a required course), you did not inquire as to the politics of your professor. Law schools use the case method; you read cases to see how the judges reasoned in coming to their rulings. These cases are then discussed in class, often using the "Socratic method," which encourages everybody to say whether they can follow the reasoning, or agree with it. But in the end, whether the professor agrees, or doesn't, should not make any difference in the fact that decisions were made, and are now the law of the land. That neutral stance may no longer be the case.

In the not-so-distant past, Constitutional Law classes were taught by discussing the various sections of the Constitution and laws that had been passed in support of those sections, and the cases that had decided the application of those laws. You relied on *stare decisis*—the principle that what has been ruled before is the basis for current law, unless it is overruled by a new amendment or a new law. Only rarely is a standing decision overruled, but it can be when that decision runs so contrary to current moral belief that it can no longer be supported by society.

ESSENTIAL

The Code Napoleon gave rise to the laws of only one state, Louisiana. The difference between this system and the Anglo-American system of common law is that the former attempts to codify all parts of the law, while common law relies on historic precedent for interpretation of most matters. The American system is becoming a hybrid of codes—like the Federal Code of Civil Procedure, or the U.S. Copyright Law, or state criminal codes—and judicial interpretations of those codes, which are as important as the codes themselves.

An example of this might be the matter of "separate but equal" schools, public accommodations, and other facilities. In 1896, in a case called *Plessy v. Ferguson*, the Supreme Court ruled that the Fourteenth Amendment meant to provide equal facilities to people of different races, but that they didn't have to be the *same* facilities. Over the years after that decision, races were often separated in waiting rooms, at lunch counters, and most particularly in schools. But it became clear that these separate facilities were seldom equal in quality, and that the idea of separating the races in public facilities was antithetical to the basic tenets espoused by the Declaration of Independence and the Constitution. In 1954, without specifically overturning *Plessy*, the court ruled in *Brown v. Board of Education* that the segregation of the Kansas City schools denied equal rights to some students on the basis of race, which ran contrary to Section 1 of the Fourteenth Amendment.

Traditionally, law professors might point out that some laws on the books might seem offensive by modern standards, but they taught that when a case was legitimately brought before the Court, such moral repugnancy provided grounds for overruling such a law. (In the absence of an actual case or controversy, the only way to overrule a law was for Congress to repeal it or amend it.) By contrast, today there are some professors who teach that judges should not find contemporary interpretations for older law when a case presents itself. This is the basis for a great schism in the ranks of those learned in the law.

Case and Controversy

A federal court—and especially the Supreme Court—cannot decide, just by looking at it, that a law passed by a state or by the federal government is unconstitutional. The case must come before the court legitimately: There must be at least two parties, and they must have a dispute that involves the enforcement of the law in question. This principle is laid out in Section 2 of Article III of the Constitution.

If there is a case with actual parties and an actual dispute, whereby one of the parties will suffer if the other is allowed to continue, the court can rule on the legitimacy of a law, or can attempt to interpret the meaning of a phrase in the Constitution that may seem unclear, and will then resolve the matter in favor of one or the other of the parties.

Finding Meaning in the Words

In the 1980s, a number of books and papers were produced by judges and legal scholars saying that the Supreme Court, under Chief Justice Earl Warren, had strayed too far from the original Constitution. The Supreme Court, for example, had ruled that there existed a "right to privacy," words that do not appear in the Constitution or the Bill of Rights. The right to privacy might extend to the control of a woman over her own body, which was a principle deciding point in *Roe v. Wade*, and in cases supporting the right of consenting adults to engage in nonviolent practices in private.

The Ninth Amendment says that just because a right isn't listed in the Constitution or the Bill of Rights, that does not mean that right doesn't exist. But many conservatives felt that if a right wasn't in the Constitution or implied by the founders in some commentary or in the minutes of Congress or of the constitutional convention, the Court should not "invent" it. Papers, books, and even some cases have upheld this principle: That the courts needed to ascertain these meanings as the founders intended, and should *not* expand on them in light of the values of contemporary society. They took this stance despite the fact that certain parts of the Constitution were necessarily vague, and had been, like the Commerce Clause, subject to various interpretations.

QUESTION

What is "judicial activism"?
Some who believe that if a right is not listed in the Constitution, it does not exist, have accused judges who find that there are such rights as privacy to be "judicial activists." However, this complaint appears to apply in many cases merely to judicial decisions the speaker does not agree with.

The Commerce Clause

In Article I, Section 8, among the powers of Congress is the power "To regulate Commerce with foreign Nations, and among the several States, and with the Indian Tribes." Over the years, there have been a series of decisions that have expanded this clause. They began with cases that determined that one state could not grant a monopoly to one shipping company on a river that constituted an interstate border. Clearly, the Constitution said that Congress had the power to regulate commerce between two states—but what about something created wholly within one state? Did it make a difference if it entered the stream of interstate commerce after manufacture, or if the materials that went into it came from outside the state? Did it make a difference if, although it was created and used totally within one state, it affected the scarcity and prices of goods in the stream of commerce among all the states? The expansion of Congressional regulatory powers based on the Commerce Clause was one of the triggers for those who felt that Congress had overreached its authority.

The Necessary and Proper Clause

The last on the list of the Powers of Congress found in Article I, Section 8, is the power "To make all Laws which shall be necessary and proper for carrying into Execution the foregoing Powers, and all other Powers vested by this Constitution in the Government of the United Sates, or in any Department of Officer thereof." That's a pretty broad mandate, but these rights are limited to those powers granted to the federal government by the Constitution, since, pursuant to the Tenth Amendment, the rest of the rights belong to the states and to the people. This clause has been the basis for the expansion of many of the powers of the federal government, but has also been used as the basis for striking down laws that couldn't be connected to the powers granted to the government.

The General Welfare Clause

This phrase "general welfare" occurs both in the Preamble to the Constitution, which sets forth the purposes of the document (including to "promote the general Welfare") and in Section 8 of Article I, which says that "Congress shall have Power . . . to . . . provide for the common Defence and general Welfare of the United States." Does this mean that, absent the interstate regulatory powers of the Commerce Clause, the federal government can regulate wages and hours and working conditions for ordinary Americans to promote their general welfare? Should it mean that Congress has the power to promote the general welfare *of the states*, rather than of their people? These are the kinds of questions that have arisen in some cases.

But what did the founders mean by what they wrote? There is a body of legal scholars who are known as "Originalists" who believe that the original meanings must be understood before a court can rule on the legitimacy of a law passed by Congress, or the rights of a person arising under that law.

Who Are the Originalists?

As with the Founding Fathers, whose attitudes were far from unanimous, those who term themselves "Originalists" may also disagree among themselves as to what "original" meaning they are seeking. Some seek "original meaning," and others seek "original intent." The former may require looking to what a word meant at the time the Constitution (or an amendment) was ratified; the latter may require exploring the correspondence, records of debate, and publications of those involved in the drafting or passage of a law.

FACT

> Several current and recent members of the Supreme Court ascribe to Originalist theories, including Justices Antonin Scalia and Clarence Thomas and the late Chief Justice William Rehnquist. Robert Bork, former judge of the Court of Appeals for the District of Columbia, whose nomination to the Supreme Court was rejected by the Senate in 1987, is a leading proponent of Originalism.

Those who subscribe to Originalism look to the original text of the Constitution, and may or may not be willing to permit judicial discretion to interpret it. Some Originalists are "strict constructionalists," seeking literal meaning in the Constitution, with no allowance for some of the ambiguities contained in that document.

One of the problems with going to original sources is that there is never a complete record of any person's thoughts throughout his life or her day. And people can change their minds in the course of the day: Think about driving to McDonald's for a hamburger and coming home instead with fries and a cup of coffee. You've changed your mind, but is there any record of that fact?

ESSENTIAL

> To see the kind of scholarship that goes into a well-reasoned Originalist court opinion, read the historically detailed majority opinion in *District of Columbia v. Heller*.

It is hard to say, more than 200 years later, whether a founder denounced a clause or paragraph in a letter that survived, but perhaps changed his mind after having an ale with a friend, and voted in favor of it after all. Can you always tell, from a letter, when someone is humoring a friend, or even being facetious?

A Living Document

Until the proponents of Originalism began to claim the Constitution had expanded beyond its founders' intentions, people were taught in law school that the Constitution was a living document; there are those who today find in this view a liberal interpretation. The fact remains that the Constitution's genius lies in the fact that it does not contain specific laws (although those laws are, when passed by Congress, incorporated into the "supreme Law of the Land"), but a *system of government*. The government creates and passes laws that vary with the times and the needs of the people.

How well does this work? There have been a number of constitutional crises in recent years. For example, there was the 2000 presidential election, decided in a Supreme Court case, *Bush v. Gore*. Other countries might have turned to bloodshed, to barricades in the streets. In the United States, the Supreme Court made a decision, and the rest of the population abided by it. It is American law and custom to wait for the next election.

In 1974, after President Richard M. Nixon was compelled to reveal tapes of calls and conversations that occurred in his office, and they revealed that he had been complicit in covering up criminal acts, it became clear that even the House members of his own party would vote to impeach him. The Nixon presidency had been unraveling for two years, following, among other things, a break-in at Democratic Party headquarters in the Watergate complex, a robbery of which the president turned out to have knowledge.

Nixon's vice president, Gerald Ford, had been appointed—pursuant to the Twenty-Fifth Amendment—to fill a vacancy after the elected vice president, Spiro Agnew, had resigned as part of a plea agreement for separate criminal charges in his home state of Maryland.

FACT

Gerald R. Ford, the fortieth vice president and thirty-eighth president of the United States, was the only president to serve without having been elected to either office. A Republican, he had represented Michigan's 5th District in Congress from 1949 to 1973, and was serving in his ninth year as House Minority Leader when Nixon appointed him to the vice presidency.

On August 9, 1974, Nixon resigned. Ford was inaugurated as president, and people pointed with pride and relief to the fact that the U.S. Constitution, a system that was, at the time, almost 200 years old, had provided for an orderly change of government, without riots, without bloodshed.

As President Ford said that day, "Our long national nightmare is over. Our Constitution works."

And so it still does.

APPENDIX A

Amendments to the Constitution

Constitutional Amendments 1–10 make up what is known as The Bill of Rights.

Amendment 1

Congress shall make no law respecting an establishment of religion, or prohibiting the free exercise thereof; or abridging the freedom of speech, or of the press; or the right of the people peaceably to assemble, and to petition the Government for a redress of grievances.

Amendment II

A well regulated Militia, being necessary to the security of a free State, the right of the people to keep and bear Arms, shall not be infringed.

Amendment III

No Soldier shall, in time of peace be quartered in any house, without the consent of the Owner, nor in time of war, but in a manner to be prescribed by law.

Amendment IV

The right of the people to be secure in their persons, houses, papers, and effects, against unreasonable searches and seizures, shall not be violated, and no Warrants shall issue, but upon probable cause, supported by Oath or affirmation, and particularly describing the place to be searched, and the persons or things to be seized.

Amendment V

No person shall be held to answer for a capital, or otherwise infamous crime, unless on a presentment or indictment of a Grand Jury, except in cases arising in the land or naval forces, or in the Militia, when in actual service in time of War or public danger;

nor shall any person be subject for the same offence to be twice put in jeopardy of life or limb; nor shall be compelled in any criminal case to be a witness against himself, nor be deprived of life, liberty, or property, without due process of law; nor shall private property be taken for public use, without just compensation.

Amendment VI

In all criminal prosecutions, the accused shall enjoy the right to a speedy and public trial, by an impartial jury of the State and district wherein the crime shall have been committed, which district shall have been previously ascertained by law, and to be informed of the nature and cause of the accusation; to be confronted with the witnesses against him; to have compulsory process for obtaining witnesses in his favor, and to have the Assistance of Counsel for his defence.

Amendment VII

In Suits at common law, where the value in controversy shall exceed twenty dollars, the right of trial by jury shall be preserved, and no fact tried by a jury, shall be otherwise re-examined in any Court of the United States, than according to the rules of the common law.

Amendment VIII

Excessive bail shall not be required, nor excessive fines imposed, nor cruel and unusual punishments inflicted.

Amendment IX

The enumeration in the Constitution, of certain rights, shall not be construed to deny or disparage others retained by the people.

Amendment X

The powers not delegated to the United States by the Constitution, nor prohibited by it to the States, are reserved to the States respectively, or to the people.

Amendment XI

Passed by Congress March 4, 1794. Ratified February 7, 1795.

Note: Article III, section 2, of the Constitution was modified by amendment 11.

The Judicial power of the United States shall not be construed to extend to any suit in law or equity, commenced or prosecuted against one of the United States by Citizens of another State, or by Citizens or Subjects of any Foreign State.

Amendment XII

Passed by Congress December 9, 1803. Ratified June 15, 1804.

Note: A portion of Article II, section 1 of the Constitution was superseded by the 12th amendment.

The Electors shall meet in their respective states and vote by ballot for President and Vice-President, one of whom, at least, shall not be an inhabitant of the same state with themselves; they shall name in their ballots the person voted for as President, and in distinct ballots the person voted for as Vice-President, and they shall make distinct lists of all persons voted for as President, and of all persons voted for as Vice-President, and of the number of votes for each, which lists they shall sign and certify, and transmit sealed to the seat of the government of the United States, directed to the President of the Senate;—the President of the Senate shall, in the presence of the Senate and House of Representatives, open all the certificates and the votes shall then be counted;—The person having the greatest number of votes for President, shall be the President, if such number be a majority of the whole number of Electors appointed; and if no person have such majority, then from the persons having the highest numbers not exceeding three on the list of those voted for as President, the House of Representatives shall choose immediately, by ballot, the President. But in choosing the President, the votes shall be taken by states, the representation from each state having one vote; a quorum for this purpose shall consist of a member or members from two-thirds of the states, and a majority of all the states shall be necessary to a choice. [And if the House of Representatives shall not choose a President whenever the right of choice shall devolve upon them, before the fourth day of March next following, then the Vice-President shall act as President, as in case of the death or other constitutional disability of the President.]* The person having the greatest number of votes as Vice-President, shall be the Vice-President, if such number be a majority of the whole number of Electors appointed, and if no person have a majority,

then from the two highest numbers on the list, the Senate shall choose the Vice-President; a quorum for the purpose shall consist of two-thirds of the whole number of Senators, and a majority of the whole number shall be necessary to a choice. But no person constitutionally ineligible to the office of President shall be eligible to that of Vice-President of the United States.
Superseded by section 3 of the 20th amendment.

Amendment XIII

Passed by Congress January 31, 1865. Ratified December 6, 1865.
   Note: A portion of Article IV, section 2, of the Constitution was superseded by the 13th amendment.

Section 1.
Neither slavery nor involuntary servitude, except as a punishment for crime whereof the party shall have been duly convicted, shall exist within the United States, or any place subject to their jurisdiction.

Section 2.
Congress shall have power to enforce this article by appropriate legislation.

Amendment XIV

Passed by Congress June 13, 1866. Ratified July 9, 1868.
   Note: Article I, section 2, of the Constitution was modified by section 2 of the 14th amendment.

Section 1.
All persons born or naturalized in the United States, and subject to the jurisdiction thereof, are citizens of the United States and of the State wherein they reside. No State shall make or enforce any law which shall abridge the privileges or immunities of citizens of the United States; nor shall any State deprive any person of life, liberty, or property, without due process of law; nor deny to any person within its jurisdiction the equal protection of the laws.

Section 2.

Representatives shall be apportioned among the several States according to their respective numbers, counting the whole number of persons in each State, excluding Indians not taxed. But when the right to vote at any election for the choice of electors for President and Vice-President of the United States, Representatives in Congress, the Executive and Judicial officers of a State, or the members of the Legislature thereof, is denied to any of the male inhabitants of such State, being twenty-one years of age,* and citizens of the United States, or in any way abridged, except for participation in rebellion, or other crime, the basis of representation therein shall be reduced in the proportion which the number of such male citizens shall bear to the whole number of male citizens twenty-one years of age in such State.

Section 3.

No person shall be a Senator or Representative in Congress, or elector of President and Vice-President, or hold any office, civil or military, under the United States, or under any State, who, having previously taken an oath, as a member of Congress, or as an officer of the United States, or as a member of any State legislature, or as an executive or judicial officer of any State, to support the Constitution of the United States, shall have engaged in insurrection or rebellion against the same, or given aid or comfort to the enemies thereof. But Congress may by a vote of two-thirds of each House, remove such disability.

Section 4.

The validity of the public debt of the United States, authorized by law, including debts incurred for payment of pensions and bounties for services in suppressing insurrection or rebellion, shall not be questioned. But neither the United States nor any State shall assume or pay any debt or obligation incurred in aid of insurrection or rebellion against the United States, or any claim for the loss or emancipation of any slave; but all such debts, obligations and claims shall be held illegal and void.

Section 5.

The Congress shall have the power to enforce, by appropriate legislation, the provisions of this article.

Changed by section 1 of the 26th amendment.

Amendment XV

Passed by Congress February 26, 1869. Ratified February 3, 1870.

Section 1.
The right of citizens of the United States to vote shall not be denied or abridged by the United States or by any State on account of race, color, or previous condition of servitude—

Section 2.
The Congress shall have the power to enforce this article by appropriate legislation.

Amendment XVI

Passed by Congress July 2, 1909. Ratified February 3, 1913.
Note: Article I, section 9, of the Constitution was modified by amendment 16.
The Congress shall have power to lay and collect taxes on incomes, from whatever source derived, without apportionment among the several States, and without regard to any census or enumeration.

Amendment XVII

Passed by Congress May 13, 1912. Ratified April 8, 1913.
Note: Article I, section 3, of the Constitution was modified by the 17th amendment.
The Senate of the United States shall be composed of two Senators from each State, elected by the people thereof, for six years; and each Senator shall have one vote. The electors in each State shall have the qualifications requisite for electors of the most numerous branch of the State legislatures.

When vacancies happen in the representation of any State in the Senate, the executive authority of such State shall issue writs of election to fill such vacancies: Provided, That the legislature of any State may empower the executive thereof to make temporary appointments until the people fill the vacancies by election as the legislature may direct.

This amendment shall not be so construed as to affect the election or term of any Senator chosen before it becomes valid as part of the Constitution.

Amendment XVIII

Passed by Congress December 18, 1917. Ratified January 16, 1919. Repealed by amendment 21.

Section 1.
After one year from the ratification of this article the manufacture, sale, or transportation of intoxicating liquors within, the importation thereof into, or the exportation thereof from the United States and all territory subject to the jurisdiction thereof for beverage purposes is hereby prohibited.

Section 2.
The Congress and the several States shall have concurrent power to enforce this article by appropriate legislation.

Section 3.
This article shall be inoperative unless it shall have been ratified as an amendment to the Constitution by the legislatures of the several States, as provided in the Constitution, within seven years from the date of the submission hereof to the States by the Congress.

Amendment XIX

Passed by Congress June 4, 1919. Ratified August 18, 1920.

The right of citizens of the United States to vote shall not be denied or abridged by the United States or by any State on account of sex.

Congress shall have power to enforce this article by appropriate legislation.

Amendment XX

Passed by Congress March 2, 1932. Ratified January 23, 1933.

Note: Article I, section 4, of the Constitution was modified by section 2 of this amendment. In addition, a portion of the 12th amendment was superseded by section 3.

Section 1.
The terms of the President and the Vice President shall end at noon on the 20th day of January, and the terms of Senators and Representatives at noon on the 3d day

of January, of the years in which such terms would have ended if this article had not been ratified; and the terms of their successors shall then begin.

Section 2.

The Congress shall assemble at least once in every year, and such meeting shall begin at noon on the 3d day of January, unless they shall by law appoint a different day.

Section 3.

If, at the time fixed for the beginning of the term of the President, the President elect shall have died, the Vice President elect shall become President. If a President shall not have been chosen before the time fixed for the beginning of his term, or if the President elect shall have failed to qualify, then the Vice President elect shall act as President until a President shall have qualified; and the Congress may by law provide for the case wherein neither a President elect nor a Vice President shall have qualified, declaring who shall then act as President, or the manner in which one who is to act shall be selected, and such person shall act accordingly until a President or Vice President shall have qualified.

Section 4.

The Congress may by law provide for the case of the death of any of the persons from whom the House of Representatives may choose a President whenever the right of choice shall have devolved upon them, and for the case of the death of any of the persons from whom the Senate may choose a Vice President whenever the right of choice shall have devolved upon them.

Section 5.

Sections 1 and 2 shall take effect on the 15th day of October following the ratification of this article.

Section 6.

This article shall be inoperative unless it shall have been ratified as an amendment to the Constitution by the legislatures of three-fourths of the several States within seven years from the date of its submission.

Amendment XXI

Passed by Congress February 20, 1933. Ratified December 5, 1933.

Section 1.
The eighteenth article of amendment to the Constitution of the United States is hereby repealed.

Section 2.
The transportation or importation into any State, Territory, or Possession of the United States for delivery or use therein of intoxicating liquors, in violation of the laws thereof, is hereby prohibited.

Section 3.
This article shall be inoperative unless it shall have been ratified as an amendment to the Constitution by conventions in the several States, as provided in the Constitution, within seven years from the date of the submission hereof to the States by the Congress.

Amendment XXII

Passed by Congress March 21, 1947. Ratified February 27, 1951.

Section 1.
No person shall be elected to the office of the President more than twice, and no person who has held the office of President, or acted as President, for more than two years of a term to which some other person was elected President shall be elected to the office of President more than once. But this Article shall not apply to any person holding the office of President when this Article was proposed by Congress, and shall not prevent any person who may be holding the office of President, or acting as President, during the term within which this Article becomes operative from holding the office of President or acting as President during the remainder of such term.

Section 2.
This article shall be inoperative unless it shall have been ratified as an amendment to the Constitution by the legislatures of three-fourths of the several States within seven years from the date of its submission to the States by the Congress.

Amendment XXIII

Passed by Congress June 16, 1960. Ratified March 29, 1961.

Section 1.
The District constituting the seat of Government of the United States shall appoint in such manner as Congress may direct:

A number of electors of President and Vice President equal to the whole number of Senators and Representatives in Congress to which the District would be entitled if it were a State, but in no event more than the least populous State; they shall be in addition to those appointed by the States, but they shall be considered, for the purposes of the election of President and Vice President, to be electors appointed by a State; and they shall meet in the District and perform such duties as provided by the twelfth article of amendment.

Section 2.
The Congress shall have power to enforce this article by appropriate legislation.

Amendment XXIV

Passed by Congress August 27, 1962. Ratified January 23, 1964.

Section 1.
The right of citizens of the United States to vote in any primary or other election for President or Vice President, for electors for President or Vice President, or for Senator or Representative in Congress, shall not be denied or abridged by the United States or any State by reason of failure to pay poll tax or other tax.

Section 2.
The Congress shall have power to enforce this article by appropriate legislation.

Amendment XXV

Passed by Congress July 6, 1965. Ratified February 10, 1967.

Note: Article II, section 1, of the Constitution was affected by the 25th amendment.

Section 1.

In case of the removal of the President from office or of his death or resignation, the Vice President shall become President.

Section 2.

Whenever there is a vacancy in the office of the Vice President, the President shall nominate a Vice President who shall take office upon confirmation by a majority vote of both Houses of Congress.

Section 3.

Whenever the President transmits to the President pro tempore of the Senate and the Speaker of the House of Representatives his written declaration that he is unable to discharge the powers and duties of his office, and until he transmits to them a written declaration to the contrary, such powers and duties shall be discharged by the Vice President as Acting President.

Section 4.

Whenever the Vice President and a majority of either the principal officers of the executive departments or of such other body as Congress may by law provide, transmit to the President pro tempore of the Senate and the Speaker of the House of Representatives their written declaration that the President is unable to discharge the powers and duties of his office, the Vice President shall immediately assume the powers and duties of the office as Acting President.

Thereafter, when the President transmits to the President pro tempore of the Senate and the Speaker of the House of Representatives his written declaration that no inability exists, he shall resume the powers and duties of his office unless the Vice President and a majority of either the principal officers of the executive department or of such other body as Congress may by law provide, transmit within four days to the President pro tempore of the Senate and the Speaker of the House of Representatives their written declaration that the President is unable to discharge the powers and duties of his office. Thereupon Congress shall decide the issue, assembling within forty-eight hours for that purpose if not in session. If the Congress, within twenty-one days after receipt of the latter written declaration, or, if Congress is not in session, within twenty-one days after Congress is required to assemble, determines by two-thirds vote of both Houses that the President is unable to discharge the powers and duties of his office, the Vice President shall continue to discharge the same as Acting President; otherwise, the President shall resume the powers and duties of his office.

Amendment XXVI

Passed by Congress March 23, 1971. Ratified July 1, 1971.
   Note: Amendment 14, section 2, of the Constitution was modified by section 1 of the 26th amendment.

Section 1.
The right of citizens of the United States, who are eighteen years of age or older, to vote shall not be denied or abridged by the United States or by any State on account of age.

Section 2.
The Congress shall have power to enforce this article by appropriate legislation.

Amendment XXVII

Originally proposed Sept. 25, 1789. Ratified May 7, 1992.
   No law, varying the compensation for the services of the Senators and Representatives, shall take effect, until an election of representatives shall have intervened.

Table of Cases

Brown v. Board of Ed. of Topeka, Shawnee County, Kan., 347 U.S. 483, 74 S.Ct. 686 (1954)

Bush v. Gore, 531 U.S. 98, 121 S.Ct. 525 (2000)

Chisholm v. Georgia, 2 U.S. 419 (1793)

District of Columbia v. Heller, 554 U.S. 570, 128 S.Ct. 2783 (2008)

Dred Scott v. Sandford, 60 U.S. 393 (1857)

Fletcher v. Peck, 10 U.S. 87 (1810)

Kelo v. New London, 545 U.S. 469, 125 S.Ct. 2655 (2005)

Loving v. Virginia, 388 U.S. 1, 87 S.Ct. 1817 (1967)

Marbury v. Madison, 5 U.S. 137 (1803)

Martin v. Hunter's Lessee, 14 U.S. 304 (1816)

McCulloch v. Maryland, 17 U.S. 316 (1819)

Miranda v. Arizona, 384 U.S. 436, 86 S.Ct. 1602 (1966)

Ozawa v. U.S., 260 U.S. 178, 43 S.Ct. 65 (1922)

Plessy v. Ferguson, 163 U.S. 537, 16 S.Ct. 1138 (1896)

Roe v. Wade, 410 U.S. 113, 93 S.Ct. 705 (1973)

Schenck v. United States, 249 U.S. 47, 39 S.Ct. 247 (1919)

Texas v. White, 74 U.S. 700 (1869)

Torcaso v. Watkins, 367 U.S. 488, 81 S.Ct. 1680 (1961)

APPENDIX C

Selected Bibliography

You can view the original United States Constitution in the Rotunda for the Charters of Freedom at the National Archives, 700 Pennsylvania Avenue NW, Washington, D.C. The entrance to the building, which is across from the National Mall, is located on Constitution Avenue NW between 7th and 9th Streets. The Bill of Rights and the Declaration of Independence are also on exhibit there.

Websites

National Archives
You can access the text of the Declaration of Independence and the Constitution (including the Bill of Rights and the rest of the amendments) at the National Archives website.

www.archives.gov/exhibits/charters/constitution

Congressional Websites
These sites contain everything from historic information about Congress to information about the U.S. Capitol, including current business, how to contact your member of Congress, and tourist information as well.

www.senate.gov
www.house.gov

The Executive Branch
A general discussion of the presidency.

www.whitehouse.gov/our-government/executive-branch

The White House
The general White House site provides all kinds of information on the current occupants of the White House, including the staff, the cost of running the White House, events open to the public, and historic information about the building itself.

The site also provides links to discussions of the other two branches of the federal government, the Constitution, a list of executive agencies and commissions, and the cabinet departments.

www.whitehouse.gov

U.S. Supreme Court
This site contains historic information, rules for appearing before the Court, and links to copies of the opinions recently handed down.

www.supremecourt.gov

Supreme Court Opinions

Partial list of publicly accessible Supreme Court opinions.

www.supremecourt.gov/opinions/obtainopinions
www.law.cornell.edu/supct/supremes

The Federalist Papers

The Federalist Papers are also known as *The Federalist*. They were written by Alexander Hamilton, John Jay, and James Madison under the joint pseudonym "Publius." You can access these essays through the Library of Congress or purchase reprints from a large number of publishers.

http://thomas.loc.gov/home/histdox/fedpapers

Publications

Beeman, R. *The Penguin Guide to the United States Constitution*. New York: Penguin, 2010.

Hall, K., ed. *The Oxford Companion to the Supreme Court of the United States*, 2nd edition. New York: Oxford University Press, 2005.

Hamilton, A., J. Jay, and J. Madison. *The Federalist Papers*. Hollywood, FL: Simon & Brown, 2010.

Nowak, J., and R. Rotunda. *Constitutional Law*, 3rd edition. St. Paul, MN: West Publishing, 2007.

Rakove, J., ed. *The Annotated U.S. Constitution and Declaration of Independence*. Cambridge, MA, and London, England: The Belknap Press of Harvard University Press, 2009.

The Mayflower Compact

The Mayflower Compact was drawn up and signed aboard the Mayflower on November 11, 1620. Signed by forty-one of the ship's 102 passengers (who were about to debark in an area outside that permitted by their patent—which was essentially a license to settle there—because they'd been blown off course). The Compact didn't change the terms of their license, but it did, in its brief text, bind the signers to governing themselves in the traditional methods used by English towns.

In the name of God, Amen. We, whose names are underwritten, the Loyal Subjects of our dread Sovereign Lord, King James, by the Grace of God, of England, France and Ireland, King, Defender of the Faith, e&.

Having undertaken for the Glory of God, and Advancement of the Christian Faith, and the Honour of our King and Country, a voyage to plant the first colony in the northern parts of Virginia; do by these presents, solemnly and mutually in the Presence of God and one of another, covenant and combine ourselves together into a civil Body Politick, for our better Ordering and Preservation, and Furtherance of the Ends aforesaid; And by Virtue hereof to enact, constitute, and frame, such just and equal Laws, Ordinances, Acts, Constitutions and Offices, from time to time, as shall be thought most meet and convenient for the General good of the Colony; unto which we promise all due submission and obedience.

In Witness whereof we have hereunto subscribed our names at Cape Cod the eleventh of November, in the Reign of our Sovereign Lord, King James of England, France and Ireland, the eighteenth, and of Scotland the fifty-fourth. Anno Domini, 1620.

The Declaration of Independence

IN CONGRESS, July 4, 1776.

The unanimous Declaration of the thirteen united States of America,

When in the Course of human events, it becomes necessary for one people to dissolve the political bands which have connected them with another, and to assume among the powers of the earth, the separate and equal station to which the Laws of Nature and of Nature's God entitle them, a decent respect to the opinions of mankind requires that they should declare the causes which impel them to the separation.

We hold these truths to be self-evident, that all men are created equal, that they are endowed by their Creator with certain unalienable Rights, that among these are Life, Liberty and the pursuit of Happiness.—That to secure these rights, Governments are instituted among Men, deriving their just powers from the consent of the governed,—That whenever any Form of Government becomes destructive of these ends, it is the Right of the People to alter or to abolish it, and to institute new Government, laying its foundation on such principles and organizing its powers in such form, as to them shall seem most likely to effect their Safety and Happiness. Prudence, indeed, will dictate that Governments long established should not be changed for light and transient causes; and accordingly all experience hath shewn, that mankind are more disposed to suffer, while evils are sufferable, than to right themselves by abolishing the forms to which they are accustomed. But when a long train of abuses and usurpations, pursuing invariably the same Object evinces a design to reduce them under absolute Despotism, it is their right, it is their duty, to throw off such Government, and to provide new Guards for their future security.—Such has been the patient sufferance of these Colonies; and such is now the necessity which constrains them to alter their former Systems of Government. The history of the present King of Great Britain is a history of repeated injuries and usurpations, all having in direct object the establishment of an absolute Tyranny over these States. To prove this, let Facts be submitted to a candid world.

He has refused his Assent to Laws, the most wholesome and necessary for the public good.

He has forbidden his Governors to pass Laws of immediate and pressing importance, unless suspended in their operation till his Assent should be obtained; and when so suspended, he has utterly neglected to attend to them.

He has refused to pass other Laws for the accommodation of large districts of people, unless those people would relinquish the right of Representation in the Legislature, a right inestimable to them and formidable to tyrants only.

He has called together legislative bodies at places unusual, uncomfortable, and distant from the depository of their public Records, for the sole purpose of fatiguing them into compliance with his measures.

He has dissolved Representative Houses repeatedly, for opposing with manly firmness his invasions on the rights of the people.

He has refused for a long time, after such dissolutions, to cause others to be elected; whereby the Legislative powers, incapable of Annihilation, have returned to the People at large for their exercise; the State remaining in the mean time exposed to all the dangers of invasion from without, and convulsions within.

He has endeavoured to prevent the population of these States; for that purpose obstructing the Laws for Naturalization of Foreigners; refusing to pass others to encourage their migrations hither, and raising the conditions of new Appropriations of Lands.

He has obstructed the Administration of Justice, by refusing his Assent to Laws for establishing Judiciary powers.

He has made Judges dependent on his Will alone, for the tenure of their offices, and the amount and payment of their salaries.

He has erected a multitude of New Offices, and sent hither swarms of Officers to harrass our people, and eat out their substance.

He has kept among us, in times of peace, Standing Armies without the Consent of our legislatures.

He has affected to render the Military independent of and superior to the Civil power.

He has combined with others to subject us to a jurisdiction foreign to our constitution, and unacknowledged by our laws; giving his Assent to their Acts of pretended Legislation:

For Quartering large bodies of armed troops among us:

For protecting them, by a mock Trial, from punishment for any Murders which they should commit on the Inhabitants of these States:

For cutting off our Trade with all parts of the world:

For imposing Taxes on us without our Consent:

For depriving us in many cases, of the benefits of Trial by Jury:

For transporting us beyond Seas to be tried for pretended offences:

For abolishing the free System of English Laws in a neighbouring Province, establishing therein an Arbitrary government, and enlarging its Boundaries so as to render it at once an example and fit instrument for introducing the same absolute rule into these Colonies:

For taking away our Charters, abolishing our most valuable Laws, and altering fundamentally the Forms of our Governments:

For suspending our own Legislatures, and declaring themselves invested with power to legislate for us in all cases whatsoever.

He has abdicated Government here, by declaring us out of his Protection and waging War against us.

He has plundered our seas, ravaged our Coasts, burnt our towns, and destroyed the lives of our people.

He is at this time transporting large Armies of foreign Mercenaries to compleat the works of death, desolation and tyranny, already begun with circumstances of Cruelty & perfidy scarcely paralleled in the most barbarous ages, and totally unworthy the Head of a civilized nation.

He has constrained our fellow Citizens taken Captive on the high Seas to bear Arms against their Country, to become the executioners of their friends and Brethren, or to fall themselves by their Hands.

He has excited domestic insurrections amongst us, and has endeavoured to bring on the inhabitants of our frontiers, the merciless Indian Savages, whose known rule of warfare, is an undistinguished destruction of all ages, sexes and conditions.

In every stage of these Oppressions We have Petitioned for Redress in the most humble terms: Our repeated Petitions have been answered only by repeated injury. A Prince whose character is thus marked by every act which may define a Tyrant, is unfit to be the ruler of a free people.

Nor have We been wanting in attentions to our British brethren. We have warned them from time to time of attempts by their legislature to extend an unwarrantable jurisdiction over us. We have reminded them of the circumstances of our emigration and settlement here. We have appealed to their native justice and magnanimity, and we have conjured them by the ties of our common kindred to disavow these usurpations, which, would inevitably interrupt our connections and correspondence. They too have been deaf to the voice of justice and of consanguinity. We must, therefore, acquiesce in the necessity, which denounces our Separation, and hold them, as we hold the rest of mankind, Enemies in War, in Peace Friends.

We, therefore, the Representatives of the united States of America, in General Congress, Assembled, appealing to the Supreme Judge of the world for the rectitude of our intentions, do, in the Name, and by Authority of the good People of these Colonies, solemnly publish and declare, That these United Colonies are, and of Right ought to be Free and Independent

States; that they are Absolved from all Allegiance to the British Crown, and that all political connection between them and the State of Great Britain, is and ought to be totally dissolved; and that as Free and Independent States, they have full Power to levy War, conclude Peace, contract Alliances, establish Commerce, and to do all other Acts and Things which Independent States may of right do. And for the support of this Declaration, with a firm reliance on the protection of divine Providence, we mutually pledge to each other our Lives, our Fortunes and our sacred Honor.

The 56 signatures on the Declaration appear in the positions indicated:

COLUMN 1
Georgia:
Button Gwinnett
Lyman Hall
George Walton

COLUMN 2
North Carolina:
William Hooper
Joseph Hewes
John Penn

South Carolina:
Edward Rutledge
Thomas Heyward, Jr.
Thomas Lynch, Jr.
Arthur Middleton

COLUMN 3
Massachusetts:
John Hancock

Maryland:
Samuel Chase
William Paca
Thomas Stone
Charles Carroll of Carrollton

Virginia:
George Wythe
Richard Henry Lee
Thomas Jefferson
Benjamin Harrison
Thomas Nelson, Jr.
Francis Lightfoot Lee
Carter Braxton

COLUMN 4
Pennsylvania:
Robert Morris
Benjamin Rush
Benjamin Franklin
John Morton
George Clymer
James Smith
George Taylor
James Wilson
George Ross

Delaware:
Caesar Rodney
George Read
Thomas McKean

Column 5
New York:
William Floyd
Philip Livingston
Francis Lewis
Lewis Morris

New Jersey:
Richard Stockton
John Witherspoon
Francis Hopkinson
John Hart
Abraham Clark

Column 6
New Hampshire:
Josiah Bartlett
William Whipple

Massachusetts:
Samuel Adams
John Adams
Robert Treat Paine
Elbridge Gerry

Rhode Island:
Stephen Hopkins
William Ellery

Connecticut:
Roger Sherman
Samuel Huntington
William Williams
Oliver Wolcott

New Hampshire:
Matthew Thornton

Selected Federalist Papers

The Federalist Papers were a series of essays on the merits of the Constitution written by Alexander Hamilton, John Jay, and James Madison under the pen name of Publius. The essays were published in various New York papers to garner support for the ratification of the Constitution by the state of New York. They remain a cogent analysis of what was intended by various sections of the Constitution and provide insight into the founders' thoughts behind the document's wording.

"Federalist Number 39: The Conformity of the Plan to Republican Principles" (James Madison)

In this essay, Madison discusses the nature of federalism and republican government and notes the ways the various parts of the new government created by the Constitution will hold other parts in check. While doing so, he makes avid arguments for ratification.

To the People of the State of New York:

THE last paper having concluded the observations which were meant to introduce a candid survey of the plan of government reported by the convention, we now proceed to the execution of that part of our undertaking.

The first question that offers itself is, whether the general form and aspect of the government be strictly republican. It is evident that no other form would be reconcilable with the genius of the people of America; with the fundamental principles of the Revolution; or with that honorable determination which animates every votary of freedom, to rest all our political experiments on the capacity of mankind for self-government. If the plan of the convention, therefore, be found to depart from the republican character, its advocates must abandon it as no longer defensible.

What, then, are the distinctive characters of the republican form? Were an answer to this question to be sought, not by recurring to principles, but in the application of the term by political writers, to the constitution of different States, no satisfactory one would ever be found. Holland, in which no particle of the supreme authority is derived from the people, has passed almost universally under the denomination of a republic. The same title has been bestowed on Venice, where absolute power over the great body of the people is exercised, in the most absolute manner, by a small body of hereditary nobles. Poland, which is a mixture of aristocracy and of monarchy in their worst forms, has been dignified with the same appellation. The government of England, which has one republican branch only, combined with an hereditary aristocracy and monarchy, has, with equal impropriety, been frequently placed on the list of republics. These examples, which are nearly as dissimilar to each other as to a genuine republic, show the extreme inaccuracy with which the term has been used in political disquisitions.

If we resort for a criterion to the different principles on which different forms of government are established, we may define a republic to be, or at least may bestow that name on, a government which derives all its powers directly or indirectly from the great body of the people, and is administered by persons holding their offices during pleasure, for a limited period, or during good behavior. It is ESSENTIAL to such a government that it be derived from the great body of the society, not from an inconsiderable proportion, or a favored class of it; otherwise a handful of tyrannical nobles, exercising their oppressions by a delegation of their powers, might aspire to the rank of republicans, and claim for their government the honorable title of republic. It is SUFFICIENT for such a government that the persons administering it be appointed, either directly or indirectly, by the people; and that they hold their appointments by either of the tenures just specified; otherwise every government in the United States, as well as every other popular government that has been or can be well organized or well executed, would be degraded from the republican character. According to the constitution of every State in the Union, some or other of the officers of government are appointed indirectly only by the people. According to most of them, the chief magistrate himself is so appointed. And according to one, this mode of appointment is extended to one of the co-ordinate branches of the legislature. According to all the constitutions, also, the tenure of the highest offices is extended to a definite period, and in many instances, both within the legislative and executive departments, to a period of years. According to the provisions of most of the constitutions, again, as well as according to the most respectable and received opinions on the subject, the members of the judiciary department are to retain their offices by the firm tenure of good behavior.

On comparing the Constitution planned by the convention with the standard here fixed, we perceive at once that it is, in the most rigid sense, conformable to it. The House of Representatives, like that of one branch at least of all the State legislatures, is elected immediately by the great body of the people. The Senate, like the present Congress, and the Senate of Maryland, derives its appointment indirectly from the people. The President is indirectly derived from the choice of the people, according to the example in most of the States. Even the judges, with all other officers of the Union, will, as in the several States, be the choice, though a remote choice, of the people themselves, the duration of the appointments is equally conformable to the republican standard, and to the model of State constitutions The House of Representatives is periodically elective, as in all the States; and for the period of two years, as in the State of South Carolina. The Senate is elective, for the period of six years; which is but one year more than the period of the Senate of Maryland, and but two more than that of the Senates of New York and Virginia. The President is to continue in office for the period of four years; as in New York and Delaware, the chief magistrate is elected for three years, and in South Carolina for two years. In the other States the election is annual. In several of the States, however, no constitutional provision is made for the impeachment of the chief magistrate. And in Delaware and Virginia he is not impeachable till out of office. The President of the United States is impeachable at any time during his continuance in office. The tenure by which the judges are to hold their places, is, as it unquestionably ought to be, that of good behavior. The tenure of the ministerial offices generally, will be a subject of legal regulation, conformably to the reason of the case and the example of the State constitutions.

Could any further proof be required of the republican complexion of this system, the most decisive one might be found in its absolute prohibition of titles of nobility, both under the federal and the State governments; and in its express guaranty of the republican form to each of the latter.

"But it was not sufficient," say the adversaries of the proposed Constitution, *"for the convention to adhere to the republican form. They ought, with equal care, to have preserved the FEDERAL form, which regards the Union as a CONFEDERACY of sovereign states; instead of which, they have framed a NATIONAL government, which regards the Union as a CONSOLIDATION of the States." And it is asked by what authority this bold and radical innovation was undertaken? The handle which has been made of this objection requires that it should be examined with some precision.*

Without inquiring into the accuracy of the distinction on which the objection is founded, it will be necessary to a just estimate of its force, first, to ascertain the real character of the government in question; secondly, to inquire how far the convention were authorized to propose such a government; and thirdly, how far the duty they owed to their country could supply any defect of regular authority.

First. In order to ascertain the real character of the government, it may be considered in relation to the foundation on which it is to be established; to the sources from which its ordinary powers are to be drawn; to the operation of those powers; to the extent of them; and to the authority by which future changes in the government are to be introduced.

On examining the first relation, it appears, on one hand, that the Constitution is to be founded on the assent and ratification of the people of America, given by deputies elected for the special purpose; but, on the other, that this assent and ratification is to be given by the people, not as individuals composing one entire nation, but as composing the distinct and independent States to which they respectively belong. It is to be the assent and ratification of the several States, derived from the supreme authority in each State, the authority of the people themselves. The act, therefore, establishing the Constitution, will not be a NATIONAL, but a FEDERAL act.

*That it will be a federal and not a national act, as these terms are under-
stood by the objectors; the act of the people, as forming so many independent States, not as forming one aggregate nation, is obvious from
this single consideration, that it is to result neither from the decision of a
MAJORITY of the people of the Union, nor from that of a MAJORITY of
the States. It must result from the UNANIMOUS assent of the several
States that are parties to it, differing no otherwise from their ordinary
assent than in its being expressed, not by the legislative authority, but
by that of the people themselves. Were the people regarded in this trans-
action as forming one nation, the will of the majority of the whole people of the United States would bind the minority, in the same manner as
the majority in each State must bind the minority; and the will of the
majority must be determined either by a comparison of the individual
votes, or by considering the will of the majority of the States as evidence
of the will of a majority of the people of the United States. Neither of
these rules have been adopted. Each State, in ratifying the Constitution,
is considered as a sovereign body, independent of all others, and only
to be bound by its own voluntary act. In this relation, then, the new
Constitution will, if established, be a FEDERAL, and not a NATIONAL
constitution.*

*The next relation is, to the sources from which the ordinary powers
of government are to be derived. The House of Representatives will
derive its powers from the people of America; and the people will be
represented in the same proportion, and on the same principle, as
they are in the legislature of a particular State. So far the government
is NATIONAL, not FEDERAL. The Senate, on the other hand, will
derive its powers from the States, as political and coequal societies;
and these will be represented on the principle of equality in the Senate, as they now are in the existing Congress. So far the government
is FEDERAL, not NATIONAL. The executive power will be derived
from a very compound source. The immediate election of the President is to be made by the States in their political characters. The
votes allotted to them are in a compound ratio, which considers them
partly as distinct and coequal societies, partly as unequal members
of the same society. The eventual election, again, is to be made by*

that branch of the legislature which consists of the national representatives; but in this particular act they are to be thrown into the form of individual delegations, from so many distinct and coequal bodies politic. From this aspect of the government it appears to be of a mixed character, presenting at least as many FEDERAL as NATIONAL features.

The difference between a federal and national government, as it relates to the OPERATION OF THE GOVERNMENT, is supposed to consist in this, that in the former the powers operate on the political bodies composing the Confederacy, in their political capacities; in the latter, on the individual citizens composing the nation, in their individual capacities. On trying the Constitution by this criterion, it falls under the NATIONAL, not the FEDERAL character; though perhaps not so completely as has been understood. In several cases, and particularly in the trial of controversies to which States may be parties, they must be viewed and proceeded against in their collective and political capacities only. So far the national countenance of the government on this side seems to be disfigured by a few federal features. But this blemish is perhaps unavoidable in any plan; and the operation of the government on the people, in their individual capacities, in its ordinary and most essential proceedings, may, on the whole, designate it, in this relation, a NATIONAL government.

But if the government be national with regard to the OPERATION of its powers, it changes its aspect again when we contemplate it in relation to the EXTENT of its powers. The idea of a national government involves in it, not only an authority over the individual citizens, but an indefinite supremacy over all persons and things, so far as they are objects of lawful government. Among a people consolidated into one nation, this supremacy is completely vested in the national legislature. Among communities united for particular purposes, it is vested partly in the general and partly in the municipal legislatures. In the former case, all local authorities are subordinate to the supreme; and may be controlled, directed, or abolished by it at pleasure. In the latter, the local or municipal authorities form distinct and independent portions of the supremacy, no more subject, within their respective spheres, to the general authority, than the general authority is subject to them, within its own sphere. In this relation, then, the proposed government cannot be deemed a NATIONAL one; since its jurisdiction extends to certain enumerated objects only, and leaves to the several States a residuary and inviolable sovereignty over all other objects. It is true that in controversies relating to the boundary between the two jurisdictions, the tribunal which is ultimately to decide, is to be established under the general government. But this does not change the principle of the case. The decision is to be impartially made, according to the rules of the Constitution; and all the usual and most effectual precautions are taken to secure this impartiality. Some such tribunal is clearly essential to prevent an appeal to the sword and a dissolution of the compact; and that it ought to be established under the general rather than under the local governments, or, to speak more properly, that it could be safely established under the first alone, is a position not likely to be combated.

If we try the Constitution by its last relation to the authority by which amendments are to be made, we find it neither wholly NATIONAL nor wholly FEDERAL. Were it wholly national, the supreme and ultimate authority would reside in the MAJORITY of the people of the Union; and this authority would be competent at all times, like that of a majority of every national society, to alter or abolish its established government. Were it wholly federal, on the other hand, the concurrence of each State in the Union would be essential to every alteration that would be binding on all. The mode provided by the plan of the convention is not founded on either of these principles. In requiring more than a majority, and particularly in computing the proportion by STATES, not by CITIZENS, it departs from the NATIONAL and advances towards the FEDERAL character; in rendering the concurrence of less than the whole number of States sufficient, it loses again the FEDERAL and partakes of the NATIONAL character.

The proposed Constitution, therefore, is, in strictness, neither a national nor a federal Constitution, but a composition of both. In its foundation it is federal, not national; in the sources from which the ordinary powers of the government are drawn, it is partly federal and partly national; in the operation of these powers, it is national, not federal; in the extent of them, again, it is federal, not national; and, finally, in the authoritative mode of introducing amendments, it is neither wholly federal nor wholly national.

"Federalist Number 51: The Structure of the Government Must Furnish the Proper Checks and Balances Between the Different Departments" (Alexander Hamilton or James Madison)

This essay explores the principle of "checks and balances," essentially saying that the Constitution is designed to keep any one branch from dominating. This so concerned the drafters that they created a system almost guaranteed to immobilize itself unless its participants were willing to compromise.

To the People of the State of New York:

TO WHAT expedient, then, shall we finally resort, for maintaining in practice the necessary partition of power among the several departments, as laid down in the Constitution? The only answer that can be given is, that as all these exterior provisions are found to be inadequate, the defect must be supplied, by so contriving the interior structure of the government as that its several constituent parts may, by their mutual relations, be the means of keeping each other in their proper places. Without presuming to undertake a full development of this important idea, I will hazard a few general observations, which may perhaps place it in a clearer light, and enable us to form a more correct judgment of the principles and structure of the government planned by the convention. In order to lay a due foundation for that separate and distinct exercise of the different powers of government, which to a certain extent is admitted on all hands to be essential to the preservation of liberty, it is evident that each department should have a will of its own; and consequently should be so constituted that the members of each should have as little agency as possible in the appointment of the members of the others. Were this principle rigorously adhered to, it would require that all the appointments for the supreme executive, legislative, and judiciary magistracies should be drawn from the same fountain of authority, the people, through channels having no communication whatever with one another. Perhaps such a plan of constructing the several departments would be less difficult in practice than it may in contemplation appear. Some difficulties, however, and some additional expense would attend the execution of it. Some deviations, therefore, from the principle must be admitted. In the constitution of the judiciary department in particular, it might be inexpedient to insist rigorously on the principle: first, because peculiar qualifications being essential in the members, the primary consideration ought to be to select that mode of choice which best secures these qualifications; secondly, because the permanent tenure by which the appointments are held in that department, must soon destroy all sense of dependence on the authority conferring them. It is equally evident, that the members of each department should be as little dependent as possible on those of the others, for the emoluments annexed to their offices. Were the executive magistrate, or the judges, not independent of the legislature in this particular, their independence in every other would be merely nominal. But the great security against a gradual concentration of the several powers in the same department, consists in giving to those who administer each department the necessary constitutional means and personal motives to resist encroachments of the others. The provision for defense must in this, as in all other cases, be made commensurate to the danger of attack. Ambition must be made to counteract ambition. The interest of the man must be connected with the constitutional rights of the place. It may be a reflection on human nature, that such devices should be necessary to control the abuses of government. But what is government itself, but the greatest of all reflections on human nature? If men were angels, no government would be necessary. If angels were to govern men, neither external nor internal controls on government would be necessary. In framing a government which is to be administered by men over men, the great difficulty lies in this: you must first enable the government to control the governed; and in the next place oblige it to control itself. A dependence on the people is, no doubt, the primary control on the government; but experience has taught mankind the necessity of auxiliary precautions. This policy of supplying, by opposite and rival interests, the defect of better motives, might be traced through the whole system of human affairs, private as well as public. We see it particularly displayed in all the subordinate distributions of power, where the constant aim is to divide and arrange the several offices in such a manner as that each may be a check on the other that the private interest of every individual may be a sentinel over the public rights. These inventions of prudence cannot be less requisite in the distribution of the supreme powers of the State. But it is not possible to give to each department an equal power of self-defense. In republican government, the legislative authority necessarily predominates. The remedy for this inconveniency is to divide the legislature into different branches; and to render them, by different modes of election and different principles of action, as little connected with each other as the nature of their common functions and their common dependence on the society will admit. It may even be necessary to guard against dangerous encroachments by still further precautions. As the weight of the legislative authority requires that it should be thus divided, the weakness of the executive may require, on the other hand, that it should be fortified. An absolute negative on the legislature appears, at first view, to be the natural defense with which the executive magistrate should be armed. But perhaps it would be neither altogether safe nor alone sufficient. On ordinary occasions it might not be exerted with the requisite firmness, and on extraordinary occasions it might be perfidiously abused. May not this defect of an absolute negative be supplied by some qualified connection between this weaker department and the weaker branch of the stronger department, by which the latter may be led to support the constitutional rights of the former, without being too much detached from the rights of its own department? If the principles on which these observations are founded be just, as I persuade myself they are, and they be applied as a criterion to the several State constitutions, and to the federal Constitution it will be found that if the latter does not perfectly correspond with them, the former are infinitely less able to bear such a test. There are, moreover, two considerations particularly applicable to the federal system of America, which place that system in a very interesting point of view. First. In a single republic, all the power surrendered by the people is submitted to the administration of a single government; and the usurpations are guarded against by a division of the government into distinct and separate departments. In the compound republic of America, the power surrendered by the people is first divided between two distinct governments, and then the portion allotted to each subdivided among distinct and separate departments. Hence a double security arises to the rights of the people. The different governments will control each other, at the same time that each will be controlled by itself. Second. It is of great importance in a republic not only to guard the society against the oppression of its rulers, but to guard one part of the society against the injustice of the other part. Different interests necessarily exist in different classes of citizens. If a majority be united by a common interest, the rights of the minority will be insecure. There are but two methods of providing against this evil: the one by creating a will in the community independent of the majority that is, of the society itself; the other, by comprehending in the society so many separate descriptions of citizens as will render an unjust combination of a majority of the whole very improbable, if not impracticable. The first method prevails in all governments possessing an hereditary or self-appointed authority. This, at best, is but a precarious security; because a power independent of the society may as well espouse the unjust views of the major, as the rightful interests of the minor party, and may possibly be turned against both parties. The second method will be exemplified in the federal republic of the United States. Whilst all authority in it will be derived from and dependent on the society, the society itself will be broken into so many parts, interests, and classes of citizens, that the rights of individuals, or of the minority, will be in little danger from interested combinations of the majority. In a free government the security for civil rights must be the same as that for religious rights. It consists in the one case in the multiplicity of interests, and in the other in the multiplicity of sects. The degree of security in both cases will depend on the number of interests and sects; and this may be presumed to depend on the extent of country and number of people comprehended under the same government. This view of the subject must particularly recommend a proper federal system to all the sincere and considerate friends of republican government, since it shows that in exact proportion as the territory of the Union may be formed into more circumscribed Confederacies, or States oppressive combinations of a majority will be facilitated: the best security, under the republican forms, for the rights of every class of citizens, will be diminished: and consequently the stability and independence of some member of the government, the only other security, must be proportionately increased. Justice is the end of government. It is the end of civil society. It ever has been and ever will be pursued until it be obtained, or until liberty be lost in the pursuit. In a society under the forms of which the stronger faction can readily unite and oppress the weaker, anarchy may as truly be said to reign as in a state of nature, where the weaker individual is not secured against the violence of the stronger; and as, in the latter state, even the stronger individuals are prompted, by the uncertainty of their condition, to submit to a government which may protect the weak as well as themselves; so, in the former state, will the more powerful factions or parties be gradnally induced, by a like motive, to wish for a government which will protect all parties, the weaker as well as the more powerful. It can be little doubted that if the State of Rhode Island was separated from the Confederacy and left to itself, the insecurity of rights under the popular form of government within such narrow limits would be displayed by such reiterated oppressions of factious majorities that some power altogether independent of the people would soon be called for by the voice of the very factions whose misrule had proved the necessity of it. In the extended republic of the United States, and among the great variety of interests, parties, and sects which it embraces, a coalition of a majority of the whole society could seldom take place on any other principles than those of justice and the general good; whilst there being thus less danger to a minor from the will of a major party, there must be less pretext, also, to provide for the security of the former, by introducing into the government a will not dependent on the latter, or, in other words, a will independent of the society itself. It is no less certain than it is important, notwithstanding the contrary opinions which have been entertained, that the larger the society, provided it lie within a practical sphere, the more duly capable it will be of self-government. And happily for the REPUBLICAN CAUSE, the practicable sphere may be carried to a very great extent, by a judicious modification and mixture of the FEDERAL PRINCIPLE.

Other Federalist Papers of Interest

There are eighty-five Federalist Papers, all of which can give you a better understanding of what the framers had in mind when they drafted the Constitution. Of particular interest, in addition to those reproduced here, are the following four.

"Federalist Number 1: Introduction" (Alexander Hamilton)

Alexander Hamilton, who would become the nation's first secretary of the treasury after the Constitution was ratified, had signed the document as one of the delegates to the Constitutional Convention. In this, the introduction to the Federalist Papers, he opens by saying flat out that the Articles of Confederation did not create a functional government, and goes on to say why he thinks, on the whole, the Constitution would be a better alternative.

"Federalist Number 2: Concerning Dangers from Foreign Force and Influence" (John Jay)

John Jay, who had served as secretary of foreign affairs (which became the office of secretary of state) under the Articles of Confederation and also during the early years of George Washington's administration, became the first chief justice of the U.S. Supreme Court in 1789. He had not attended the Constitutional Convention but participated in these efforts to obtain the Constitution's ratification.

This second of the Federalist Papers contains an interesting statement of how the Founding Fathers viewed the country, and why there were omissions such as a provision that English would be the official language of the United States: They didn't think they had to state anything so obvious. He describes Americans as "one united people—a people descended from the same ancestors, speaking the same language, professing the same religion, attached to the same principles of government, very similar in their manners and customs. . . ."

"Federalist Number 12: The Utility of the Union In Respect to Revenue" (Alexander Hamilton)

Fittingly, Hamilton discusses revenue and commerce in this essay, which includes an impassioned argument that the United States should be one nation, rather than separate states or smaller confederacies, thus avoiding the kind of tariffs between state borders that had stymied commerce and productivity in Europe, especially in France.

"Federalist Number 78: The Judiciary Department" (Alexander Hamilton)

Although the founders saw Congress as the most important branch, and the courts the least important, Hamilton makes a strong argument here for the checks and balances that can be provided by an independent judiciary. He also explains how precedent governs the law, and how judges who would be serving for what is essentially a lifetime would be able to use the length of their tenure to become very knowledgeable about those precedents.

Index

We Have

EVERYTHING®

on Anything!

With more than 19 million copies sold, the Everything® series has become one of America's favorite resources for solving problems, learning new skills, and organizing lives. Our brand is not only recognizable—it's also welcomed.

The series is a hand-in-hand partner for people who are ready to tackle new subjects—like you!

For more information on the Everything® series, please visit *www.adamsmedia.com*

The Everything® list spans a wide range of subjects, with more than 500 titles covering 25 different categories:

Business	History	Reference
Careers	Home Improvement	Religion
Children's Storybooks	Everything Kids	Self-Help
Computers	Languages	Sports & Fitness
Cooking	Music	Travel
Crafts and Hobbies	New Age	Wedding
Education/Schools	Parenting	Writing
Games and Puzzles	Personal Finance	
Health	Pets	